RV Travel in Mexico

RV

Travel in Mexico

by

John Howells

Gateway Books
San Francisco

Printed in the United States Of America

GATEWAY BOOKS

San Francisco

Edited by Sherry Pastor
Illustrated by Dorris L. Quinn
Cover design by Ed McElligott

Other books by John Howells:
Choose Mexico, 1985, 1988
Choose Latin America, 1986
Retirement Choices, 1987

ISBN 0-933469-08-X

10 9 8 7 6 5 4 3 2 1

Acknowledgments

Thanks to Ferne Holmes and Sherry Pastor for their help and editorial assistance in putting this book together. Also, thanks to Alan and Estelle Cohen, Teal Sewards, Don and Judy Merwin, Shirley Miller and Mexico West Travel Club, Walter Mueller and Vagabundos del Mar plus all those wonderful RV travelers in Mexico who responded to questionnaires, gave advice and shared their experiences with other RV enthusiasts.

239

D. QUINN

Contents

Introduction   **11**

Chapter One
A Mexican Experience   **13**
RVs in Mexico, Good and Bad Points • RV Budgets • Why Mexico? •
Bargains ?

Chapter Two
The Third Mexico   **23**
Getting Involved • Three Mexicos, Three Prices? • Bargaining Game • What
About the Future?

Chapter Three
Is Mexico Travel Safe?   **31**
Low Crime Atmosphere • Travelers' Warnings • Drugs and Crime • Law 'n
Order • Getting Sued • RV Travels for Singles? • Children in Mexico •
Mexican Roads

Chapter Four
Driving in Mexico   **39**
Right-of-Way • Don't Drive at Night! • Traffic Signals • Traffic Cops •
Insurance • Accidents • Gasoline Stations • Mechanics • Green Angels •
Maintenance

Chapter Five
Getting Started   **55**
What to Take • Tools • Flotation Tires • Water and Electricity • Mail? •
Money Exchange • Legal Details • Mordidas: The Bite • Guns • Boat
Permits, Fishing licenses • Telephone Calls • CB Radios • Pets

Chapter Six
Parking Your Rig   **69**
RV Park Variety • Parking Lot Boondocking • Auxiliary Transportation •
Buying an RV Lot • Rating RV Parks

Chapter Seven
Fabulous Baja   **75**
Desert and Ocean • Retirement • The Free Zone • Mobile Homes •
Ensenada • San Felipe •Bahía de Los Angeles • Bahía de Concepción •
Loreto • Puerto San Carlos • La Paz • Bahía de Palmas • Todos Santos • Los
Cabos • Baja vs. the Mainland

Chapter Eight
Catching the Ferry   **95**
Economics of Ferry Crossings • How to Get Aboard • Reservation
Philosophy

Chapter Nine
Mexico's Mainland   103
West Coast • Gold Coast • Isthmus • Yucatán • East Coast • Central Plateau • Mexico's Interior

Chapter Ten
Keeping Healthy   133
Good Cooking Practices • Ice Cubes and Bulk Ice • Eating in Restaurants • Drugstores and Prescriptions • Vitamins • Doctors in Mexico • Hospital Care

Chapter Eleven
Shopping and RV Cooking   141
Menu Planning • Shortages • Supermarkets and Native Markets • At the Butcher Shop • Favorite RV Recipes • Kitchen Items to Check

Chapter Twelve
Retirement in Mexico?   149
Winter Retirement • Full-time RV Retirement • Thinking of Retirement? • Legalities of Mexico Retirement • Buying Property • Trying It Out

Chapter Thirteen
Buying Insurance   157
Boats and Trailers • Group Insurance • Insurance Brokers

Chapter Fourteen
Getting Involved   163
Volunteer Work • Helping the Needy • Christmas Gifts

Chapter Fifteen
Travel Clubs and Caravans   169
Mexico West Travel Club • Vagabundos del Mar • Monarcas and Club Deportivo • Professional Caravans

Chapter Sixteen
Speaking the Language   173
Total Physical Response • "Castilian" Spanish • Why We Can't Understand • It's not in the Dictionary! • Speaking 'Pidgen' Spanish • Spanish-English, English-Spanish

Chapter Seventeen
Questions and Answers   179

Recreation Vehicle Park Guide   A-1

Appendix   A-31

RV Travel in Mexico

Five years ago, my friend Don Merwin and I co-authored a book on retirement in Mexico. We thought we had a good subject but we had no idea the book would be so well-received. The first edition sold over 90,000 copies. We received hundreds of letters from readers pleading for more information. We got busy with our research, and in early 1989 we placed a revised and expanded edition of CHOOSE MEXICO in the bookstores. The new book was equally well-received by the reading public. Obviously, long-term living in Mexico is a popular subject nowadays.

As we were going through the stack of questions from our readers, one thing stood out clearly: people wanted to know about recreation vehicle (RV) travel and retirement in Mexico. Frankly, this hadn't occurred to us when we were researching CHOOSE MEXICO. We were thinking in terms of permanent living in apartments, condos or houses—not RVs. Readers asked questions like:

What about taking my motorhome into Mexico? Is it safe?

Can I find a winter location for my fifth-wheel somewhere around Puerto Vallarta? What about mobile home living?

These questions, and many more, deserved answers.

As it happens, I know something about RV travel in Mexico. I own a small motorhome and I've taken other RVs over many miles of Mexican roads during the past 30 years. So, it seemed logical that I should embark on another journey of research and write yet another book. This led to more thousands of miles through Mexico—retracing old trails and revisiting favorite places—this time from the viewpoint of an RV traveler. It was work, but fun, too! My wife Sherry and I handed out questionnaires and tabulated responses as we toured the country, wheeling our way from boondock to RV park. Our interviews paid off in the form of invaluable travel tips, advice and in-depth experiences from hundreds of RV enthusiasts. From this information and my own knowledge, I tried to cover just about everything you need to know about RV travel in Mexico.

Foreign Travel

For most people, a trip into Mexico—by any form of travel—is something special, something out of the ordinary. After all, it's a foreign country and it's a long drive. It's an even *longer* drive in an RV! When you drive or tow a heavy rig a thousand miles or more, you sort of like to sit there for a while before making the trip back, don't you? Therefore, it's no surprise that most RVers in Mexico tend to stay much longer than other tourists. Many stay the whole winter and return season after season. In large part then, this book is directed towards the longer-term RV tourist in Mexico. Yet any traveler, with or without an RV, long-term or short-term should benefit from the information presented here.

I make the assumption that most readers of this book are familiar with RV travel. Words such as *boondock* (to camp free of charge), *snowbirds* (who fly away from winter) or *fifth-wheels* (type of travel trailer), may appear from time to time, but I trust they won't be confusing to the non-RV owner. The term *gringo* is used in the neutral sense accepted by most people in Mexico when referring to a citizen of the United States. For most Mexicans, it's easier to say *gringo* than the tongue-twisting *estadounidense* or the inaccurate *norteamericano* (Canadians are also *norteamericanos*, and technically, so are Mexicans since we all live in North America).

This book tries to synthesize information, concepts and advice on traveling in Mexico that you cannot find in any other single publication. However, it isn't simply another travelogue or motoring atlas. There are any number of excellent travel publications that will give you full descriptions of travel in Mexico, places to go and points of interest for tourists. Instead, we focus on topics specific to travel by *recreation vehicle* in Mexico. Yet, equally important as learning about RV travel in Mexico, is knowing and understanding something about how and why Mexico differs from our country, and ultimately about the Mexican people and how we can relate to each other in friendly, positive ways. Hopefully, this book will give you a feel for Mexico and clear the way for you to enjoy your travels to the fullest.

Chapter One

A Mexican Experience

For most North Americans, the only foreign country they'll ever visit (or can afford to visit), is Mexico. But, what about Canada? Isn't Canada a foreign country? It's a separate country, true, but is it really a *foreign* country? Canadians and U.S. citizens look alike, mostly speak the same language, read the same books and watch the same television shows. With the exception of Quebec, most Canadians share a common culture and world view with their neighbors in the United States. It really isn't *foreign* in the strict sense of the word. Taking your RV to Mexico may be your only chance to enjoy foreign travel in your wonderful "home on wheels."

Mexico is different. It's a genuine foreign country, make no mistake about that. As a matter of fact, Mexico is even more foreign than most European countries you might visit. This is because Mexican culture and ambiance are a blend of medieval Spanish, native American and 20th Century civilizations. Beneath all this lies ancient Aztec, Zapotec, Toltec and Maya civilizations and their beliefs and customs. This merger of traditions, religions, philosophies and architectures makes Mexico unique among nations, its people unique among peoples.

Europe isn't nearly as foreign because it has been, from very earliest times, the main source of our values, beliefs and customs. Early European settlers in North America all but eliminated the native American. But in Mexico, settlers married into the indigenous population, blended their blood lines and accepted new approaches to life. That's why you see all those brown faces in Mexico.

When you travel in Europe (and Canada) things are rather predictable. People behave and react pretty much as they would back home. Customs and beliefs, in general, are the same. Not so in Mexico. Mexico is another world, an exciting cosmos of contrasts. Its world-view is existential and mystical, as opposed to our materialistic and pragmatic concepts. Mexico is as different from the mother culture of Spain as gold is from silver.

Mexico offers RV enthusiasts some real cultural adventures if they desire to take the opportunity to learn and participate. One goal of this book is to make you aware of the differences in Mexico, enabling you to step through some of the doors that can open for you and to enjoy your Mexican interlude to the fullest.

Taking Your RV To Mexico?

At first glance, it doesn't make sense to tow a tin box or to wheel a wide motorhome through narrow streets and over winding highways. Not when hotels are so inexpensive, and restaurant food so tasty and reasonable. There's no question that Mexican roads aren't nearly as good as ours, plus, facilities for parking aren't as plentiful or as convenient. So why take an RV into Mexico?

Many arguments against recreation vehicle travel can be made here at home, nevertheless, millions of Americans swear by RVs. Everywhere you look, you'll see these little houses on wheels toodling about the highways. Therefore, it should be no surprise that those of us who enjoy the concept of RV living "back home" also delight in adventures "south of the border." Ask anyone who travels by RV in Mexico, and you will hear the simple answer: "Because it's fun!" But clearly, RV travel in Mexico is a totally different game; therefore this book.

My first Mexico RV adventures began in Baja California about 30 years ago. Pulling a 16-foot Aristocrat behind our brand-new Edsel was a snap, at least as far as Ensenada. South of Estero Beach, it was a different story. There, the road abandoned all pretense of pavement and turned into a treacherous washboard, meandering tortuously toward La Paz. In those days, four-wheel-drive was the sensible way to travel most of Baja. (I did my share of that, also. Once I made it to La Paz in only 10 days, trailing thick clouds of dust and bouncing through potholes the size of bathtubs.)

On this first RV trip to Ensenada, over Christmas holidays, we quickly discovered how different RV travel in Mexico was from our usual apartment-hotel mode. For one thing, the people we met seemed different. Partially this was because RV travelers tend to be friendly anywhere you go; the level of friendliness is immeasurably higher in a trailer park than in the Hilton. Those of you who travel in RVs will understand. This is especially true in Mexico, where North Americans tend to stick together anyway.

Group Activities

In the United States, when RV parks depend on folks returning each season, park management often tries to provide something extra to lure you back next year. They'll have holiday parties, barbecues, potlucks, bingo, and just about anything they can think of to get people to mix and enjoy themselves. If you have fun, you'll remember the park next season. Since many of the better RV parks in Mexico are owned or operated by North Americans, it isn't surprising that the same kinds of things happen down there. When the park management doesn't offer the extras, the RV folks tend to do it on their own.

For example: during this first RV trip, our children were treated to a Christmas *piñata* party and we parents organized a terrific potluck. It happened that grunions were spawning that night, so, after the party, everyone went "grunion-running" on the beach, kids and all. We collected a bucket of the delicate-tasting little fish for next morning's breakfast. We made many new friends, and of course, made plans to return next year. Christmas vacations in Baja became a semi-tradition in our family until the children developed other interests.

We probably would have had just as good a time in an ordinary RV park in Florida or Arizona, but we enjoyed the extra adventure of being in Mexico. It was fun wandering about Ensenada, shopping for onyx chess sets, imitation leather purses, hideous green piggy banks and other "Mexican curios" to drag back as gifts for unfortunate friends. But it was different from our usual Mexican vacation, where we would rent an apartment or a house someplace like in Puerto Vallarta or Acapulco. It was a *different* kind of fun. Through the years, we mixed both modes of travel, enjoying both.

RVs in Mexico: Good and Bad Points

Recreation Vehicle travel in Mexico has a dissimilar flavor from conventional auto, bus or air travel. There are some good aspects about it and also some drawbacks. Let's check out both sides of the picture.

From my point of view (feel free to argue), the biggest drawback to RV travel is that we *norteamericanos* tend to cling together, choosing our companionship almost exclusively from among fellow English-speakers. Although we like Mexicans, we seldom mix with them.

We usually can't help it, because all Mexican RV parks cater to "gringos." You can be 99% sure that your neighbors will not be Mexican. This is true simply because RV travel among Mexican families hasn't caught on; rarely will you see a travel trailer or motorhome with a Mexican license plate. Therefore, most RV travelers' contacts with Mexicans are limited to shopping and asking directions to the bathroom. This isolation is exaggerated when parking facilities are away from the center of town (often far out on the outskirts) and away from the town's cultural and social activities. Since few of your RV neighbors speak or understand Spanish, you won't find much opportunity to brush up on your language skills.

On the other hand, those North Americans who live in neighborhood apartments or houses tend to make more frequent contact with their Mexican neighbors. They have greater motivation to learn the language, to make friends among the Spanish-speaking community, and to savor the cultural and philosophical differences. Neighborhood-dwellers tend to eat out more often, sampling native dishes and trying restaurants that RV folks seldom think about. In short, neighborhood living offers closer contact with Mexico and things Mexican than does RV living. It doesn't have to be that way, as we will see later on in this book.

RV meals are usually cooked "at home," using the same ingredients and recipes as you used back in Minnesota, so you may not get the chance to sample authentic "Mexican cuisine." (Mexican food is much more than a taco-enchilada combination plate, as far as I am concerned.) Many RV parks have "grocery trucks" coming through on regular basis, so people really don't *have* to leave the park until it's time to go back home.[1] Some travelers do exactly that: set up their rigs, put out the lawn chairs and umbrella, open a beer and— that's it for the season! This lack of cultural and physical involvement in Mexico is (to me, at any rate) the major disadvantage of RV travel in Mexico.

What Drawbacks?

Yet, what I consider "drawbacks" to RV travel in Mexico turn out to be "attractions" for others. Many RV enthusiasts emphatically disagree that these traveling conditions are "drawbacks" at all.

Why? Because, as one couple pointed out: "We don't come here for a cultural experience or to learn a new language. We are here to get away from winter, do some fishing and meet our friends who come here every year."

The typical couple returns to the same location every winter.

---

1 This is not to say that RV folks don't eat out. On the contrary, they contribute significantly to the local restaurant economy, especially with their customary weekend group dinners. Some places, it's wise to make dinner reservations on weekend nights.

They pull their 24-foot trailer from Nebraska or Missouri every January and stay two months. They drive onto the beach or into the park, back into the same space they had last year, and before long, old friends from last "season" are exchanging greetings and helping set up camp. "It's like a family reunion or a school homecoming," one lady said. "I look forward all year to seeing my friends again."

Is Mexico a Cheap Place to Live?

Living and traveling in Mexico, in general, is inexpensive. In our book CHOOSE MEXICO, Don Merwin and I show how it is possible for a retired couple to get by on as little as $400 a month. That's for an inexpensive apartment or small house, with part-time household help, not including automobile costs. Of course, most North Americans spend more than $400, but whatever their budget, they can live far better than they could live in the United States on the same money. So, conventional living in Mexico is relatively cheap.

Why is long-term living in Mexico inexpensive compared to the United States? Because you save on the two items that chew up most of your budget back home: rent and utilities. For example, when you pay $500 a month for rent in the Midwest, plus $250 a month to heat the place, you're $750 in the hole before you start buying food, clothing and beer. But in Mexico (where few houses need furnaces) you can usually rent an acceptable place for $200 or less, with utilities around $20. That's rent and utilities for less than just fuel oil bills back home! So, out of that $750 figure that you need to keep from freezing in Chicago, you could enjoy a nice place with a view of the beach plus $530 a month left over to buy groceries, gasoline, clothes, restaurant dining and perhaps an occasional weekend in Acapulco.

Another factor is low wages in Mexico. Many Americans living there hire a lady to do house-cleaning and laundry for about $5 a day, a gardener for $8. A skilled building tradesman earns from $10 to $15 a day.

What about RV Travel Expenses?

Sounds good, doesn't it? However—that big however again—while conventional living is by far cheaper in Mexico, RV travel is *not necessarily* cheaper. It can be, but most RV travelers report little difference between the cost of travel in Mexico compared to costs back home.

This surprises many folks who assume that everything is inexpensive in Mexico. You see, the major expenditures of driving or pulling an RV are gasoline and overnight parking fees (unless you boondock, of course). Gasoline costs about the same in Mexico as it does in Michigan. Mexican parks (because they have captive American clients) often charge as much as similar places in the United States. Hookup charges average between $8 and $10 a night, but can run $15 to $20. Oddly enough, in some towns, the cost of an overnight hookup is as high or higher than a room in the local hotel! (This is not true everywhere, but you need to know how and where to go.) Furthermore, the low cost of household help doesn't figure dramatically into the average RV owner's budget. So far, I have met remarkably few motorhome owners who employ live-in maids or gardeners.[2]

Also, since most RVers like to cook at "home" and use the same ingredients (often stocking up on groceries before crossing the border), the cost of meals isn't going to be significantly different. Your insurance costs and vehicle payments go on, no matter where you travel (and even if you don't travel). Additionally, you must have extra insurance for Mexico. Some people report spending as much as $30 a day just for insurance. Later in this book, you'll discover how to buy it more economically.

So you see, major RV expenses in Mexico aren't much different from expenses north of the border. As a matter of fact, when doing a survey in San Felipe (Baja Calif.), most people said that costs were just about the same as in Yuma, Ariz., the closest place in the United States with a similar climate.

Why Mexico?

"Well, why take an RV into Mexico," you may be asking right about now. But let's be fair: the same question can be asked about RVs *anywhere*. Depending on how you travel, they can be economical or expensive. I remember looking at a motorhome—the giant, deluxe size—and wondering if I could ever afford payments on something so splendid. When I asked the salesman what kind of gas mileage the monster delivered, he replied haughtily, "If you have to ask that question, sir, you can't afford to buy one."

He was correct. Anyone who drives an RV to "save money" must have some secrets the rest of us haven't learned. When you get eight miles per gallon (as I do), drive long distances, stay one night, then move on, RV travel can turn out to be a rather expensive proposition. It's cheaper to fly and rent a car when you arrive.

---

2 While they may not have FULL-TIME help, many RV people who stay the winter hire Mexican cleaning ladies once or twice a week. Teenagers pick up extra money washing trucks, motorhomes, etc. A friend tells of one lady with a 24-foot trailer who hires a cleaning lady as her way of contributing to the Mexican economy.

If you already own a motorhome or travel trailer, you don't have to be told this. RVs are for longer, more leisurely trips. That's when the cost-per-day drops.

When used for extended trips, doing some boondocking, and cooking most of your meals, there isn't a more inexpensive way of traveling, whether in Mexico or in the United States. Looking at it from that point of view, we can hardly expect it to cost significantly less in Mexico. It's already cheap, provided your non-driving days outnumber driving days by a good margin.

The advantage of RV travel is convenience and the fun of traveling this special way. Many places you can't even hope to vacation if you don't have a camper or trailer. This is true in the United States, and even more so in Mexico. Therefore, the good news is: if Mexico RV travel is done right, it can also be quite economical.

Bargains in Mexico?

Does everything cost the same as in the U.S.? Nope. Some things are downright cheap. Vehicle maintenance, for example. A few months ago, I had work done on my motorhome by a mechanic in Bahía de Los Angeles. He charged $5 to replace a thermostat (I supplied the part) and to repair the horn. This would have cost at least $50 back home, since my local garage charges $50 an hour to fiddle around under my hood. A year earlier, in San Miguel de Allende, I wanted some dents on my VW's fender rolled out and painted. The dent-and-body man studied the car, and shook his head woefully. "But, señor, you also need paint on this scratch, and on this one, and on that one. Also, your wheels are a disgrace, they're so rusted. They also should be painted." He shook his head again, saying rather defiantly: "I couldn't possibly do all of that work for less than $25." Of course, I agreed. Later I discovered that the VW dealership would have painted the entire car for $125! A similar quality paint job would have cost $800 at home. Later on, we'll talk about maintenance and Mexican mechanics.

Another area of bargains is food. Local food, that is. Imports are prohibitive. If you check prices in most Mexican *mercados* (markets) you'll find that some things are expensive, other items incredibly cheap. Vegetables and some meats, are bargains. Eggs are fresh and tastier than we get at home. Carrots are often so sweet that you'd think they had sugar added, and tomatoes are heavenly to those of us in California who are used to the leather-hard variety they sell there. Mexican steaks are tough and chewy, that's true, but they come from delicious, grass-fed beef. Pork comes from free-foraging pigs, who produce tasty and lean red meat rather than bland, white cuts from our penned up, forced-fed animals (which are also loaded with dangerous antibiotics).

Okay, load your camper with hard-to-get U.S. goods, but use them as treats for your friends who have been in Mexico long enough to run out of things or as gifts for your Mexican friends. For some reason, items like cornflakes and canned soups are worth their weight in pesos. (Maybe triple the weight, considering the 2500 to the dollar rate at time of writing.) Meanwhile, you can save by buying from *supermercados* or dealing with farmers in person at open-air markets.

Clothing is inexpensive, unless it's imported, but the quality isn't super. Shoes are real bargains in Mexico. Many name brands you buy in the United States are manufactured in Mexico, so the quality is the same, but the prices are significantly lower.

Traveling on a budget

Let's review some interviews with people living long-term in their RVs.

One couple lives full time in Cabo San Lucas, one of the most expensive areas in Mexico (for tourists). When asked how much they budgeted for living expenses, they replied: "We budget *all* our income. That's $300 a month!" Explanation: a few years ago, this couple went in with two other couples to purchase a piece of land in Cabo for about $6000. The large lot had electricity, water and a septic tank already installed, an ideal place for three RV pads. After a couple of years, our couple decided to hang up their battle swords and opt for early retirement. They towed a trailer to Cabo San Lucas and arranged for their bank to send $300 each month. "We've never regretted it," they said, "and we've never had a problem living within our $300-a-month budget."

Many other couples interviewed failed to live quite *that* economically, but several manage for under $500 a month, living with gorgeous beaches 20 feet from their back doors. "There's nothing to spend money on," said one lady who camps with her husband at Santispac Beach in Baja every year. "We pay $2.27 a day for parking (about $70 a month), and solar-electric cells on our roof charge the batteries to power our lights and our radio. A water truck comes around every week to fill our tanks with good water for $1.50." Fresh vegetables, clams, freshly caught fish and occasionally lobsters and scallops are delivered to their door by local people. Once a week they drive into town for shopping and dump their holding tanks. "We'd have to try hard to get rid of $500," the lady said. "And, we've been spending three months each winter here for the last five years."

Understand, these aren't people who *have* to live on such a tight budget, it's just that they've found a situation where they simply don't need a big cash outlay. When you aren't driving all over creation, you aren't paying out a lot of money for gasoline. These are illustrations of one particular style of RV travel. Other styles, of course, can be much more expensive. Some people would go bonkers "just sitting." I'm afraid that I'm one of those. Planning a trip and getting there are the most enjoyable aspects of traveling for me. As soon as I get there, I get busy planning my next move. As Robert Service said in one of his poems: *". . . for theirs is the curse of Gypsy Blood; They don't know how to rest."*

Other RV life-styles can be expensive by contrast. One park we looked at, for example, was quite spiffy, with an elegant, country-club atmosphere. There, you must buy a space (on a 30-year-lease) for $5,000, and then pay $200 a month for maintenance, utilities and the right to park your rig under a thatched palapa, whether you are there or not. Most people visit from two to three months per winter; almost no one stays year around except the managers. So, two months of winter vacation amortizes to over $90 a day, plus what it costs to bring the motorhome or trailer down and back. (That's figuring the lost income a $5,000 investment could return from Treasury Notes at today's interest rates.)

However, "buying" your space in a park can be a very positive thing, depending upon your situation. You can leave motorhomes, campers or trailers in your park (by bonding them) and either drive, fly or sail a boat to your Mexican winter home. It's your special hideaway, any time you need it. Where summers are milder and year-round living is practical, a permanent RV location can even become a retirement base. Later on in this book, we'll take a look at long-term living or retirement living in Mexico in your RV. It definitely can be done.

Chapter Two

The Third Mexico

One theme from the book *CHOOSE MEXICO* is that there are two different Mexicos: one for tourists and one for residents. The typical tourist on a two-week vacation thinks nothing of paying $60 to $100 a day for lodgings. This looks like a bargain. He couldn't find a similar vacation hotel this cheap at home. With such a short time to stay, the tourist is interested in deriving maximum enjoyment from each day; shopping around for bargain accommodations eats into vacation time. Cutting corners to save money wastes time that could be spent on a beach or in a cocktail lounge.

But people who intend to stay in Mexico for several months— those residents or retirees who rent houses or apartments, or who take RVs—can't afford a "sky's the limit" attitude. At $100 a day for a condo, most of us would head home before long. Somehow, we must match living costs with purses. Fortunately, inexpensive apartments and houses are available, making budget living possible in most parts of Mexico. Instead of dining at overpriced tourist restaurants, a resident or RV traveler chooses inexpensive restaurants (where the food is usually far better), or shops in local markets and cooks at home. Some couples report that they spend as little as $100 a month on food, most come closer to $150 or $200.

But a more important difference between the tourist's Mexico and the resident's Mexico is *social life*. Tourists associate almost exclusively with other tourists, and on an extremely limited basis. Mexican hotels bubble over with people from Des Moines, Duluth and Dodge City. Same at the beaches. Yet, tourists rarely talk to one another during their two-week sojourn; they socialize even less with the Mexican people who wait on them in hotels and restaurants or who sell souvenirs on the streets. Vacation time is too short to bother making friends. The typical resident, on the other hand, enjoys a full circle of friends, not only North Americans, but Mexicans as well. Instead of spending evenings alone in a hotel restaurant or bar, residents entertain in their homes and accept invitations from others in the community.

Why is this so? An interesting aspect of living in a foreign country is the way North American expatriates so easily join together into intimate social groups. It's as if they suddenly feel an instinctive need for the companionship of fellow Americans. People who seldom speak to strangers in the United States or Canada find themselves forging close, lifelong friendships when meeting in a foreign country. Newcomers are eagerly sought out and invited to dinners, to card parties, asked to join clubs and to participate in local activities. By taking Spanish lessons, doing volunteer work with the local American groups or just lounging around the town square, a newcomer soon gets to know just about every foreigner in town as well as acquiring Mexican friends.

This *Second Mexico* of the resident is a major attraction for living there. Inexpensive living is the icing on the cake, but only the icing, because most foreign residents of Mexico say they would live there even if it were more expensive than in the United States. That's how pleasant many people view the *Second Mexico*.

RV Travel: The Third Mexico

People who travel to Mexico by recreation vehicle enjoy yet *another* world. They combine the unique style of traveling by RV with the advantages of the residents' *Second Mexico* and come up with an exciting travel mode all their own: the *Third Mexico*.

Those of you who travel by recreation vehicle in the United States or Canada already understand the advantages of RV living. You have freedom to go where you want, and to stay and where and when it's convenient. You can park your rig in some of the prettiest locations in the world and enjoy the scenery from your living room window. Stay overnight if you like. Often for free. You aren't fettered by motel reservations or having to make a rigid, predetermined number of miles before dark. If you choose to have lunch beside a mountain stream, you don't have to drive about, hoping to find an appropriate restaurant. You simply park, haul out the folding chairs and fire up the stove. You needn't spend time in a restaurant, waiting for a table, waiting for a waitress to come your way, waiting for your meal and then waiting for the check. Probably you can't get a window table anyway. But with your RV, if you feel like it, you can lunch in a supermarket parking lot and take a well-deserved nap afterwards. Right?

Of course, it's the same in Mexico. Some of the most magnificent scenery is located where there are woefully inadequate tourist accommodations. But, with your RV, you simply back up to the beach, unload the boat, push it into the water and send your husband after bait. You can stay overnight, a week, or loaf away the entire winter in places that others only glimpse through automobile or bus windows as they speed past. The RV traveler has immeasurable advantages over the ordinary traveler, whether tourist or resident in Mexico.

Just as residents of the *Second Mexico* have that instinct for collecting friends in a foreign country, so do RV travelers. But there's a difference. The minute RV people step out of their rigs, they find an instant network of English-speaking friends parked on either side of them. Contrast this with people who rent a house or an apartment; they need to spend time building a social life. Instead of English-speaking people scattered throughout town, maybe one in the next block and another six blocks away, RV travelers encounter English-speaking neighbors just a few feet on either side of the parking space. My experience is that within minutes of "docking" there is almost always someone talking to you, offering information about the location, probably helping you get set up, whether you need help or not. We RV travelers are friendly folk.

All the Amenities

Tourists, during their three-week vacation, pay through the nose to stay at a hotel with "all the amenities." The more features the hotel offers, the higher the room rate. Should RV travelers care to go "deluxe" they have plenty of options in their *Third Mexico*." Listed below are some advertised features of one Mexican RV park (in Baja California):

- Full hookups, with concrete drives and patios.
- 20,000 sq.-ft. clubhouse, with rec room, game room and library.
- Dining room and cocktail lounge with ocean view.
- Swimming pool and spa, sauna and steam room.
- Volleyball, tennis and horseshoes.
- Laundry, grocery store, and satellite TV hook-ups.
- Walled in grounds, with 24-hour security.

Not too rough, is it? That's one way to go. The cost of this park is around $18 a day, compared to $100 a day that ordinary tourists might expect to pay in a hotel that offers such amenities. I have to admit that this is a bit *too* deluxe for my tastes. I am just as happy in an ordinary park or a plain beachfront location. My experience has been that the more spartan the parking facilities, the more friendly the tenants, and the more *Third Mexico* you experience. It's all a matter of what you prefer.

Getting Involved

In Chapter One, I mentioned the fact that RV travelers mix with fellow Americans so much that they miss many cultural adventures available to them. It doesn't have to be this way.

On our questionnaire, we asked: "What do you like best about RV travel in Mexico?" Almost all mentioned something about "the people." (We found the same thing on our questionnaires for our *CHOOSE MEXICO* book.) Typically, the reply to the question was: "the people—both American and Mexican." Or, "People are friendly everywhere." When we asked the question: "Do you feel safe traveling in Mexico," *all* replied "yes," and when asked why, many said, "People are friendly, always willing to help."

Now, curiously, very few of the respondents know more than a smattering of Spanish words, therefore their contacts with the local people couldn't have been very extensive. Clearly, encounters with tradesmen and service people are pleasant, for rarely do you find them otherwise. And, no doubt, if you smile at someone while walking along the street, you'll receive a smile in return; that's the way most people are everywhere. I believe that what happens is: when RV travelers pick up a sense of Mexicans being friendly, warm people, it's because they, themselves, are warm and friendly.

Therefore, if RV travelers like Mexican people without really having much contact with them, I submit that becoming involved will make the experiences even more pleasant and interesting. If you plan on staying in one place for a month or so, I urge you to think about broadening your contacts with the world outside the RV park. There are many opportunities—usually very satisfying—to further enjoy the *Third Mexico* by making Mexican friends. More about this later on.

Three Mexicos, Three Prices?

A common belief among North Americans is that Mexico has different price structures for different customers. That is, a tourist pays one price, while local people pay another. They believe a tourist is handed one menu, while a Mexican gets quite another. I've heard returning tourists swear they were charged more just because they were Americans. I won't argue that they couldn't be short-changed (that happens occasionally in the United States), but as far as there being two standard sets of prices, that's not the case.

In Mexico, many items and services are controlled by government regulations. Hotels and RV parks must conspicuously post a list of officially approved prices. In order to raise the price of meals, a menu must be submitted and approved by the Ministry of Tourism and decorated with the proper rubber stamp. (Mexican officials love rubber stamps.) Confidence in the system is very important, from the government's viewpoint, so they try to police these controls.

Now, obviously, it would be impossible to have inspectors teeming through the country checking prices. Violations do occur, often. Sometimes the law is blatantly ignored and price lists not posted. But where over-pricing happens, it's almost always in a sphere where competition would force prices up anyway. When a restaurant decides it can't make money serving steaks for $5.50, and raises the price to $7.50, that's a matter of business judgment. Should other restaurants find they can make money at $5.50 and don't raise the prices, they will get the customers instead of the higher-priced place. Soon prices drop back to the $5.50 level.

Repeat Customers Valued

All of the above is understandable. But the myth about separate menus for locals and foreigners is just that: a myth. Restaurants that depend on repeat business would be cutting their throats to over-price customers. Mexican restaurants and stores are just as anxious for repeat clients as are U.S. businesses— particularly the non-tourist enterprises—so they aren't going to overcharge you if they expect you to come back and shop again. If you look at most price lists, you'll find prices are usually *below* the maximum set by law, except in periods when inflation has heated up so fast that the bureaucracy cannot keep pace in granting changes. During times like this, price lists come down and it won't do any good asking to see them. Yet, it's during times of inflation that the dollar buys the most, because we get more pesos for the dollar.

There are some areas of commerce where you can expect to pay more than a local person. For example, suppose you ask someone to change the oil in your truck. I never bother to ask beforehand how much it's going to cost. I know that it's going to be a fraction of what I pay in the United States, even if I'm charged double. A Mexican might have to pay the equivalent of two dollars, whereas I'm asked for three, or maybe four. I'm sure that if I negotiated in advance, and insisted, I could save that extra buck. To me, that dollar means very little. To the man who crawls on the dirt under my truck, burns his hands wrenching the oil filter loose, then burns them again on the drain plug, and finally smiles proudly when the job is done—that extra dollar or so means a lot. It puts extra food on the table, buys something special for his kids.

Bargaining Game

That old game of bargaining is tradition in some parts of Mexican business life, as you've probably heard. Some businessmen feel obligated to quote an unrealistic price because they expect the customer to counter with an unrealistic offer, no matter what the asking price. Both sides sometimes feel cheated if it doesn't work out this way. If this seems strange, think about the way we buy new RVs in this country. The dealer's list price is about as realistic as Alice in Wonderland's Queen of Hearts. So is our Mad-Hatter counter-offer. It takes several hours of hard bargaining before you drive out in your new rig. Right?

It's the same way in Mexico, only it can be done even on small items. While living in Tequisquiapan, we had a maid who liked to shop for groceries. She always embarrassed us by bargaining over things like tomatoes or oranges when the asking price already seemed ridiculously low. Our maid would argue obstinately until she shaved a penny off the asking price, and then begin another round of arguing until the shopkeeper agreed that a dozen consisted of 13 instead of 12.

That's fun for Mexicans, but bargaining over pennies isn't enjoyable for me. What earthly difference can it make if I pay ten cents for a dozen tomatoes or nine cents? Now, if you're talking about something worth $100 and I can get a similar discount, I'm saving ten bucks! That buys dinner for two in most Mexican restaurants. But if you enjoy the thrill of bargaining, go right ahead, nobody will think it strange. (Whenever you see price tags on items, they probably mean it; don't bother to bargain unless it's a big money item).

What About the Future?

Since 1982, prices in Mexico have been extremely favorable for Americans. Sometimes prices are so low they are embarrassing. Two years ago, while doing an article on *ejidos* (government-sponsored farm cooperatives), I spent some time interviewing farmers and field workers. I discovered that many of them worked a ten-hour day for what I typically paid for lunch.

Everything is relative. Prices seem low to us because the dollar is so strong. Prices seem high to Mexicans because the peso is weak. On the other hand, Japanese tourists flock to the United States for their vacations to take advantage of the strong value of the yen. They are amazed, because everything is so *cheap* here!

How much longer can this favorable dollar-to-peso exchange rate last? Looking toward the future in my crystal ball doesn't help. I can't even see the past very clearly in it. Especially not after a couple of margaritas. But my guess, along with many other people's guesses, is that low prices will be with Mexico for an extended time.

In the past couple of years, prices (in dollars) have risen sharply, sometimes doubled. But this is due partly to the sharp decline in the dollar's value in the world money market. If this decline of the dollar is purely a political move, rather than a realistic valuation, then the dollar should rise again, and prices in Mexico fall in relation to the dollar. If this is not to be the scenario in Mexico, then we can expect a long, slow period of "gap narrowing" between prices there and up north.

Inflationary Hot Spots

There are inflationary hot spots in Mexico. Particularly overheated is the economy around the tip of Baja, around the "Los Cabos" area. There, prices have doubled and doubled again over the past five years. This is partly due to the influx of Americans bidding up prices. They are standing in line to buy condominiums for $150,000 which wouldn't fetch $50,000 in Florida or $25,000 in Acapulco. The hotel where I usually stay in San José del Cabo has risen from $4.50 a day to $23 a day in five years, whereas the hotel I use in Mazatlán went from $8 a day to $10. Both hotels are still bargains, compared to U.S. prices. The $23 hotel in Cabo would cost $60 in San Diego, and the $10 hotel (across from the beach) would be worth $75 in a similar location in Florida.

How does all of this affect RV travelers? Not a whole lot, actually. Since RV people don't patronize hotels, they couldn't care less if room rates go up. RV people cook many meals "at home" so rising restaurant prices don't matter as much. Gasoline and park rent cost about the same as at home anyway, so you aren't out anything there. As stated earlier, RV travel in Mexico costs about the same as in the United States. Therefore, should inflation skyrocket wages and prices in Mexico up to U.S. levels— squeezing out marginal American residents, driving away the three-week-vacation tourists—RVs can still enjoy their *Third Mexico*. After all, if they can afford to travel in the United States and Canada, they can afford to travel in Mexico!

Is RV Travel in Mexico Safe?

Here's a quote from Carlos Mélendez A., the founder and director of Monarch Camping Club (based in Guadalajara), concerning safety in Mexico:

"About safety, we can truthfully report that during the ten years our club has existed, none of our members has ever had a single serious matter to report . . . We have traveled with and assisted countless caravans, have camped in trailer parks or parked in streets, vacant city lots, sports complexes, on beaches, next to gas stations or in the open country (always in groups). This adds up to thousands of days/nights without a single tragedy."

Flying with the Green Angels

From Monarcas Travel Club: "If you are uneasy about traveling alone on Mexican highways, here's a tip. Cross early into Mexico and find out where the Green Angel base station is located. Get there by 7:45 am, and tell them you'd like to tag along with the patrol truck that morning. The Green Angels won't mind, but they will stop every time they find a broken down vehicle, and they drive 45 miles per hour. About halfway to the next big city, you'll meet another Green Angel coming from the opposite direction. Both will turn back to their original bases. Follow the one you meet, all the way to your night's stop. Is there a safer way to travel, anywhere? Most people follow the Green Angel only their first day into Mexico. After that, they travel faster by themselves, secure in the knowledge that the Green Angel they passed a while ago will eventually catch up with them in case of trouble."

Chapter Three

Is Mexico Travel Safe?

Since I was a teen-ager, I've lived in and traveled through all imaginable parts of Mexico. That's more than a couple of years. My unequivocal opinion is: I feel just as safe if not safer anywhere in Mexico than in similar locations in the United States. I've driven more miles south of the border than any North American I've personally met, and more miles than most Mexicans I know. I can state categorically that I have never been hassled, never felt threatened or uneasy, and I have never been treated with anything but respect. Yes, I've had my share of run-ins with traffic cops, but in each instance, I was willfully violating a traffic law (and didn't realize a cop was around to catch me.) No problem. I simply negotiate the amount of the fine, shake hands and we both depart with smiles on our faces.

When I say I feel safe, I mean personal safety. When you read about random shootings on our freeways and turnpikes—from New York to California—you might wonder where we are heading in this country. Recently, I read a newspaper report that a man was murdered because he was driving too slowly to suit another driver. The killer's girlfriend had to go to the bathroom, so he simply put a bullet through the victim's head to get him off the road. Extreme? Yes, but the level of hostility among U.S. drivers is frightening. One drive through downtown New York, Chicago or Los Angeles demonstrates this clearly.

Let's face it, the United States is a violent country. In Washington D.C., an average of one person a day is murdered. That's violence! According to *Time* magazine (2/5/89) 8,092 people in the U.S. were murdered by handguns alone in 1985. Compare that to just 59 in *all* of Canada, Great Britain and Japan for the same year. Isn't that astounding? That makes the U.S.A. *137 times as dangerous* as those combined countries! (Handguns are strictly prohibited in Mexico, by the way.) Murder and violence are so common here that a killing seldom makes the newspapers or TV news, not unless the crime was committed with extra ingenuity or against some famous person. There was a murder in my area last week. It made news on page 17. Page one was devoted to the question of property tax increases. Yet, in Mexico, a crime against an American citizen not only makes headlines all over Mexico, but throughout the United States as well.

I've talked to several criminologists in this country, trying to get some kind of comparative statistics about crime in Mexico. Unfortunately, Mexico doesn't keep many statistics, so there's no way to make valid comparisons. But the criminologists agreed that the level of violent crimes is infinitely lower in Mexico.

Low Crime Atmosphere

When doing the research on this book as well as my other books on Mexico, we interviewed hundreds of North Americans living in Mexico, both in person and through questionnaires. Retirees and long-time residents overwhelmingly pointed to the low crime atmosphere as one of the attractions.

RV owners agreed. Almost every RV owner in Mexico who filled out a questionnaire or who consented to an interview said he or she felt perfectly safe in Mexico. That isn't to say that they aren't careful about not leaving valuables in plain sight in their cars, or that they don't lock their doors. You certainly have to do that in the United States. But, it's comforting to be able to walk along darkened streets at night without feeling waves of fear lashing at your imagination. It's almost like it used to be at home when I was a kid.

Travelers' Warnings

Not too long ago, the State Department issued a series of "travelers' warnings" about travel on Mexico's highways. The Associated Press immediately sent newsmen to the border to find out what was going on. Law enforcement officials knew nothing, neither did the insurance companies who cover American tourists. So, reporters went to the American Embassy in Mexico City to find out who had been robbed or murdered. They were told by the embassy staff that "we don't keep statistics." After intense pressure, the embassy finally released the names of a "couple from California" who had been robbed and murdered on Highway 15 (west coast highway).

Now, since murders occur with such alarming frequency in the United States, it shouldn't come as a surprise that they could happen in Mexico from time to time. Still, we don't issue travelers' warnings because people are murdered on U.S. highways, do we? But the interesting thing is: the murdered couple *weren't* American citizens. They were Mexican *brazeros* who had been working as field hands in California's Sacramento Valley, and were returning home "from California" with their savings. Needless to say, the reporters were miffed at the misinformation.[1]

Why the travelers' warnings? A government official in the Nixon administration, in an interview for the *San Francisco Chronicle*, supplied a possible answer. He spoke of the time he was in charge of "Operation Intercept," an anti-drug campaign involving Mexico. He told of how travelers' warnings and border crossing hassles had been used to put pressure on Mexico to conform to State Department policy that had nothing to do with drugs. Just a couple of weeks of bad publicity was enough to get the Mexican government to toe the line. Mexico cannot afford the loss of tourist dollars.

Regarding the last travelers' warnings, it seems rather obvious to me that they were imposed to punish Mexico for not supporting the State Department in its Nicaragua-Contra policy. I traveled through that part of Mexico immediately afterward, and talked to as many Americans as I could, and questioned Mexican law enforcement officials. I found no one who had heard of any unusual problems. But the publicity was devastating for Mexican tourism. American newspapers played up the warnings with huge headlines. Few newspapers printed the AP wire stories about the basis for the travelers' warnings.

Anything bad that happens in Mexico grabs headlines. Example: a few years ago, some Boy Scout campers at Punta Banda (Baja California) were robbed at knifepoint of some camping equipment. (It was never made clear whether the delinquents were Mexican or American youths.) This made headlines all over California, and presumably in other parts of the country. Yet thousands of robberies were committed around the nation that same day with no mention in the newspapers. The interesting thing is, that very same week, in Northern California, three campers were attacked as they lay in their sleeping bags, stabbed and rolled over the edge of a cliff. Two died, and the third, a young girl, was paralyzed (and remains so today). Predictably, front-pages featured the Boy Scout robbery and stuck the murder story on the inside pages.

It's the old story of "dog bites man" not being news. When certain crimes are common they don't make good headlines, but when it's *uncommon*, then it's news. What does that say about crime in Mexico?

---

1 Technically speaking, the Embassy was correct in that they didn't specifically say that the victims were U.S. citizens, merely that they were coming "from California."

Drugs and Crime

Once I asked a law-enforcement official about the drug problem in Mexico. He looked startled. "Drug problem? We don't have a drug problem! True, drugs are raised here, processed here and sold to distributors in the United States. No problem. But *you* have a problem, because your government permits you to *use* those drugs!"

It's a serious offense to be caught with drugs in Mexico. Very few people are willing to take the chance of going to prison, so drugs are simply not generally in demand or available. I've heard estimates that 80% of American crime is drug-related. If this is so, then the scarcity of drug abuse in Mexico explains this relative lack of crime, particularly violent crime, there. But there is another element: law and order.

Law 'n Order

The whole philosophy of law and order is different in Mexico from the United States. Up here, it's difficult to convict a suspect, because you must convince a jury of 12 people to vote unanimously for guilt. Even if a criminal is convicted, chances are he'll get probation, or at worst, a short sentence in an air-conditioned cell, color TV and recreation programs. In the United States, a life of crime is a viable way to earn a living. Beats working eight hours a day, according to many Americans.

Not so in Mexico. There, the accused goes before a magistrate and has to convince this *one man* that he is innocent. If he cannot, he takes the consequences. There is a system of appeals, but the point is, a jury system isn't part of the philosophy. Neither is probation and parole. Furthermore, should a person be convicted *twice*, he is classified as an "habitual criminal," and upon the third conviction, he is given 20 mandatory years in prison. No parole, no color TV. In many cases he must buy his own food and pay rent for his cell. Mexican taxpayers think our system of providing free room and board for criminals is a bit silly.

Three strikes and you're out! I'm convinced that this three-strike rule is why we see low levels of crime in Mexico. Juvenile delinquency and youth gangs are practically unknown. Few kids are willing to waste one of their three strikes on foolishness like spray-painting graffiti or fighting in public.

The legal system in Mexico is known as the *Napoleonic Code.* Used in most countries of the world, this set of laws does *not* presume innocence until proven guilty beyond a reasonable doubt (as we do in North America and Great Britain). People raised under our system often look with repugnance at the Napoleonic Code, but they cannot deny its efficiency. While occasionally an innocent person may be accused, the guilty rarely escape. Because of this code of justice, people tend to be very cautious that nothing they do might be interpreted as being suspicious. I'm not saying that this system of law is preferable to ours, but it seems to work better than ours. The way things are going, almost any system works better.

The Brother-in-law Syndrome

While I've never had problems in Mexico, I am forever meeting someone whose brother-in-law's cousin had some horror story to tell about his or her trip to Mexico. Now, clearly, bad things can happen anywhere; they certainly do happen up here. But the odd thing is, I've never personally met one of these brothers-in-law or cousins so that I could get the story first-hand.

A frequent tale concerns being stopped by "bandidos." This is funny, and about as likely as being attacked in Arizona by hostile Apaches. Bandidos and hostile Indians went out at about the same period of history. Some novice travelers become frightened when stopped by army patrols or customs officials as they check for contraband. Mostly, the soldiers are concerned about drugs and weapons, two things the government is fiercely determined to intercept. The soldiers are actually there for your protection. Any time a patrol is discourteous to tourists, the officer in charge is taking a chance with his career. The Ministry of Tourism takes a very dim view of things like this; the government refers to the flow of tourist dollars into Mexico as their "green oil pipeline" and are quite sensitive to any complaints.

I suspect what happens is that the brother-in-law's cousin becomes paranoid when stopped by a military or customs patrol, and immediately begins shelling out money, thinking that's what they want. All they really want to know is whether you're smuggling in guns or television sets, or bringing out marijuana. Moral of this story: don't give money to strangers who haven't done anything to deserve it. You probably should follow the same rule in the United States as well. I certainly do.

Getting Sued

Another horror story I've heard several times is about people being sued over an accident in Mexico. I hear people say: "You must be careful when driving down there, because someone will run into your vehicle, and then sue you for damages!"

This is absurd. When you hear someone passing this rumor along, you know that he obviously doesn't know the first thing about the Mexican legal system.

First of all, protection against liability is why you have insurance. If someone's car is damaged, the insurance company pays. Since they don't try the case before a jury as we do, you can be sure the insurance company isn't going to pay any more than it has to: the actual amount of damages. Huge settlements for damages and punitive assessments don't happen in Mexico; payments are limited by the actual losses. (You'll find comparatively few wealthy lawyers in Mexico!) Personal injury compensation is based on the daily minimum wage in Mexico City (about $4 a day right now) and is limited to a fixed number of days. If a person isn't satisfied with this, he can appeal the insurance company's decision, but it's the insurance company's problem, not yours. However, if there is an injury due to criminal action, such as driving under the influence of drugs or alcohol, or if a death occurs, the problem is more serious. Still, the problem is between the offender and the court; the injured party can't sue.

Where you can get into real trouble is driving *without* insurance. If you have an accident *without* insurance, you are likely to be arrested until you can post a bond to assure the police that you can pay for the damages. The reason for this is obvious, otherwise, you would be a fool not to skip across the border. We talk about this further later on in this book.

RV Travels for Singles?

Many singles who travel in the United States hesitate going into Mexico on their own. This is understandable, although those who do go report they have wonderful times. If you are single and feel like you don't want to try a solo RV trip into Mexico, there is a way it can be done. There is an organization for single RV folks, called Loners on Wheels (LOW). (See address in appendix.) This is a national club devoted to helping single people enjoy RV travels. Their newsletter comes out once a month and is full of club members' travels and proposed trips.

Occasionally the club will form a caravan for Mexico, but individuals don't have to wait. There's a section in the newsletter called TOURS/CARAVANS in which members place notices for intended trips and solicit other members to caravan with them. One thing the club is strict about is, that the club is for *singles*, and not for two people in the same unit. This isn't prudishness, it's just policy. Many couples have met this way, and there is a regular column entitled "Committed Matrimony" listing those RV campers who fell in love and fell out of the club.

Children in Mexico

In the winter—when tourists usually travel to Mexico—it seems that most RV travelers are adults, the majority of them retired. You'll see very few children because most kids are in school and can't get away for extended winter vacations.

This is truly a shame, because children not only have a wonderful time in Mexico, but they learn a lot. They gain first-hand lessons in economics (how international monetary markets work), Spanish, sociology, anthropology and geography. What better way to learn about foreign lands than to actually travel through them? If you have kids or grandkids you'd like to take with you, by all means, talk to their teachers and explain this. My granddaughter went with us on our last trip; her teacher loaded her with a stack of books plus an outline of lessons and homework for a two-month trip. In addition to math, English and spelling, the teacher assigned a daily diary and an essay on the cultural and social differences between Mexico and the United States. It was a wonderful learning exercise for all of us as we discussed these subjects, each from our own viewpoint and experience. She became the expert at peso-to-dollar conversions.

While she found few other American kids to play with, she soon discovered that English isn't necessary to make friends with Mexican children. She spent hours helping other tykes build sand castles, decorate coloring books or playing catch with the old tennis balls she brought along for gifts. Invariably, the children would begin pointing at objects and asking what they were called in each other's language. Since Mexican children play very gently and quietly, we had no worries about letting them have the run of the beach.[2] If you can possibly bring a child to Mexico, do it!

Driving on Mexican Roads

While I believe Mexico is personally safe, road conditions and accident potential are another story. Later in the book we'll cover the hazards of driving or pulling an RV over Mexican roads. Suffice it to say at this point, that people who drive safely in the United States and Canada, who never have accidents at home, will likely have the same experience in Mexico. Careful driving pays off anywhere.

2 The contrast between the way American and Mexican kids play is very interesting. American children are typically boisterous, shoving and chasing each other, laughing and shouting at the top of their voices as they play, and are very competitive. Mexican kids don't run about as much, and laugh quietly or giggle instead of screaming. They play gently, particularly with children smaller than they are, and favor cooperative games that don't involve physical contact.

In most parts of Mexico, local drivers drive slowly, sometimes excruciatingly so. The older the automobile, the slower it travels, in the belief that slow driving makes the car last longer. This is one of the best pieces of advice we can offer: slow down to a Mexican pace. The second best advice is: don't drive at night. Never, never. Chapter Four deals with this in detail.

Just as Mexicans are courteous to one another in social contacts, I find Mexican drivers equally courteous on the road. They seldom blow horns simply to express annoyance, they'll frequently pull over to allow you pass, and I've even seen some stop for pedestrians! (When a pedestrian, don't count on it, though.)

None of the foregoing remarks about courtesy apply to Mexican bus drivers. In answer to the question: "What do you like least about Mexico?" many included reckless bus drivers as their pet peeve—ahead of rough roads. Bus drivers are infamous for taking chances, passing where they shouldn't, pulling any stunt to try and make the schedule. I always get a little nervous when one is riding on my tail; I'll slow down and wave him around the minute there is a straight stretch where he can make it safely. I like to drive fast, but not *that* fast!

Mostly, you'll find courteous drivers. A few years ago, while driving a rental car in Villahermosa during a rainstorm, I went through a red light and slid into the rear fender of a brand new Volkswagen Rabbit. The damage was slight; in the U.S., probably less than $200, in Villahermosa, less than $20. But damaged it was, and unquestionably my fault. I must have looked awfully sheepish as I apologized and volunteered that the rental car was insured, because the driver and his wife both laughed. "Don't look so worried," the man said. "Let's see what the damage is." He inspected the dent and shrugged his shoulders. "Oh, that was probably there all the time. Forget it." We shook hands and he drove away, leaving me quite relieved. He apparently didn't think it important enough to stand around in the rain discussing it.

One place where I dread driving: Mexico City. I've never seen traffic congestion so thick, so gridlocked or so frustrating. When driving into Mexico City, I plan on entering and leaving before 6 a.m. on Sunday mornings, the only time I find the streets anywhere near deserted. Maybe you are braver than I, but my recommendation is to avoid taking your RV through Mexico City during rush hour traffic, preferably not through there at all! (There aren't any RV accommodations there, anyway.) There are ways to circle the city via the *periferico* (beltway, or expressway), and I urge you to study the maps and to coordinate your trip to not only bypass the center, but to do it on a quiet Sunday morning!

Chapter Four

Driving in Mexico

S o, you feel you know all about driving an RV, and can handle any situation? Then you shouldn't have any trouble driving in Mexico. The basic difference between RVs in Mexico and RVs on your own turf is the level of caution required. If you use common sense and drive defensively, you should be okay on any road. This holds true whether you're driving a conventional auto or an RV.

In the United States there is a comfortable predictability about road conditions. If something unusual lies ahead, we know there'll be a road sign or a flagman to alert us. If a gang of workmen is patching the pavement, a flagman will slow us down. If last night's flood washed away a bridge, you can be fairly certain that someone will have barricades and flashing lights to save you from an unscheduled dip in the river. Not so certain in Mexico. It's your job to drive defensively.

In the United States, when an animal gets mauled by an automobile in the night, someone mysteriously comes and takes it away. In Mexico, dead animals lie alongside the highway until they disappear by thoroughly disgusting processes. It seems like every mile of U.S. highway has somebody responsible, watching over it. Not so in Mexico. With taxes at a starvation level, the government can't spare money to hire well-equipped road crews as we do. The philosophy is: let the driver beware. I recall one time in Ajijic, driving along and noticing that a manhole cover was missing in the middle of the street. Concerned that someone might get hurt, I stopped at a nearby restaurant, and informed the owner of the potential disaster in front of his business. He shrugged his shoulders and said, "It's been missing for two years now. There's nothing I can do, señor; it is not my manhole."

The biggest headache with Mexican roads is the lack of shoulders. Where the pavement ends, the roadbed ends. Erosion sometimes takes away sand or soil at the edge, leaving a dropoff of from one to several inches. This is bad enough when driving an ordinary automobile, but when your vehicle is a wide motorhome or when you're hauling a 30-foot trailer, it becomes crucial to stay on the pavement. Surprisingly enough, a few miles of this and you become an expert. Your eye can judge to within an inch or so, precisely where your tires are. I just finished doing over 4,000 miles over typical Mexican roads, and my motorhome wheels never dropped off the pavement once.

Getting the Right-of-way

One of Mexico's driving customs works out to make driving somewhat easier. I often wish we had this custom at home. That is: the car in front of you always has the right-of-way. No matter how stupidly he is driving, it's your job to watch him and not collide with him. Simply assume that the driver in front is going to do something wrong at any moment, and you'll find yourself driving very cautiously, as you should.

Why does this make driving easier? Because the driver behind you is watching out for any stupid move *you* might make. If you make an illegal turn, or swerve sharply to miss a pothole, the guy behind you is supposed to give you room. Of course, coming from the United States or Canada—where we are responsible for the person behind us as well—gives us an edge on defensive driving. It is refreshing not to hear a claxonic chorus of angry horns after making a dim-witted move. The driver behind expects something stupid anyway, so he is neither surprised nor angry.

One important rule worth stressing is that a driver attempting to pass has the right-of-way. It doesn't matter if he is in gross violation of the law and/or common sense, once he starts to pass, you must be prepared to help him get around. Should an accident occur, you are just as guilty as the other car if you didn't yield.

Don't Drive at Night!

Lack of highway shoulders becomes critical when driving at night. Anyone who knows anything about driving in Mexico will caution you: *don't drive at night!* Darkness changes a beautiful landscape into a scary nightmare. No shoulders are the biggest scares; you can't tell if the pavement ends with a gentle stretch of gravel, or with an eight-inch dropoff. During the day it's easy to judge, but at night, particularly on a road without a white center-line, it's pure guesswork.

Not only that, suppose you were to suddenly get a flat tire? Since there is no place to pull over, you are stuck with making repairs in the middle of your lane. At night. In the dark. Hopefully, your tires are good and not likely to give out on you. But don't let this give you confidence. When *someone else* gets a blowout, they'll be blocking a lane in front of you. And if they neglect to put out any warnings, or if it happens around a curve in the mountains—well, you get the picture.

Another problem with night driving is animals on the pavement. Since most of Mexico's countryside is open range, cows, horses, burros and assorted livestock wander about freely. They love the highway because during the day it soaks up the sun's heat and by night it makes a wonderful, toasty place to snooze. When you encounter a one-ton black bull sleeping in the middle of a black asphalt pavement—at 60 miles an hour—you know how the losing bullfighter must feel.

Horses and burros are particularly dangerous, since they sleep standing up. They are perfectly balanced to flip up over the hood and to come sliding through the windshield—at 50 miles an hour—several hundred pounds of rawhide and bone.

Bandidos again?

If you drive in Mexico very much, particularly through the mountains, some day you'll run into a mysterious line of boulders blocking half of the road. Sometimes about 20 yards further on, there's another barrier of rocks obstructing your path. This isn't particularly serious in the daylight. You simply slow down, and when nobody's coming in the opposite direction, swerve around them. But at night—when oncoming headlights temporarily blind you—you can have problems. A 30-pound boulder can bend your tie rods and steering mechanisms into rather interesting shapes.

Where do these rocks come from? I've heard puzzled tourists speculate that perhaps "bandidos" placed the barricades in order to rob motorists. Oh, sure—bandidos again—sure. Remember my scenario about having a flat tire or motor trouble and not having a shoulder to pull onto? Well it turns out that Mexican truck drivers prefer to drive at night. (They're not only fearless but they make better time in the sparse, after-dark traffic.) They drive old diesels for the most part, and their fuel pumps and injectors are forever getting clogged with dirt or water in the fuel lines. They have to stop every once in a while to clean out the system. With no shoulder to park on, they're forced to stop on the pavement. They may or may not have emergency blinkers, but in any case, they want to be sure no one comes along and clobbers them from behind.

So, they walk back a few yards and place large rocks across their half of the highway to warn other drivers out of that lane. By making the rocks big enough, they ensure that the warning message won't be lost on an unwary driver who doesn't happen to see the message. So much for the bandidos. So much for you if you go driving through the darkness.

Another related problem is when the fuel pump balks while driving uphill through the mountains. Even if the driver doesn't place a boulder barrier across the road, he will place large rocks behind his rear wheels. This way, when he is ready to roll again, he won't have to juggle the clutch and brakes to get that uphill start. He simply lets the weight of the truck rest against the stones behind the wheels and he doesn't have to worry about rolling backward. But, when he gets underway, the stones are left in the middle of the lane for you to crash into in the dark of night.

As if all of this isn't bad enough, the buses roll at night and the drivers are bound and determined to make their schedule on time. When they come to a hill or curve, some of them turn off the headlights to see if anyone is coming. If they don't see any oncoming headlights, they'll pass, no matter what. They assume that you know the rule about giving right of way to a passing vehicle, and that you will slow, or stop to let them get around. But suppose there's a bus coming the other way without headlights?

By the way, in the cities, you'll sometimes see people driving with only their parking lights on. Ask them why, and they'll reply, "Because it's safer that way, we can see better without headlights glaring in our eyes." As kinky as it sounds, it makes sense. Think about it, you don't need lights to walk around most city streets, and you have no problem seeing. But unless *everyone* drives with low lights, I prefer to use my regular headlights. This shouldn't particularly worry you in the first place, since you aren't planning on driving at night anyway. Are you?

Have I scared you sufficiently about night driving? I hope so, because this is the only really dangerous thing about Mexico. Enough said about night driving. *Don't even think about it!* Driving daylight hours is pleasant, as safe and as leisurely as you care to make it. You won't miss any scenery and your trip will be much more congenial.

What do the Signals Mean?

You're driving along the highway, getting ready to pass this slow-moving truck, when suddenly his left-turn signal flashes on. This doesn't necessarily mean he's turning left. If there is no side road ahead, what he probably is saying is: "Okay, I see you, and I think it's safe to pass. If someone comes over the hill or around the curve, I'll slow down enough so you can get around me." Sometimes, a trucker will use his *right turn signal* to say the same thing. However, this applies only on the open highway. If you are coming on an intersection or when you are in town, a right or left-hand signal probably means just that. The most interesting signal of all is the emergency blinker, which means: "Watch out, I'm going to do something weird!" So, when you see both signals flashing, be sure and stay back until the situation clarifies.

The whole matter of signals can be confusing if you don't know the conventions. If an oncoming car flashes its lights and the driver gestures at you with an open palm or acts as if he is waving gnats away from his ear, it means that a traffic cop is sitting in his car just ahead of you. If a driver holds up the second finger of his hand and waves it at you, he is probably a fellow-American offering a critique of your driving.

Traffic signal lights are the standard kind—red, green and yellow—but sometimes they'll be suspended overhead, in the center of the intersection, so keep your eyes open for them.

I know a man who pulls a trailer with a passenger car, and who likes to bring his aluminum boat with him. On one trip he thought he discovered a perfect solution for carrying his boat. He strapped it on top of the car. Upside down, with the bow projecting out over the windshield, it streamlined through the wind and cut drag on the trailer. The only problem was, when he stopped at a red light, the boat stuck out so far he couldn't tell when the overhead light turned green. He had to wait until a chorus of honking horns urged him forward.

Roadside Signs

As far as stop signs and speed limit signs go, they often have little rationale for being. As a result, many drivers pay scant attention to them. This is where I get into trouble. Since there are seldom traffic cops around, I tend to drive what I believe to be a safe speed, regardless of what the signs say. Then, I forget what I'm doing when the cops *are* around. Do as I say, not as I do; it doesn't slow you down that much to obey the signs.

One important consideration when driving in town is the system of one-way streets and directional arrows. These signs are usually posted on the corner of a building, almost never on sign-posts as we anticipate. Sometimes they are difficult to locate, but you'd better get used to looking for them, because a cop won't accept the excuse: "I didn't see the arrow!" The arrows show two things: The direction of traffic, and who has the right-of-way at that intersection. If the arrow you see on the corner facing you is red, then you must stop for cross traffic. If it is black, it means the first car in the intersection has the right-of-way, and if it is green, then cross traffic should stop for you. Don't count on it though. Always approach these intersections ready to stop; you never know if the other vehicle is driven by a tourist who doesn't know how to read the arrows.

Important: when you see a large "E" with a line slashing

through it, that means "no parking." It doesn't matter if others are parked there; don't park there yourself. Before long, a cop will amble along with a screwdriver and pliers and begin removing *placas* (license plates). Then you have to go to the police station and pay a small fine. The inconvenience causes more aggravation than the fine.

VADO is another sign you are likely to see in the desert. This is a dip in the highway to allow water to cross during infrequent rainstorms. (Cheaper than building a bridge.) During dry weather, they don't mean a thing, but in a rainstorm, be very cautious. Sometimes there are measuring devices that look like yardsticks that indicate how deep the water is. If it's too deep, just wait. The water can go down as quickly as it rises. Rushing water is dangerous as it sweeps through a vado.

One more important sign: *TOPES*. You will see this sign often at the entrance to small towns and villages. This is a warning that there are speed bumps installed across the road to slow down traffic. Pay attention, because these *topes* can jolt your teeth out of your head should you hit them at speed. There can be more than one, so be careful.

Traffic Cops and the Bite

Seeing a cop in your rear-view mirror, closing in on you relentlessly, always seems to get the old adrenaline flowing. It's no different in Mexico. For most people, it's even worse in Mexico. After all, they speak little or no Spanish, and the thought of spending time in a Mexican jail isn't particularly soothing. *"What did I do wrong? What is he going to do to me?"*

This has happened to me so many times in Mexico that I've lost my fear, but I can appreciate the feeling. A year ago, I was driving through Alabama when a siren pulled me over. I knew I had done nothing wrong, yet I was sure that the first thing the cop was going to say (after spitting out a chaw of tobacco) was: "Boy, you shore iz in a heap o' trubble." (That's what they say on TV.) I was shaking so hard I could hardly find my car registration. It turned out that my out-of-state license plate looked as if it were expired. "Sorry to have bothered you, sir," he apologized pleasantly as he waved me on. Whew!

In most parts of Mexico, chances are you won't be stopped unless you've definitely done something wrong, something so obvious that you can't or won't argue about it. The reason for this is, the cop is hoping that you will agree that you've been speeding, or whatever, and that you will give him the fine rather than insist on taking a ticket and paying the fine at police headquarters.

Now, most Americans become highly indignant when they

think about a cop accepting money and pocketing it. After all, cops in the United States are usually well-paid; to take money under the table for doing a job they are paid to do is the sleaziest kind of graft.

But police in Mexico are different. They come from the lower socio-economic classes, have little or no training and are pitifully underpaid. Typically, traffic cops earn about $80 U.S. a month. Nobody in his right mind can expect a cop to feed and clothe his family on that, not even in Mexico. It is understood that he will earn the rest of the money he needs to live on from collecting fines. Dr. Jorge Klor DeAlva[1] compares this to a waiter collecting tips to fill out his minimal salary. If you ask Mexican taxpayers why they don't pay their police a living wage, you'll hear: "What? Spend my taxes to pay a cop to chase speeders? Let the foolish speeder pay the cop's wages, not me. If I ever get caught speeding, then I'll pay. Not before!"

We may not like this, but that's the way it is in Mexico, and it isn't up to us to change the system. Raising hell with the cop will do nothing but aggravate the situation. Seriously aggravate it. What do you do when you're stopped? Act pleasant, determine what the problem is, and then decide whether to pay or not to pay. Generally, the cop is right, you were speeding, or you did miss that stoplight. If this is the case, it is easier to bargain for the fine and be on your way. If you insist on taking the ticket, the cop might keep your driver's license and/or your license plate until you pay the fine at the station. They're supposed to escort tourists to the police station to collect the fine rather than take the license plates, but this consumes a lot of time they could put to better use chasing speeders.

But do bargain. I always ask, "How much will this fine be?" And if it's anything over five dollars, I roll my eyes painfully, as if I've just been stabbed with a rusty pitchfork. Then I try to work him down to five bucks, or less if possible. When you give him the money, it's customary to make it unobtrusive. Either hand it to him with your license, or in a fold of paper. I try to keep $5 worth of pesos folded in my license, just in case. Yes, I could avoid all of this simply by obeying speed limit signs, but then, no one else does.

Sometimes cops are known to "invent" traffic infractions, or they greatly inflate the amount of the fine and stick with it. That's not playing the game fair. Should this happen, you should insist on taking the traffic ticket and paying at the station, either this or

1. A Mexican philosophy professor and the holder of a law degree from U.C. Berkeley

demand a signed receipt. If the violation is trumped up, the cop doesn't dare take you to the police station (*delegación*), nor will he want to give a receipt (*recibo*). Remain calm, reasonable, but insist on either the *delegación* or the *recibo*.

In the long run you'll save money and you'll be doing a favor for the next tourist who might be eyed as an easy mark. The official fines are ridiculously low when you measure them against what you might pay back home, so don't worry about paying at the police station.

According to the Attorney General for the Protection of Tourism in Baja California, the following fines are official for Tijuana and northern Baja.[2] Running stoplight, or driving the wrong way, $5.29; Speeding, $10.57; Driving with liquor on your breath (*aliento alcoholico*) $66.08; Drunk driving, $77.09. Just as traffic fines vary in different localities in the United States, so they do in Mexico. But you can safely use these figures as a gauge to see if you're getting ripped off or not. I've never paid more than $5 to a policeman for speeding (my favorite violation). But should a cop demand $30 or $40, then I'd insist on taking the ticket. So far, that's never happened. I've been guilty every time and knew it.

It would seem that there would be a great temptation to make arrests for no reason, but this seldom occurs (although they tell me this happens more often closer to the border). Why not? Because if the motorist feels he is innocent, he will demand a ticket and pay at the police station; the cop collects nothing for all his trouble. It's more profitable catching people who won't argue about the offense, but who will only argue about the amount of the fine.

Should you feel you are being hassled unfairly, or if you feel the fine is exorbitant, in addition to demanding the ticket, make a note of the policeman's badge number or the license plate on the car, the time and location, anything to make an identification of the cop, and make a report to *La Procuraduría de Protección* (the Attorney General for the Protection of Tourism). They take their jobs seriously, and you can be sure they will put pressure on the offenders. In Tijuana the phone numbers are: 84-21-81 or 84-21-38, from 9 am to 4 pm weekdays, or the national Ministry of Tourism "hotline" at 5-250-0123 (24-hours a day).

Insurance, a Must!

The best way to keep out of legal trouble in Mexico is to have Mexican insurance. (U.S. insurance isn't recognized there.) Yet, I am continually astounded by the number of Americans who dare

2. From *Mexico West Newsletter*, April 1989.

travel in Mexico without insurance. People who should know better. It's as if they think they are immune from accidents and from Mexican laws. You must have the liability insurance, and if your equipment is expensive, you should consider full coverage.

On my last trip to Mexico, my rig was parked next to a large, late-model motorhome, at least $40,000 worth of rolling stock. In the middle of the night, an electrical problem in a gas furnace blower motor started a small fire, and before the occupants realized what was happening, the blaze grew larger. The owner came pounding at my door asking for a fire extinguisher. (He hadn't bothered to buy one). By that time, it was almost too late. Other campers came running to assist with hoses, but the water pressure was too low to do any good (typical of Mexico). Within an hour, the $40,000 investment was reduced to a pile of twisted steel and ash. I tried to console him and his wife by saying, "Everybody I've ever interviewed has had nothing but praise for Mexican insurance companies. I'm sure you'll have no problem collecting on your loss." He looked at me with sad eyes, replying, "I didn't buy insurance."

Even more important, without liability and property damage insurance you can be in deep, deep trouble in case of an accident. All parties to the accident can be held in jail until fault is determined and the guilty party proves his ability to pay up. However, with insurance, the problem becomes the insurance agent's. As one travel writer puts it, "An insurance policy is your 'get out of jail free' card."

It's true, all motorists I've interviewed who have had dealings with insurance companies were satisfied with the way their cases were handled. "The agent found us a place to stay," said one man, "and he watched over the repairs to make sure everything was done properly." Another man reported that he had an accident in Mazatlán and the police assessed a fine even though the accident wasn't his fault. (It's common for both parties to be fined for "damaging the road.") The fine was less than $10, but when paying off the damages, the insurance adjuster wrote our friend a check for the fine. It seems that a clause in his policy covered legal expenses, including fines.

Of course, this is Mexico, and you can't always bank on finding an English-speaking adjuster (any more than a Mexican tourist might expect to find a Spanish-speaking adjuster in Omaha), so be prepared to use sign language and a dictionary. Better yet, don't drive at night, and you probably won't need an insurance adjuster.

Mexican insurance rates are controlled by the government, so ostensibly, all policies should cost the same. But this isn't necessarily true. Several Mexico travel clubs have persuaded insurance companies to grant low-cost package rates to their members. This is a real bargain for anyone who plans on staying in Mexico for more than a couple of weeks. As an example, the travel clubs *Mexico West* and *Vagabundos del Mar*[3] offer their members a one year policy with full coverage on a vehicle with a value of $15,000 for $165 a year plus membership fees of about $35. Compare that with full coverage in your home town! An extra $13 buys legal services: $500 lawyers fees, $2,000 in bonds and up to $50 in fines. $15 more buys emergency road service, towing, hospital and medical benefits, emergency transportation and emergency cash of $300. Liability alone is around $100 or less for the year. The *Club Deportivo* of San Carlos Bay (near Guaymas) offers similar coverage. There may be others (write and let me know). There are area restrictions on the insurance coverages; they're not good everywhere in Mexico without an extra premium (see chapter 16 for complete details).

Low Risks

I asked one broker, who sells this low-cost insurance, how such rates could be possible. It turns out that insurance companies have very good experience with RV owners. After all, we are mostly mature, safe drivers. We rarely use our rigs for drag racing or hill-climbing events. The comforting thing is that these low insurance rates are an indication of overall safety in Mexico; if there were a lot of accidents and claims, the rates would be much higher, you can bet on that.

Another factor is that Mexico doesn't have a legal system that awards enormous damages for minor accidents. As mentioned in the last chapter, there isn't an "adversary" type of legal system in Mexico, so insurance companies only have to pay actual damages. They aren't plagued with long jury trials and ambulance-chasing lawyers demanding compensatory and punitive damages.

Yes, insurance is important; the man with the $40,000 rig could have been covered for a full year for a little over $200. He could have been covered by Sanborn's or other companies for about $15 a day. Today he would have an additional $40,000 in his pocket.

Sanborn's, by the way, is my favorite American company for short term insurance, because they hand out marvelous log books which detail the road in a very accurate and readable manner. American Automobile Association also has great log books plus excellent maps, but you must be a member to obtain them for free.

3. See Chapter 15 for addresses and more information about these organizations.

Sitting in a Park

Many RV people insure their rigs only for the amount of time it takes to get to their destination. They feel that while it's sitting in the park, they don't need liability or collision, just good fire extinguishers. For someone who is going to be in Mexico for several months, insurance costs drop considerably doing it this way. Some tow cars behind their rigs, or bring bicycles or small motorcycles to run around town and to do their shopping so they don't have to drive the RV. When they are ready to return home they buy just enough insurance coverage to get them back to the border. Many larger parks will have someone in the park or nearby who can sell these one- or two-day policies. I still like the full year coverage for the price. Sanborns (and maybe other companies) offers special fire and theft coverage for trailers or motorhomes which are going to be parked for long periods of time and not taken out on the road.

What if You Have an Accident?

It's a good idea to make copies of the insurance policy, vehicle registration and the entry permit and keep them separate. In case of an accident, bring these papers out immediately. Next, call the nearest agent and put him to work. Call as quickly as you can. It's a mistake to walk away from an accident, leaving your vehicle unprotected, presuming that it's the insurance company's problem now. The insurance company may try to deny payment for vandalism or theft of parts if you fail to report within a reasonable time. One agent said the limit is six hours, assuming that you can get to a phone within that time. However if you're driving an RV and this is your living quarters, you aren't likely to just walk away from it as you might a rental car. If you have to leave, get someone to watch over it for you, even if you have to pay a small fee. Do not, under any circumstance, wait to make a claim until you return to the U.S. The insurance company can legally refuse to pay.

Gasoline Stations

Here is another place where legend has it you will be cheated. The fact is, gasoline stations in Mexico are no more likely to cheat you than those in the United States, not if you watch what you're doing. Of course, that's damning with faint praise. On my way back from my last trip to Mexico, an Oceanside, California attendant tried to shortchange me ten bucks! So much for honesty. Seriously, most Mexican attendants are honest, but you can be sure they remain that way by taking a few precautions. Follow my advice, and you'll never lose a centavo at a gas station.

First of all, always get out of your vehicle and watch carefully all that is going on. Even if you don't understand what's going on, you will appear to, and that's enough. Get out immediately and make sure the pump has been turned back to zero. By standing around with your calculator in your hand, even the most brazen con man will think he's up against an expert. Calculators are intimidating.

Secondly, *never* ask him to fill the tank. I don't know how it's done, but there seems to be a way to keep the meters running after the tank is full. I imagine that the gasoline recycles back through the hose, or something like that. Ask for a specific amount of fuel that you know will fit in the tank, then you can't be cheated.

If you're like me, and have a hard time converting dollars to pesos and liters to gallons at the same time, it's best to figure out in advance how many liters your tank will require. Then multiply the liters times the price of fuel per liter. (All stations charge the same.) Round off the sum to the nearest 1,000 pesos and order that amount to be pumped into the tank. The point is, by ordering an even peso amount rather than filling the tank, you see exactly how much is going into the tank, and you pay with the exact currency. There is no way to be short-changed using this system. On my last trip, I stopped at many, many gas stations during those 4,000 miles and didn't get cheated once. Not until I got back to California, that is.

One thing to be cautious about is when a gang of cute little kids come running up to pump the gas. They know how to keep you distracted with questions or jokes while they fill the tank. When it's filled, they quickly turn the pump back to zero before you have a chance to see what is going on. Then they'll quote you a price for more gasoline than your tank could possibly hold. Also, they could pump the wrong kind of gas, or even put diesel into the tank. Try to wave them away from the pump if you can, and wait for a grownup. Should this fail, keep your eye on the pump's gauge and insist upon paying the money to a grownup. A single youngster could be the regular attendant; it's the gang of lovable little tykes you have to watch out for. By the way, diesel fuel always comes from a RED pump, not silver or blue.

Washing your windshield is not a service of the station. But there are usually some boys hanging around who are eager to do it for you. If you don't want it done, simply say no, very firmly. But I usually let one wash the windshield even though it might not need it. This is the only way they have of earning money, and I don't begrudge them a quarter's worth of pesos. But don't let half a dozen get busy, or you'll be besieged by a half a dozen hands asking for pay!

Leaded and Unleaded Gas

There are two kinds of gasoline in Mexico and only one brand, the government's PEMEX. The unleaded gas is called Extra and the regular (leaded) type is called Nova. Occasionally, you'll find a third category, Nova Plus, which is also leaded but with a slightly higher octane rating. Since it has a lower lead content, the Mexican government would like to see it used for ecological reasons. But you don't see it often because Mexicans don't think it's worth the extra money.

Unleaded gas (Extra) is sometimes difficult to find, particularly away from a city. The problem is, most Mexican drivers prefer to use Nova because it is cheaper, therefore many small-town stations don't bother to carry Extra. Our recommendation is to keep your unleaded tank "topped off," just in case. Recently, because of pressure exerted by travel clubs and caravans, the government has ordered its stations in high tourist-traffic areas to carry more no-lead. It's a good idea to carry a gas can, just in case you run out because Mexican PEMEX stations almost never have one to lend. If you have a can and a siphon hose, you'll find Mexican drivers generally willing to let you borrow from their tanks.

The one time I ran out of gas in Mexico, several cars with U.S. license plates passed me by while I was hitch-hiking in the rain, gas can in hand. But soon, a couple of Mexican cars stopped. They flagged down other Mexican drivers until they found someone with a siphon hose and someone else with a can. Eventually, five cars and a truck stopped, while a dozen or more Americans cars whizzed past. One of the Mexicans crawled under my car to prime the fuel pump with gas (in the rain, yet), and before long, I was on my way. Nobody would accept money, not even to pay for the gallon of gasoline they gave me.

Carburetor Adjustment

Both the leaded and non-leaded gas are low octane, 80 and 87, respectively. I burn Nova (the cheaper, leaded gas) in my Dodge engine, and it runs fine. If it begins pinging going up hill, I mix in half a tank of unleaded Extra. The only problem I have is that the engine doesn't want to quit when the ignition key is turned off. This is easily remedied by adjusting the idle jets to a leaner mixture and cutting idle speed down.

These are easy adjustments, and can do no harm to the engine. If you are hesitant to do it yourself, then have a mechanic take care of it for you, or show you how. Having him retard the timing a little can help, although it might rob you of a little power. Some folks swear by gasoline additives, although I've never felt the need for them.

Mechanics and Repairs

Suppose something happens to your rig? The motor conks out, or the transmission begins howling in anguish. It's scary enough in the United States, isn't it? So what happens in Mexico? Fortunately, Mexico has some of the most ingenious, innovative mechanics in the world. They have to be. Otherwise they'd never be able to keep the all those old junkheaps running. There is a term used in Mexico, probably invented by some grateful motorist, called *Mexicaneering*. This refers to the imaginative ways their mechanics make repairs, without fancy tools and often without spare parts. They are masters of innovation.

A few years ago, a friend was driving his new Dodge van when a piston blew on a steep grade near El Rosario. Despondent, facing a long delay until the Los Angeles dealer could either bring down a new engine or haul the warranted vehicle back to L.A., my friend resigned himself to a boring three- or four-day wait. Then, a local mechanic approached him with a proposition.

"For $100, señor, I can fix your engine by tomorrow morning. If I fail, you owe me nothing. *Nada!*"

My friend didn't believe it could be done, but he had nothing to lose, so he agreed. Since there were no Dodge engines in the local junk yard, the mechanic removed a piston and connecting rod from a *Ford* and started to work. All through the night, using primitive tools, mostly files and whetstones, the mechanic toiled away. Sure enough, the engine was running by dawn, with old Ford parts churning about in the bewildered Dodge engine. When my friend arrived in Los Angeles, the dealer didn't believe him, so he disassembled the engine to see for himself. He was so impressed at this "Mexicaneering" that he cut the engine block away and put the engine on display as a tribute to mechanical innovation.

Every time I've had automotive problems in Mexico, I've been pleasantly surprised. First of all, surprised at the level of competence and native ingenuity of the auto mechanics, secondly, surprised at the mechanics' honesty and candor. I'm not used to that back home. One of the questions asked on the interview questionnaire was: "Have you ever had mechanical work done in Mexico?" and "What was your experience?" About half of the respondents had work done; none reported any bad experiences. Most said things like: "They fixed our problem with no delay— Very friendly people, and very inexpensive bills."

Miracle Workers

Another man told of traveling with friends, when one of his group broke a crankshaft on an almost new RV. They were in a small village near the ocean. The garage sent away to Guadalajara for new parts (a one-day wait), but, because it was fiesta in the village, there was another three-day wait until the vehicle was ready to hit the road again. "We found a great place to park our RVs on the beach and joined in the fiesta fun," said the respondent. "The total (including a $20 tip) for a new crankshaft, main bearings, oil gaskets, coolant and labor, came to under $300."

Other examples of mechanical repairs from respondents: a broken shock absorber mounting, $4 to weld on a new one; replace pressure hose on an automatic transmission, $5. New factory engine for VW camper, $475.

Even though mechanics seem to work miracles, you can help them by carrying spare parts and supplies you might need. Fan belts, oil filters and parts you might want changed can be tucked away in your rig for future reference. I always carry my own oil, because I like to know what quality I'm using. For $2 to $5, almost any mechanic will change the oil and filter for you. They'll drop whatever they are doing to pick up the easy money. Instead of customers being excluded from the garage area, as we are in the United States, you are welcome to watch over the mechanic's shoulder as he works. He might even ask you to help. And, instead of a "garage area," you could be working under the shade of an avocado tree.

Other considerations: many RV rigs use half-size tires, which are odd-size for Mexico. You'd be wise to carry a spare if you are going over some back-country roads. A gallon of antifreeze comes in handy should you have problems with the cooling system and need to replace the coolant.

Green Angels

No, they aren't heavenly messengers who've had too many margaritas. The Green Angels are employees of the Mexican government, whose job is to patrol the highways, looking for tourists to help. They drive bright green trucks (hence the name Green Angels) which are loaded with spare parts and gasoline. The drivers are experienced mechanics and at least one on each crew speaks English (or is supposed to). Should you have a problem, the Green Angels will change a tire, make minor repairs to your engine, give you gasoline, whatever it takes to get you rolling again. Their only charge is for the gasoline and parts; labor is compliments of the Mexican Tourist Bureau. Every major highway is supposed to be patrolled at least once a day. So if all else fails, just sit back and relax; one will be along before long.

But don't let this lull you into a false sense of security. Make sure your rig is in good working condition before you take it into Mexico. If you lose a transmission or something else serious, the best the Green Angels can do is help get you to the nearest garage.

Routine Maintenance

Since "full service" stations don't exist in Mexico, you're expected to watch crankcase and transmission levels yourself and to be aware of the water levels in your radiator and battery. Keeping proper air pressure in the tires will prolong the tires' life expectancy as well as improve handling on rough roads. As an experienced RV driver, you don't have to be told these things—just a reminder.

Everything is measured by the metric system in Mexico, including gasoline and air pressure. Gasoline is easier, since you will be stopping often and will have plenty of practice converting liters to gallons. Air pressure is another matter; it's harder to convert and you don't need it as often. If an air hose has a gauge, it will be in kilograms per square liter, or something like that. Below is a conversion chart to figure pounds-to-kilograms, but it's a good idea to carry your own air gauge with pressures in the traditional pounds-per-inch.

TIRE PRESSURE		
U.S.A		Mexico
LBS.		KILOS
22		1.6
24		1.7
26		1.8
28		1.9
30		2.0
32		2.1
34		2.2
36		2.3
38		2.4
40		2.5

GASOLINE		
GALLONS		LITERS
1		3.8
2		7.6
3		11.4
5		18.9
6		22.7
7		26.5
8		30.3
9		34.1
10		37.9
11		41.6
12		45.4
13		49.2
14		53.0
15		56.8
16		60.6
17		64.4
18		68.1
19		71.9
20		75.7
21		79.5
22		83.3
23		87.1
24		90.8
25		94.6

Getting Started

What kind of rigs are best for Mexico travel? There doesn't seem to be any "best kind." You'll see everything from VW vans all the way to $250,000 mansions on wheels. Each has its own advantages and disadvantages. The biggest advantage of VWs and older rigs is that parts are available everywhere and mechanics are very familiar with keeping them going. The pluses for the larger units are added comfort and room to entertain. The bigger the unit, the more difficult to drive. But that doesn't seem to matter, because you'll see rigs so long that it seems a miracle they can turn the corners of some narrow streets. Of course, there is a limit, because anything over 40 feet requires special permits enveloped in tangles of red tape.

Where I would draw the line is against taking *mobile homes* into Mexico. With few exceptions, dragging one of those monsters is highly impractical. Mexican roads were simply not designed to accommodate 12-foot wide vehicles. If you try to take one through towns where the streets were designed for horse and carriage some four hundred years ago, you'd better have a unit that bends in the middle when turning corners.

What to take

For those used to taking RV trips through North America, you pretty much know what you're going to bring with you. There are a few items which you might think about which are not so necessary back home.

For instance: you'll find that while many RV parks have washers, too often there are no dryers. (Or they haven't been in working condition for years.) So, bring a clothesline and plenty of clothespins. By the way, if you're going to be traveling a lot, it's handy to have a large plastic container to use as a washer. We put the dirty clothes in the container, and when driving fill it with water and detergent. When we arrive at our destination, all the laundry requires is rinsing and drying. Washing in cold water? Get used to it. You might want to bring a supply of detergent that you know works well with cold water. A trailer park with a washing machine is one thing; one with a washing machine *and* hot water is another. To find all that and a dryer that works too, well, that would be your lucky day.

Another good investment is in a 20-foot sewer line. For some reason, the hookups seem to be inconveniently placed (at least for my rig), either on the wrong side or about three-feet away from the end of my inexpensive 10-foot line. It's quite a nuisance having to disconnect everything and turn the rig around every time you need to empty the tanks. If you haven't already done so, stock up on holding tank deodorant. It's impossible to find in Mexico. No Mexican RVs, remember?

A Complete Tool Kit

When something breaks down and you need a tool to repair it, a wrench can be worth double its weight in gold. Even if you don't know how to make the repairs yourself, a set of tools will enable a good samaritan to help. Without tools even a simple repair job can be hopeless. My advice: bring a full set of tools.

Not just auto repair tools, but also the kind of tools you might need around the house. A hammer, pair of pliers, a small saw, a chisel, and other common tools like that can make life infinitely easier. If you decide to stay for a while, a hammer and saw, plus a few nails will permit you to take the initiative in building a ramada, or perhaps an impromptu outdoor table to hold the barbecue.

These tools needn't be the best in the world, preferably your "second best" set. Then, when you decide to return home, you can give some or all of the tools you brought to someone who has been particularly nice to you. In Mexico, tools are almost worshipped, particularly by those who don't have them and can't afford to buy them. Tools are unbelievably expensive there. The $4.89 socket set with a ratchet wrench on sale at our local auto parts store is never sold on special in Mexico. A set like that might cost $30—a week's wages for many. So, if someone does something real special for you, a few tools will be accepted gratefully whereas offering money might be insulting.

Other items that should be in your tool kit: a tow cable and a set of jumper cables. Maybe you won't need them, but they might come in mighty handy for helping someone else. If there's still room left, a set of emergency flares is a good addition. Should an emergency occur that forces you to drive at night, and should you have to stop on the highway, a couple of flares on the highway will make you feel much better. However, since you're never going to drive at night, maybe you don't have to worry about this. Right? In the mountains, flares are good even in the daytime, to warn drivers that you are stopped to fix a tire or to overhaul the engine.

Flotation Tires

A potentially valuable tool to add to your kit is an air pump, the kind that operates from your cigarette lighter socket. Why would you need it when your tires are in good shape? Because you might need it to make "flotation" tires should you get stuck in soft beach sand. Flotation is a trick four-wheel-drive people use. Here's how it works: when tires are up to 35 pounds of pressure they are as hard as rocks and might as well be solid steel as far as getting a good grip in sand. They just dig deeper. By lowering the air pressure, the tires become pliable and widen to place a wide footprint on the sand. The soft tire spreads out and climbs over the sand instead of digging in.

To determine how much air should be released, you measure from the ground to the rim of the wheel. For proper flotation, you want to retain 75 percent of this height. That could mean taking the pressure down to as low as five pounds. If this doesn't get you out of trouble, better look for help because you aren't going to get out by yourself. After you are back on solid pavement, be sure and replenish the air in the tires with your air pump. Driving very far with low pressure can damage them. If you didn't bring a pump, drive very slowly until you can fill up with air.

Water and Electricity

Other travelers often advise you "Don't drink the water." Until you find out differently, take that advice. Don't take a trailer park employee's word for it; ask some of the long-term residents to see if it's okay. Many parks have pure water, particularly in Baja and in isolated locations. The farther away you are from town, the less likely wells are to be contaminated.

Mexico's water problem stems from having too many people with septic tanks and cesspools feeding sewage into the water table. Eventually it contaminates the wells. Gradually, cities are coping with the problem by supplying good drinking water, but this requires tax money, always short in supply in Mexico. In some places, such as Mexico City, the situation is aggravated by frequent earthquake activity which plays havoc with sewer and water lines, permitting them to leak.

If you are one of those who have an efficient routine when

hooking up in a new park, best break some habits while traveling in Mexico. I learned this the hard way once. I backed into a nice space and jumped out to complete the docking. I automatically reeled out the electric cord, hooked up the sewer line and without thinking, connected the water hose. My wife discovered the mistake when she turned on the water and was treated to a display of detergent suds pouring from the faucet. The well in this case was located near the septic tank that collected the water from the laundry room. It took a long time to clean out and sterilize the tank when we returned. Meanwhile, we had to do with bottled water. More about the water situation in Chapter 11.

Electrical Hookups

As you might guess, the electrical hookups are interesting, to say the least. You never know what kind of receptacles you might have to plug into. Be prepared and have adapters that can fit either the three-pronged small socket or the old-fashioned two-pronged socket as well as the larger, heavy-duty three-pronged socket.

Electricity in Mexico is of the 110-120 variety, at least in theory. In fact, the voltage varies depending on the time of day you use it. During slack times, it can come pretty close to the 110 volt level, but other times it's far less. For most appliances, this won't make much difference, although your TV may look weird. Most RVs in Mexico use 12-volt TVs partly because of that.

Some parks—especially more remote ones—only have electricity for part of the day. Sometimes it starts at 7:00 in the morning, shuts off for siesta, and then comes back on from 5:00 to 10:00 in the evening. So forget about TV after that unless you have a 12-volt job. However, unless you have a satellite dish, there's no reception in remote areas anyway. By the way, some of the better parks provide TV hookups via their satellite dishes. And, it's surprising to see so many smaller dishes perched atop the rigs. Maybe not so surprising, considering the American addiction to TV.

Some of the most scenic locations—beaches and mountain settings—have no electricity at all. You must depend on your auxiliary batteries. Solar-electric cells are great for these locations. They come in panels that sit on top of your roof. Several people reported that the sun supplies more than adequate power to run radios, tape decks and even some television. This is important when you're spending several months on your own at a public beach.

While low AC voltage may not hurt most appliances, I've been told that exceptionally low voltage can damage the AC-DC converters (battery chargers) that many units use to keep the auxiliary battery up to capacity. You know low voltage is happening when you hear a loud buzzing coming from the converter instead of the normal low humming noise. I've heard this noise many times in Mexico before anyone told me it might be damaging. Still, my converter works fine, so I wonder if the damage is only caused to units that are on the verge of going out anyway? It doesn't hurt to shut off the 110 current when this happens.

What About Mail?

Mexico is a large country, with post offices scattered hither and yon. It's an absolute miracle that mail gets delivered at all, given the complicated logistics of the situation. The truth is, Mexican mail is very slow. You can figure two weeks or more for mail to reach your home town. The same for the return trip.

As you drive towards the border, on your way home from your trip, people will often hand you packets of letters. "Please mail these when you get to El Paso," they'll say. They know that they can cut down the delivery date by at least a week.

But, what do you do about receiving mail in Mexico? Unless you are planning on staying in one place for a considerable period of time, you had best forget about receiving mail. Simply tell your family and friends that you'll contact them when you return. But if you plan on staying for a time in a predetermined town, mail delivery is possible. You can get a post office box (*apartado postal*) for one thing. Or you can have mail sent to you general delivery. Tell your friends to mark on the envelope: *Lista de Correos*).

In some towns, names of all people who have mail waiting is posted on a wall. You check to see if anything has come. If you are expecting something important, it doesn't hurt to make yourself known to the postal clerk; that way he will remember you and be on the lookout. Frankly, I haven't had much luck with this system, but friends tell me they've never missed a letter.

What About Money?

Be sure to take a stack of dollar bills; they make good tips and people love them. There is something magic about a dollar bill, because the recipient can drop it in his dresser drawer, and tomorrow it could be worth more than it's worth today! That's the way a Mexican looks at it, at any rate. From our perspective, it loses value and besides, it doesn't draw interest in a dresser drawer.

Most businesses accept dollars, and closer to the border, prices are often quoted in dollars rather than pesos. But having pesos in your pocket is better because of confusion in mentally converting exchange rates. If you know the price in pesos, you simply peel off that amount and don't have to wonder if you got the right change.

Changing dollars into pesos is easy. It can be done three ways, at a bank, at a *casa de cambio* (a money exchange office) or in a store or hotel. Banks give the official exchange rate, which can be a fraction higher than a casa de cambio. But banks have restricted hours. Often they will cash dollars only between the hours of 9:00 and 11 a.m. Sometimes they won't change money until *after* 11:00 a.m. It all depends upon when the official rate is figured, then they close at 1:00 p.m. A *casa de cambio* has more flexible hours. Sometimes they are open on weekends. Usually the rates are slightly lower than a bank, but the convenience of not standing in long lines at the bank is worth it. And finally, stores often change dollars, sometimes at a higher rate than a bank; they do it to get your business. Of course you must buy something. If you exchange money at a hotel, or pay your bill by traveler's checks or dollars, watch them closely, because sometimes hotels offer the worst exchange of all.

Supermarkets often change money at bank rates or slightly below. I'm not sure why; it may have to do with needing dollars for buying foreign goods. This is my favorite place to cash money. It's fast and you don't have to hang around a bank. The last time I cashed money at a bank, I waited in lines for over an hour, and I figured I had saved 47 cents over what the supermarket would have charged to cash $100. My time ought to be worth more than 47 cents an hour. (Feel free to argue.) Banks, being government-operated, are very bureaucratic. Usually, you must wait in one line to have the transaction approved, then move to the end of another line to collect. For traveler's checks, be sure to have your tourist card for identification.

Traveler's Checks or Cash?

Whichever you prefer. For some mysterious reason, banks seem to pay a fraction more for traveler's checks, maybe an additional 10 cents on $100. Some stores will cash them if you buy something, but mostly they would prefer dollars or pesos. Personally, I prefer to bring all cash except for a few traveler's checks "just in case." You see, I watch television ads for traveler's checks, and according to the commercials, people are always losing traveler's checks. In airports, at the opera, even in hot tubs! But you never see anyone losing *cash* on the TV commercials, do you? Only traveler's checks. In all my years of traveling I've never lost any cash. Las Vegas excepted.

Firewood

If you're planning on doing a lot of beach boondocking, and you have room in your truck for firewood, pile some in. It's scarce. On beaches and the more rustic camps, there is nothing more satisfying than to have an evening campfire blazing cheerfully by the back door. It's magic. Strangers and friends alike begin drifting irresistibly toward the flames like moths toward a porch light. The problem is, Mexico is terribly short of firewood so many campfires never come into being.

"People don't know how to find firewood," remarked one experienced beachcomber. "They look for logs, and they look in the wrong places. Any logs near a campsite were burned long, long ago. The best place for wood is someplace they never think of looking. A dump, for example." He went on to explain that for some unknown reason, shipping boxes are often discarded in the local dumps. "They make fine firewood, and when broken up, they take up little storage space."

Another tip he passed on is that when returning from shopping in town, he takes side trips onto the many roads leading away from the highway. "Here's where you'll find plenty of brushwood. Sure, it's small, but I pick up anything that's thicker than my thumb, break it up and drop it into a gunny sack. By the time I return to camp, I have enough wood for a half-dozen campfires." As an aside, desert wood often makes wonderful barbecue coals, particularly sagebrush; it gives the meat a spicy flavor. Sniff the smoke before you drop a steak on the grill, though; some types of desert brush give off an odor of burning creosotes. Makes your steaks taste like roofing compound. Not good.

Legal Details

Since Mexico is a foreign country, expect some red tape to slow down your entry. Don't let this frustrate you, but at the same time, be prepared by bringing all the pertinent documents with you. To enter Mexico, you need a tourist card. This is free and can either be obtained in advance at your local Mexican consulate, or at the border. If you get it at the border, it's still free, but the man issuing it may hint that he deserves a tip. I usually give a dollar for each card he fills out. (It's not really a card anymore, but rather a folded piece of paper.) To get this document you need proof of citizenship, either a birth certificate or a passport is best. The passport can be expired; it doesn't matter. Sometimes they'll accept a voter's registration or other ID.

By law, you are supposed to carry this tourist card with you at all times, but I've never been asked for it, other than when stopped for a traffic violation. If they suspect that you're overstaying your limit, you could be asked. Try not to lose it, because it's your only proof of when you entered Mexico. Also keep the document you used to obtain the card handy (the birth certificate or passport) because they could insist on seeing that as well. Sometimes you need your tourist card to cash traveler's checks.

Being in the country on an expired tourist card can be a problem. So make sure, when applying for your card, that you get one with enough time for your stay. If you don't say anything, they will give you a 90-day tourist permit. If you might stay longer than 90-days, ask for the six-month card. It doesn't cost anything to get the longer permit, and who knows, you might need it, should you discover a new fishing secret.

Next, you need a vehicle permit. That's supposed to be obtained in Mexico. This could be right at the border, or it could be several kilometers away from the border. The reason you can't get it at the consulate is that your vehicle is supposed to be inspected before the permit is issued.[1] The man who pastes a sticker on your windshield usually expects a tip (I usually give him 50 cents) and the man who inspects your rig also likes a tip (another dollar). Since you are obviously a tourist, the inspector usually sticks his head through the door to see if you've loaded the inside of your rig with washing machines and TVs (favorite contraband). Since you haven't anything in plain sight, he will wish you a good trip and you're on your way.

Mordidas: The Bite

Don't be upset by border officials hinting for tips. It's the same principle as we discussed in Chapter Three with the police: they earn very low wages, and are expected to earn the rest of their living from tips. For very little you are getting good service and occasionally some smiles. After all, they could make us wait in line like their countrymen have to do. If you don't feel like tipping, by all means, don't do it.

A word of warning about entering south of Sonoyta, Sonora. Many California and Arizona travelers cross the border at Tijuana, Mexicali or south of Yuma. They drive along the border (a wonderfully scenic road) all the way to Sonoyta, then turn south toward Guaymas. To this point, no car permits or tourist cards are needed, because you've been traveling just a few miles south of the border, in the *zona libre*. No one asks for your papers until you hit the inspection check point a long way south. The bad

1. Some travel services offer to get the permits for you, you might check one of them listed in the Appendix.

news is (unless things have changed lately) they don't issue papers at the check point, they only check for contraband. To avoid a long trip back to the border, be sure and turn to the *left* at the Sonoyta junction (toward the U.S.) and pick up your entry papers and vehicle permits. The turnoff is marked, but it's easy to miss seeing the sign. I'm not aware of any other problem spots, but I'd appreciate readers letting me know if there are.

Make sure that your car permit is good for the same period of time as your tourist card. Six months is the maximum, and I mean maximum. If you are caught one day after it's expired, the vehicle could be confiscated or a heavy fine imposed. Should you decided to leave your trailer or motorhome there all year, you'll need to have it "bonded" with Mexican Customs. Many trailer parks can do this for you without any hassle. Should something happen to your car so that you can't drive it out on time, go to the nearest *Oficina de Turismo* (Tourist Office) and explain the problem. They can either give you an extension or bond the vehicle for you.

Shooting Deer out of Trees

The Mexican government is very touchy about firearms. It discourages Mexican citizens from having anything other than shotguns and small-caliber hunting rifles. I recall one evening in the mountains above Mazatlán when my car broke down and my wife and I spent the night with an Indian family. They set up cots in front of their little house and invited us to share some beans and tortillas with them. I asked them how they acquired their food, and they answered that what they didn't grow, they hunted. The husband showed me an ancient single-shot .22 rifle. He said, "I shoot wild pigs and rabbits, and I shoot deer out of the trees." I thought I had misunderstood about the deer.

The next day he showed me his hunting technique. With his low-powered .22, he positions himself near a large fig tree, a tropical type that grows on a slant with roots growing straight down from the trunk to buttress the sloping tree. It turns out that deer love to eat the leaves and fruit of this tree. They carefully climb up along the slanted trunk to feed. This gives my friend time to get off several shots before the deer has a chance to turn around and make an escape. He wasn't kidding; he shoots deer out of the trees!

No Handguns, Please

The point is, Mexico doesn't want high-powered weaponry floating about freely. Don't even *think* about taking a handgun in your rig! The police are really serious about this one, so don't speculate that you would get away with a little *mordida* if caught.

If you feel you can't travel without a pistol, then you should make travel plans that don't concern Mexico. Believe me on this one.

Shotguns are about the only firearms permitted across the border. You're better off to rent one when you get there, because the red tape involved is bizarre. Besides proof of citizenship, you need character references (in duplicate, of course) from your local police department, the serial numbers, calibers and makes of your guns. You will need 14 passport-size photos, and you can plan on several days visiting Mexican consulates, Military Comandante and Mexican Game Department offices. Fees, stamps and papers will cost at least $120 plus mucho time and energy.[2]

Boat Permits, Fishing licenses

When renting a boat and fishing gear from professional fishermen, they usually get you a permit as part of the fee. Taking tackle into Mexico is okay. But you will need a license. You can either get it yourself, or better yet let clubs like Mexico West or Vagabundos del Mar do it for you. One year licenses cost about $19 and a one-week license $10.

Sometimes U.S. Customs check for fish in ice chests, and if they find fish they'll want to see a Mexican license. If you don't have one, you will be cited for contraband fish, and the Mexican customs officers will cite you for fishing without a license. This is being done under a treaty between the U.S. and Mexico for wildlife conservation. So, get your license!

Boat permits can be obtained from travel clubs or from one of the several agencies that specialize in Mexico.[3] The cost is about $20 for a boat permit for boats up to 23 ft.; boats from 24 ft. to 36 ft. are $32. Anything over that is considered a yacht and needs special documents. If you'd rather not deal with a travel club or agency, and you have at least three weeks lead time, you can deal directly with the Mexican Department of Fisheries in San Diego. The downtown address is 1138 India St., San Diego, CA 92101. Be sure to call first to see what is required (619) 233-6956.

Making Telephone Calls

The Mexican telephone system leaves much to be desired. Making telephone calls home can be absolutely hilarious. I recall once, in a small village on the Yucatán Peninsula, trying for two days to get a call out. The village telephone was booked solid and the almost blind telephone owner was extremely slow. We had to write the numbers two inches high so he could read them.

Finally, at the end of the second day, my turn was next. While

2. See Apendix for people who can obtain shotgun permits for you.
3. See Appendix for addresses.

I waited, a lady tried to get me to use my turn to call information in New Jersey for her. "Ma'am, I've been waiting two days for this phone, and I'm not about to call New Jersey information!" Then, just as the caller ahead of me was about to hang up, he turned away from the wall and accidentally pulled the handset wire from its socket. Furious, the telephone owner chased everyone from his store and went out of the telephone business for a few days to sulk properly. I had to drive 38 kilometers for the nearest phone and get in line again.

Usually, when making a call, you look for a store or restaurant where they place the call for you. In smaller towns, telephone booths are unknown. Anyway, for years, the value of money changed so often, that there were never any coins to use in a pay phone. Finally, many, if not most towns stopped charging for pay phones; coins aren't worth the trouble of collecting them.

Sometimes it takes an hour or more to get a line through to the 'States, and other times, the call goes through as if you're calling across the street. The confusing part is the system of telephone numbers. You'll see them listed in the standard form: (555) 353-2242, or six numbers, hyphenated in pairs: 55-23-97. Sometimes a phone will be five numbers: 2-09-21, or 5-0921. Other times simply two numbers.

It can certainly be baffling. If calling from the United States, to Tijuana, for example, you can sometimes dial 1-706-555-1234, just as you would to make a long distance call in the United States. However, this doesn't always work. The operator may tell that you have to start the call with 011. Theoretically, every Mexican phone number should have a three-digit area code and a seven-digit number, just as we do. On top of that is the 011 international area code. The confusion arises when you discover that you needn't dial all the numbers when calling from a local Mexican telephone exchange. Since there aren't enough people in an exchange to need all those numbers, they only dial the important last ones and forget the rest.

When calling from Mexico to the United States or Canada, a good method is to place the call collect. That way you only pay a modest fee for making the call, usually not more than 50 cents or a dollar. But if you make it an ordinary call, you have to pay whatever the owner of the telephone claims the charges are. Hotels are famous for gouging on telephone calls. I understand that an AT&T credit card is also accepted. This also saves the extra charges of a collect call.

CB Radios in Mexico

Citizen band radios (CBs) have always been popular with RV

fans, partly because they are fun to pass long stretches of driving time by chatting with other rigs and truckers, and partly because they are an "ace in the hole" in case of trouble. Should you have a break-down out on the highway, there's a good chance you can contact someone and get help.

In Mexico they serve yet another function. CBs substitute for the local telephone system. In a country where you can wait up to two years for telephone installation, it's obvious that few RVs ever stay in one place long enough to have their own telephone. So, a CB radio becomes your telephone. When you set up in a park, instead of having a telephone number, you have a "handle." Each area has its own protocol for channel usage. Check with local RVers when you get set up.

The law in Mexico says that you must have a license for a CB radio. The law rarely has been enforced, but lately I've heard of people having CB's confiscated. Licenses can be obtained at any Mexican Consulate, and they cost a little less than $3.00, but few people ever bother to get one. My advice is to either go to the trouble of visiting the consulate, or else keep the CB out of sight when you hit the customs inspection. I've personally crossed the border numerous times with a CB and nobody's ever mentioned it. Maybe it's luck.

Taking Your Pet With You

Traveling with your pet is easy in Mexico, since almost all parks accept them. There are some legalities, however. To enter or return from Mexico requires a current vaccination certificate, preferably an International Health Certificate, form #77043, signed by a veterinarian to show that your pet is in good health. Mexico also requires a pet "visa" for dogs, although I don't know of anyone who's ever been asked to show one. It costs about $15.00 and can be picked up at any Mexican Consulate. Good idea to get one.

Bring plenty of pet food, because it's difficult, if not impossible to find. You see, in Mexico, pets don't generally enjoy "family-member" status as in the United States or Canada. Dogs, in particular, are regarded as nuisances and are fed table scraps, if at all; they mostly forage for themselves. As an illustration of how differently animals are viewed in Mexico, separate words refer to animal body parts and human body parts. For example, it would be highly amusing to refer to a dog's foot, for example, as *pié* (a human foot) rather than *pata* (an animal foot). And it would be highly insulting to imply that a person had a *pata* instead of a *pié*. Seriously insulting. You would be implying that the person is less than human.

Mexicans are often puzzled at our personification and love for pets. About the only attention the average dog gets is a kick in the rump if he ventures too close. They are careful not to get too close to strangers.

Keep Them Leashed!

Just as you are considerate about keeping your pet under control in U.S. campgrounds, you surely will do the same in Mexico. This is not only good manners and neighborly, but also for the well-being of your pet. There are some good reasons why you should keep your dog leashed, and not to allow your cat to run free.

The biggest reason is that Mexican dogs are seldom leashed and run almost wild. While they are very timid and cowardly around people, they can be quite brave with another dog, particularly if the strange American dog invades what the Mexican dog perceives as his territory. You'll notice Mexican dogs are not only lean, but often display multiple battle scars. As long as your dog hangs around the RV, he's okay, that's considered his territory and the Mexican animal instinctively respects this. But if he wanders afield and challenges some other pooch's turf, he'd better enjoy a good fight.

You'll notice very few cats in Mexico, at least not running around loose. I suspect that one reason for this is the multiplicity of dogs. So keep your cat inside, or on a leash when outside. Birds, by the way are not allowed. Well, you'll have no trouble bringing them into Mexico, but bringing them out can be impossible if you are caught at the border returning. Particularly serious is bringing parrots back to the U.S., because of disease control. Don't try to slip one across, no matter how cute he looks, or you will be in deep trouble with U.S. Customs.

Remember that your pet can get sick from bad water or food, just as you can. So make sure Fifi drinks the same water that you do. The last thing you need is a pet with "tourist trots" wandering around your vehicle!

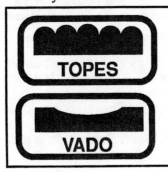

TOPES—Sharp bumps across road for speed control. Often used in small villages where there are no police. Very effective. Hit 'em at 60 miles an hour and you wish you had slowed down to five miles an hour.

VADO—A dip in the pavement to allow water to run across in place of a bridge. Used in dry, desert country where it seldom rains. During rainstorms, be careful, unless you are exceptionally good at treading water.

Road Lingo

alto-inspección	inspection stop	*highway junction*	empalme
aduana	customs inspection	*hombres trabajando*	men working
		licencia de manejar	driver's license
asfalto fresco	fresh asphalt	*no estacionar*	no passing
bajada	downgrade	*no hay paso*	do not enter
bordos a 100 metros	dips, 100 feet ahead	*no rebase*	no passing
		no voltear a la derecha	no right turn
camino en reparación	road under repair	*no voltear a la izquierda*	no left turn
camino ondulado	wavy road	*no voltear en U*	no U-turn
camino sinuoso	winding road	*parada*	bus stop
ceda el paso	yield right-of-way	*parado obligatoria*	mandatory stop
chalán	ferry	*paso superior*	overpass
conserve su derecha	keep right	*peligro*	danger
cruce de caminos	crossroad	*placas*	license plates
cruce de peatones	pedestrian crossing	*precaución*	caution
		puente angosto	narrow bridge
cuidado con el ganado	watch out for cattle	*solo derecha*	right turn only
curva forzada	sharp turn	*solo izquierda*	left turn only
curva peligroso	dangerous curve	*subida*	upgrade
despacio	slow	*título de propiedad*	vehicle registration
desviación	detour	*topes*	speed bumps
entrada	entrance	*poblado próximo*	town near
escuela	school	*vado*	dip in road
fin del pavimento	end of pavement	*zona de derrumbe*	landslide area
grava suelta	loose gravel		

(No Parking)   **(Parking Okay)**   **(1-Hr. Parking)**

Most traffic signs are self-evident. A picture of a trailer with an arrow, obviously indicates an RV park in that direction. A circle with "100 MAXIMA" means 100 km.-per-hour speed limit. A picture of two cars passing with a line slashing across them: no passing, and so on. But, there is one sign too often misunderstood: the no parking sign. The "E" stands for *"Estacionar"* (parking). This is one sign most frequently enforced in Mexico. Pay attention, or you'll be making a trip to the police station to collect your license plates.

Chapter Six

Parking Your Rig

Not too long ago, trailer parks in Mexico were rare. Not that many RVs were on the road. Mostly, people "boondocked" or stayed in hotel parking lots for a small fee. The few parks that were available were often rustic, "dry-camp" affairs.

Things have changed, with some rather elaborate parks accommodating an astonishing number of RVs. On my last trip to Mexico, it seemed like most of the vehicles on the road with U.S. or Canadian plates were RVs. Sometimes motorhomes and travel trailers outnumbered trucks and buses. With this much business, it's small wonder that new parks are constantly springing up.

The popularity of commercially-organized RV caravans has grown remarkably. People who are apprehensive about going on their own, feel better about going in a crowd. Several regular visitors to Mexico told me their first experience was by caravan. But once RV drivers see that Mexico travel is non-threatening and is easier than expected, they tend to return by themselves. The pressure RV caravans put on existing RV facilities is a major factor in park development. Parks are expanding and new ones appear, as if by magic, in an effort to satisfy the growing demand.

Commercial caravans range from Baja to the Yucatán—a great way to see Mexico by RV—although they are relatively expensive. More information on commercial caravans is found in Chapter 15. With a little initiative and a sense of adventure you can organize your own caravan with friends or a join a club, and go just about anywhere you want to.

But you don't need a caravan. You can "do-it-yourself" and save money while enjoying freedom from regimentation. If you're comfortable doing RV travel in the United States, you'll have a great time in Mexico.

RV Park Variety

The better parks are fenced, and many provide 24-hour security. Concrete pads, with sewer, water and electrical hookups are just about standard. Some have satellite TV hookups so you can watch your favorite game show or soap opera. Camping just isn't what it used to be.

For some Americans, accustomed to staying in clean, well-managed parks, the sight of a dirty restroom or an electrical connection that doesn't work, is a turnoff. But that's just how things are in Mexico. No matter where you go, it seems that *something* doesn't work, is broken, or was installed wrong. This is the land of *mañana* when it comes to making repairs or doing maintenance. *Mañana*, by the way, doesn't necessarily mean *tomorrow*, but rather "when I get around to it, possibly never." So, bring your sense of humor along and laugh when something doesn't work. It isn't up to you to change the system.

Boondocking vs RV Parks

Most guidebooks advise against camping along the highways in Mexico. I surely would advise against camping alongside U.S. highways as well. But, both in the U.S. and Mexico alike, there are some delightful "boondocking" places for those who want to get away from commercial parks or who want to visit places with no formal RV facilities. Sometimes a temporary boondock is convenient when several hours from the nearest park and in need of an overnight stop.

I have absolutely no hesitation to boondock any place in Mexico where others boondock. (There are locations in the U.S., however, where I wouldn't think of *parking* my rig while I ate lunch.) I feel perfectly safe in Mexico, particularly when there are 10 or 20 others parked for company. However, many wouldn't consider boondocking at home, and they won't be doing it in Mexico. If you feel apprehensive, perhaps you'd best not do it, and it isn't necessary, since there are almost always parks within easy driving distance. If you do want to boondock, just make sure to ask first. You might be asked for a small fee. In Chapter Seven and Chapter Nine, I'll mention special boondocking locations.

Many people prefer the more rustic settings to spiffy parks. In some parts of Mexico, particularly in Baja California, it's possible to simply choose a nice location off the road or on a beach and park. The Baja government permits boondocking on any of its "public" beaches, although there may be a $1 to $3 charge for the people who clean up the beach. Anywhere in Mexico, you can usually make an arrangement with a farmer who owns land, maybe next to the beach, to stay for a very small consideration. I know one family that brings Christmas gifts and groceries every time they come to Mexico and the farmer's family welcomes them with open arms, treating them as part of their own family. They park their RV in the yard in front of the farmhouse.

I met one couple from Oregon who travel to a small bay on the east coast of Baja every year and boondock the whole winter. The husband is into woodworking; some local *indios* taught him how to find ironwood and how to work it into superb carvings. He has his woodworking equipment set up behind his trailer in an improvised, outdoor shop. With a solar panel on the roof for electricity and a solar-powered desalinator for fresh water, they are just about self-sufficient. Some of these newer salt-water converters are advertised at 12 gallons or more a day, using the sun's energy to bring you fresh water. Others advertise one to two gallons. I'm not at all sure that they are worth their very substantial cost , the space they take up, and the weight they add to your RV.

Parking Lot Boondocking

On the mainland, particularly away from major tourist areas, RV parks are difficult to find, or non-existent. If you're just passing through a town, you probably are not interested in luxury accommodations anyway, not just for overnight and an early start in the morning. Many hotels and motels have special places where you can park and hook up to electricity and water. Sometimes they even have sewer connections or a dumping station. It's nice to have dinner at a hotel restaurant, have a few drinks, perhaps dance a bit (many of the better hotels have a small combo or piano player-singer entertaining in the cocktail lounge) then retire to your suite in the parking lot.

By the way, city parking lots are great places for urban boondocking in Mexico. They are always fenced, sometimes with 12-foot stone or adobe walls which shut out traffic noise. Guarded around the clock, they are centrally located and they are cheap. On our last trip, we boondocked in a downtown Los Mochis parking lot. For a small tip, the attendant kept an especially sharp eye on the motorhome while my wife and I strolled about downtown. Had we stayed at one of the local trailer parks, we would have been several miles from the center of town. We couldn't have enjoyed dinner, a movie and then dancing afterward without violating my rule against driving at night.

We decided to go to *Cañon de Cobre* by train for a few days, so we left our rig in the parking lot with full confidence that it would be watched carefully for the days we were gone. By the way, we weren't the only ones boondocking in that parking lot. Two other motorhomes and a small travel trailer were our neighbors.

Auxiliary Transportation

A fact of life about RV parks in Mexico is that they are usually on the outskirts. In smaller towns, this is no problem, because shopping is usually just a pleasant walk down the road to the village center. But in the larger towns and cities, count on being isolated. To solve this problem, some folks strap bicycles or motorbikes on the back of their rigs. This can be handy in some instances, but I'd be very leery of bicycling unless there were wide shoulders by the road. I'd want to get out of the way of speed-thirsty bus drivers and truckers. There's barely enough room for them to pass each other, much less space for me and my bike. The same thing goes for a motorbike, unless it goes fast enough to keep up with traffic.

The interesting thing about Mexico is its network of buses. Almost anywhere you are—on sandy desert roads or overgrown jungle trails—before long you'll usually see a bus come jolting and bouncing along. So, if you're stuck out in the country in an RV park and you need to get to town, just wait for the old jitney to lumber by. They're often ancient, rattling and slow, but they take you where you need to go. Often, there aren't any formal bus stops, you just wave your hand and the driver pulls over to pick you up.

It's customary for someone who is driving into town for shopping to ask if neighbors need anything from the store. In some parks you'll find grocery and vegetable trucks making the rounds. You might not have to unhook your rig as often as you might expect.

Your Own Place in Mexico

An interesting alternative to RV parks is leasing your own piece of land, then setting up your trailer or motorhome in your own private park. Since zoning restrictions in most parts of Mexico are zilch, there is often no objection to having a lot with a trailer or motorhome right in town. The advantage to this is that you have neighbors who can keep an eye on things should you leave your rig sitting empty for the time you're back home.

I know of cases where several families have gone in together and leased a piece of land. Since you only need one septic tank, one water and electric connection, basic expenses are cut sharply for each party. Placing a secure fence around the property isn't as expensive when shared by several people. Some people use their RVs on this property as an interim thing, planning on building a substantial home someday—for retirement. Others actually live there year around in their RVs.

Living in the heart of a small village is an excellent way to become a "part" of the local community. As a neighbor, you have a chance to get involved with "real" Mexicans. (This is also a super way to learn Spanish—by complete immersion.)

One couple I interviewed discovered that their neighbor's sister had two children living in a distant village where there was no high school. The sister couldn't afford to pay to send them away to school, so the children were doomed to end their education at an early age. The American couple decided to sponsor the children. They took them into their home and made sure the kids had the chance to finish high school. Since the children are bright, chances are they'll go on to the university. "Yes, it's crowded, but it's a marvelous feeling to know that you can make a difference in people's lives," said the wife.

Since many desirable RV-lot locations are found near the ocean where it is illegal for a foreigner to own land, you'll have to do a bit of soft-shoe routine to bypass the restrictions. That's why it's called a "lease" (*fidecomiso*) rather than a purchase. Actually, you must put up the purchase price of the land, so in effect, you're buying it. (Cash, of course, because time payments are unthinkable in a country where money loses value every year.) The rules for leasing land are the same as for houses. The land is purchased through a bank, then the bank leases it back to you for a small fee. Since you hold the mortgage, it is actually your property for the length of the lease. Leases are good for 30 years, and can be sold like ordinary property, or willed to heirs.

In some places, notably Baja, the law used to be that the property must be sold to a Mexican citizen at the end of the 30-year period. That rule was changed on May 17, 1989. Now, you can add 30 years to the length of the lease for a total of 60 years. That's a big change, because if someone did the "lease-buy" thing ten years ago, for example, then the lease only had 20 years to go, not 30. If they kept the property 10 years and sold it, the new buyers would have to sell to a Mexican citizen in another 10 years. But even if they hadn't liberalized the laws, I don't think this would be disastrous.The way Baja is attracting gringos, at the end of the lease, ten years from now, there would have been plenty of Mexican citizens willing to buy so they could turn around and re-sell to the next gringo in line. But this extra 30 years is a comfortable cushion, to say the least

Anyone considering buying property, RV lot or home, must go through a respectable lawyer and must do everything just right, or risk losing the investment. Before making any commitments, ask around the American community for a good lawyer. Don't just take the salesman's word for it that everything is in order. I've met salespeople who start selling property two weeks after they arrive in Mexico; they know less about Mexican laws than you do. See chapter 13 for more information on buying or leasing land.

Another way of having your own place: rent a part of a family's land. The problem with this is that any improvements you make to the land, such as a septic tank or cement pad, becomes part of the land, and you can never recover the investment. The advantage is that you needn't lay out any money in advance, and if the family lives nearby, they will take care of things in your absence.

Rating RV Parks

Trying to make comparisons of RV parks in Mexico is next to impossible. There are too many personal factors. The questionnaires asked respondents to name their favorite and least favorite parks. To our astonishment, parks that several people listed as their favorites were listed as the *worst* by others!

In an effort to develop a scientific evaluation system, I employed Teal Sewards to conduct an on-the-spot survey. Teal is my 11-year-old granddaughter and is very critical of just about anything that doesn't suit her fancy. Her ratings were based upon such considerations as: the presence of a swimming pool, its size and temperature, and whether the park had a satellite dish. Beaches with pretty sea shells raised the rating of nearby parks, as did the presence or absence of RVs with friendly dogs she could play with. She rated the shower and restroom facilities on a scale of *okay, I guess*, to an emphatic *yucko!*

The problem was, her ratings varied widely from mine. When I rated a park at "nine" because it was convenient to grocery shopping and there was a good bar-restaurant across the highway, Teal gave it a "one" because the swimming pool looked "abysmally gross" without a diving board. At that point, I gave up trying to do a scientific evaluation.

The list in the back of this book is simply a compendium of all information I could glean from a stack of RV newsletters, publications, guide books, questionnaires and personal interviews. If you take a look at the number of them—175 cities, towns and villages with 410 RV parks—you'll understand why I didn't visit all of them personally. However, during the research on CHOOSE MEXICO and its recent update, I made it a point to visit as many parks as I could during my travels, even when I was using rental cars. When passing through or stopping in a town, I made an effort to visit all facilities even when I wasn't staying there.

Chapter Seven

Fabulous Baja

If you ask anyone who has traveled Mexico by RV, chances are, one of their first trips involved Baja California. I have no statistics to back this up, but I believe more people travel Baja by RV than any other mode of land transportation. On my last trip (spring, 1989) I counted between 30 and 50 percent of the vehicles on the road to be RVs. They outnumbered trucks most of the time.

It wasn't always that way. Until just a few years ago there were no paved roads in most of the peninsula. Back then, Baja was four-wheel-drive country. The opening of the 1000-mile long Transpeninsula highway coincided with a boom in RV travel, so it was only natural that RVers investigate Baja. They loved it. They have been returning in increasing numbers every year since.

Just what is the attraction?

Because of its isolation over the years, Baja California has become a legend of mystery and romance for those who love rugged desert landscapes, formidable peaks of jagged granite and gorgeous stretches of empty beach. While parts of Baja are in a period of boom and construction, most of the peninsula is too harsh for people to live in permanently. Except for a few enclaves of civilization then, Baja is largely desert—unspoiled, unpopulated, natural desert. Ordinary tourists head for civilized places in Baja where they can secure a condo with hot and cold running water, electricity, air-conditioning and taxi service for shopping. Too bad. They miss the best parts of the peninsula that we RV folks get to keep for ourselves.

Fortunately for RVers, some of the most magnificent scenery imaginable lies miles away from plentiful sources of drinking water, not to mention air conditioning and taxis. No problem; RV's are self-contained. Some incredibly attractive beaches are enjoyed only by tent-campers and RV travelers who bring their own water and electric systems.

Beaches totally deserted 20 years ago, save for an occasional tent, now support small (and not-so-small) populations of pick-up-campers, travel trailers and motorhomes. In some locations, RVs line up along the beach—close to one another as if seeking company—with the Sea of Cortez splashing at their back doors. On some beaches, it costs a couple of dollars a day—providing someone comes around to collect—other locations are totally free. Where sufficient drinking water permits towns or villages to exist, Baja travelers find trailer parks ranging from primitive to country-club posh.

Desert and Ocean

Because the peninsula is so narrow, you're seldom more than 30 miles from either the Pacific on one side, or the Sea of Cortez on the other. Due to a series of fortuitous conditions, fishing is fantastic on both sides. Deep ocean currents well up from the depths of the Pacific, rich in nutrients that provide bountiful sustenance for fish. On the peninsula's Sea of Cortez side, strong tidal currents churn food-rich nutrients to support abundant sea-life there. The sea becomes a virtual hatchery, nurturing amazing varieties of sea life, producing huge game fish for the sportsman, and tasty fillets for our tables. Some of the largest shrimp in the world come from the Sea of Cortez, as well as swordfish, sailfish and giant sea bass.

You needn't be a fisherman to enjoy Baja's beaches. Personally, I seldom fish, but I do spend some time collecting (and eating) oysters and clams. However, I cheerfully accept any gifts of fish from neighboring campers who always seem to catch more fish than they can eat. The problem comes in trying to eat it all before the freezer gets full.

Whale-watching is another attraction, with people coming from all over the world to observe the unfrightened animals frolic in their natural environment. (January and February are the best months.) At Scammons Lagoon you can boon-dock and spy on the whales through your binoculars from the shore. For a set fee, boats take you out among the whales, who are as curious about you as you are about them. (Private boats are banned at Scammons.)

Often with small calves at their sides, the animals approach the boats without trepidation to stick their enormous heads out of the water and stare for a moment. At Laguna San Ignacio, whales sometimes come so close you can actually scratch their backs.

Baja isn't all activity. Many people are sublimely satisfied simply to sit in a folding chair by their rig's back door, read a paperback, and, from time to time look up and take in the gorgeous panorama of mountains, cactus and blue water. Here is a time and place for self-congratulation.

Land Time Forgot

Baja California is a strange place. A long, narrow peninsula, it juts out to parallel the mainland, stretching almost 900 miles south. Geologists say that originally it was part of the coast near where Manzanillo and Puerto Vallarta are today. A humongous earthquake fault follows the coastline, easing Baja steadily northward. Supposedly, the whole peninsula is moving north at the rate of an inch per year. To get where it is today has taken many millions of years. You folks in Los Angeles needn't worry, not just yet.

This long isolation from the mainland produced strange ecological effects. Flora and fauna, distinct from anywhere else in the world, evolved here. Zoologists and botanists pilgrimage to Baja, doing research in this wonderland of curiosities.

Yet, you don't have to be a zoologist or a botanist to enjoy Baja. You'll see cactus, trees and desert shrubs so distinct that you would have to be blind not to notice. You'll see "bojuum trees," looking like huge carrots growing upside down. There are "elephant trees," with wide, thick trunks that resemble elephant skin and that bleed an eerie red sap that looks like real blood when you stick a knife into the soft, flesh-like trunk. You'll see "smoke trees," salt pines, and ironwood trees. Numerous varieties of barrel cactus grow short and fat on the ground, while giant saguaros tower overhead. Hike just about anywhere and it's like walking through an outdoor desert museum. Many Baja California species can be found growing no where else in the world.

Even though the desert may appear void of animal life in the daytime, if you study the ground at your feet you'll know it's inhabited. A bewildering variety of animal tracks, from kangaroo rats to mountain lions, lead off in all directions, scribing signatures in the sand. Baja even boasts a population of wild burros who seem perfectly content to munch on desert shrubs, happy not going to work every day like their unfortunate domesticated cousins.

Traveling in your RV, you can pull over to the side of the highway whenever you feel like it, enjoy lunch, and then hike through this enchantment—stay overnight if you choose. People who travel by airplane miss so much!

Baja's economy, also isolated from the mainland, evolved its own characteristics. Only one highway crosses over to the peninsula, up north near the border, and the single railroad line ends at Mexicali. Therefore, all Mexican goods and merchandise must travel either by truck, across the narrow highway and down the peninsula, by airplane, or else by boat from Mexico. What cannot come from Mexico has to be shipped from the United States, and

naturally costs more. Therefore, prices and wages are higher than on the mainland and some Mexican consumer goods aren't always found in stores. Despite this, Baja California is still Mexico, and some prices are still bargains. Baja Californians are the same friendly people as you'll find on the mainland.

Introductions to Mexico

For many people living in the western United States, Baja California is the only part of Mexico they know. This is particularly true of Californians. They fondly recall long stretches of beach where large, tasty Pismo clams clustered so thickly just under the sand that clam forks hit "paydirt" just about anywhere. It was a great place for moonlit grunion runs, camping, fishing, soaking up sunshine while drinking Tecate beer flavored with lemon and salt. Pismo clams are scarcer today, due to too much commercial collecting and the proliferation of sea otters, but everything else remains pretty much the same.

Generations of teenagers from California towns like Pasadena, Fresno or Sacramento had first adult adventures in Hussong's Cantina in Ensenada. Hussong's is a landmark, a grungy, clapboard bar that boasts that it has changed nothing in the last 100 years but the sawdust on the floor. As a rite of passage from juvenile to young adult, teenagers flock there to order tequila cocktails or Carta Blanca beer, hopeful they won't be refused because of stateside technicalities like not being 21 years old. It's not all youngsters, though; you'll find a marvelous assortment of compatriots hanging over the bar or leaning elbows on the rickety tables. You'll meet fellow RV enthusiasts, yachtsmen stopping off on their way to Acapulco, stylishly-dressed Yuppies, rugged-looking 4-wheelers exchanging adventure tales of the back trails, as well as Ensenada residents wanting to practice English.

Yet, Baja is more than simply a place for tourists to let off steam. More and more it has become a mecca for season-long RV travel, RV retirement, and retirement in general. In recognition of this movement, and to encourage it, the Mexican government made special rules for North Americans who want to buy property here.

Long-term Living in Baja

A good reason for long-term RV living in Baja California is simple convenience. For someone living on our West Coast, having a trailer in Ensenada means being able to drive north to visit the grandchildren any time they choose. It means friends are more likely to come down for a weekend visit than if they had a similar place in Puerto Vallarta or Lake Chapala.

Another reason given by RV people for long vacations or retirement in Baja is the weather. When snow blankets Montana and cold winter rains plague Florida, Baja can almost guarantee pleasant, sunny weather. To be perfectly fair though, summers often heat up to pizza-oven temperatures along the inland sea. But the west coast, maybe 80 miles away, offers pleasant relief, with California-type summer days. This explains why so many RV travelers do Baja's east coast exclusively in fall, winter or spring.

Nevertheless, some *do* stay year around, even in places like Loreto, Mulegé and San Felipe. Particularly so in the Los Cabos area at the southern tip of the peninsula, where cooler Pacific waters make summer livable. Since the air is so dry, temperatures around 100 degrees are perceived by the human body as much lower. Personally, I love hot, dry weather; I feel comfortable and energetic at anything below 100 degrees. (I wilt at 80 degrees in humid Florida!). Over 105, on goes my air-conditioner and something cold comes from my fridge.

Friendly People

We've discussed two reasons for long-term travel and/or retirement in Baja: convenience and weather. There is a third reason, mentioned by almost all answering our questionnaires: friendly people. Both Mexican and American.

The local people openly welcome North American visitors. And in return, many RV people go out of their way to become involved, sometimes doing community service and charitable works. Many bring gifts of clothing and food for less fortunate families, Christmas gifts for children. This gives North Americans a very positive image.

For example: American businessmen in Ensenada have undertaken some rather innovative projects which serve the entire community, with beneficial consequences for the Americans living there as well. They sponsor Christmas pageants, Easter parades, a wine festival, children's choirs and musical ensembles, plus library and charity events to assist the poor and needy.

The local people recognize that American residents are behind these events. As a result, we are viewed in a much more favorable light than if we were withdrawn and snobbish. This feeling of goodwill rubs off onto us lucky RV travelers. An excellent English-language newspaper *Ensenada News & Views* is helpful in keeping residents informed and active in local affairs.

The Free Zone

The northern part of Baja is known as the *zona libre* or the *free zone*. The government deliberately makes this area quite relaxed as far as immigration and customs are concerned. It isn't necessary to have tourist papers to enter. You can usually cross the border without even saying "Hello" to Mexican customs and immigration officials. Don't misunderstand; this doesn't give you rights of residency or any legal status at all. By law, your stay is limited to 72 hours, even though the law is seldom enforced—not unless you are a troublemaker.

If you plan on buying a piece of land for your rig, or purchasing a trailer already in place, you'd better pay attention to this law. Many Californians own weekend places here and seldom stay long enough to need tourist papers or visas; after all, 72 hours is three full days. But, if you plan on staying longer, I recommend that you follow the entirely reasonable rules of the Mexican government. There are several ways to do this, all of which are covered in the chapter on legal matters. Getting a tourist card is simple, free for the asking. A multiple-entry card allows you to come and go at will. (Also free.)

Sure, there are people who ignore the rules and who are seldom if ever hassled, but most feel that if you are a guest in a country, the least you can do is to comply with its entirely reasonable rules.

Driving in Baja

My suggestion would be to pick up a guidebook with a detailed log which shows landmarks; that way you know exactly where you are at all times. Also, the extra information and history about the landscape makes for interesting driving. I particularly like Tom Miller's *Baja Book III*, AAA's *TravelGuide* or Sanborn's *Motorlog*.

The rules for driving in Baja are no different from other parts of Mexico: don't drive at night, have insurance and drive carefully. The roads here are average for Mexico, which in itself is an astounding development. Until a few years ago, most Baja roads were nothing more than rough trails liberally spotted with deep potholes brimming with powder dust. To drive this trail required day after day of 10-mile-an-hour jolting and bouncing, with bandanas tied across our faces, making us look like dusty bandits.

Today, driving the Transpeninsula highway is a piece of cake. But make no mistake, it wasn't designed as a high-speed highway—as road signs frequently remind you. Some stretches can be safely covered at 60 mph, other parts are best navigated in the 45-50 mph range. One factor that eases driving strain is relatively light traffic. The flow seems to be mostly trucks and RVs, with a sprinkling of passenger cars and an occasional bus.

You can drive long intervals seeing no other vehicles. Some stretches afford visibility for miles ahead and behind. When this is the situation, I relax and move into the center of the road, no longer bothering with keeping my wheels close to the edge of the pavement. However, when going through the many mountainous stretches, I slow down and drive as though someone were coming around every turn.

Driving Baja Alone?

In a recent article by Shirley Miller, entitled *Baja Alone?* *
Shirley describes her trip driving alone from San Diego to the tip of Baja and back. She reports, "Well, all I can say is that a woman alone driving the Baja highway from Tijuana to Cabo San Lucas is safer than she would be driving into downtown Los Angeles. Nary a problem with gasoline, my trusty 1980 Chevy pickup, the roads, or anything else, for that matter." Her only caution is that one should bring plenty of cassette tapes for the tape deck, because radio reception on the car radio fades rapidly away from civilization.

Shirley is director of *Mexico West Travel Club*, one of two very popular organizations for those who regularly travel in Baja. The other California club is *Vagabundos del Mar*. (You needn't live in California to belong. See chapter on travel clubs for details.) As mentioned earlier, by joining a travel club, you can buy insurance at a fraction of what it costs elsewhere.

These clubs also send out newsletters covering trends and

_____

* from *Mexico West Newsletter*, June, 1988

events in Baja and give updates on new RV parks and boondocking spots. If you are interested in boating and fishing or perhaps
in the social aspects of Mexican RV travel, then these clubs offer
more than just inexpensive insurance. They sponsor fishing con-
tests, tours, caravans, and they hold club get-togethers—both in
Mexico and in the United States (mostly California)—where
members can rehash and compare their Baja adventures.

Mobile Homes in Baja

Hauling mobile homes through Mexico is generally an exercise in futility. As mentioned in chapter five, mobile homes are far
too wide for Mexican highways, they cost more than new home
construction in Mexico, and they look out of place. Nevertheless,
in Baja, as far south as Ensenada (also to Guaymas, on the mainland), people have done some rather interesting and creative
things with mobile homes. Since it's four-lane highway that far,
transportation isn't out of the question, although not easy. You
can't move a wide load yourself; it's a professional job that requires warning cars front and rear.

Sometimes Americans will move a unit down from San Diego
and set it up with an ocean view. Next they construct a masonry
shell around the unit, complete with arches, ceramic tile inlays
and a tile roof. When finished it looks very Mexican, picturesque,
with little or no clue as to its origin as a sheet-metal box on wheels.
The advantage of this arrangement is that you have instant
plumbing, bathrooms, electricity and built-in appliances—all
working and easily repaired by buying standard parts across the
border in a mobile home supply store.

Still, it seems foolish to me. By the time you purchase a mobile
home, pay for having it transported to your lot, pour cement
foundations and put up a roof—you could have a contractor build
you a *real* house. With just a little more work, you could have the
fun of designing your own place. Good carpenters and brick-
layers in Baja work for $12 a day or less, so the cost of building a
house—a really nice one—is less than what most people pay just
for an average-size mobile home in the 'States.

God and Mr. Gómez

Readers of *L.A. Times* columnist Jack Smith's adventures with
Mexican plumbing and electrical connections will understand
how important these things can be. Smith managed without running water for many long months while his contractor, Mr.
Gómez, struggled with the plumbing. Finally, the long-promised
mañana came. Mr. Gómez proudly turned on the water connections. They worked fine! One small problem was: only cold water

flowed from the kitchen and bathroom sinks. Ditto the shower and the bathtub. On the other hand, the toilet had plenty of steaming, hot water.

Since there are few if any building standards or contractor license requirements in most of Mexico, electrical wiring usually looks as dubious as the plumbing, as if neither electrician nor plumber could have been serious about the whole thing. Yet, it always seems to work. (Well, maybe not *always*. Nothing in Mexico *always* works.) Be forewarned about this should you decide to buy or lease an RV lot and need to have wiring and plumbing work done. Doing anything like this in Baja or anywhere in Mexico isn't something to be undertaken by the impatient, the fussy, or by those who possess anything less than an enormous sense of humor.

Ensenada South

A few miles south of Ensenada is a small community called Punta Banda. It's mostly Americans, living in motorhomes or trailers, most part-time, some year-around. Some have rather elaborate places that evolve in an interesting manner. It typically begins with something like a 20-foot travel trailer. The first year, the owners lay down a flagstone patio and put up a picket fence. Since a 20-footer is a little cramped, the next year they add a living room so they can spread out a little, and perhaps a storage room. Then, as the grandkids start coming to visit, they tack on a bedroom or two as well as a larger bathroom. By this time, the old travel trailer is beginning to fall apart, so they pull it out and replace it with a kitchen. In its final stages, the compound rambles all over the place and has no relationship to its origin as an RV.

End of the Zona Libre

Near Punta Banda, the *zona libre* ends. From here on you need tourist papers. Sometimes there is an immigration station at Maneadero for tourist cards, but lately it's been closed. So, if you're planning on going south, be sure and stop at the border crossing and get your tourist cards (or have them processed there, if you already have the forms). Understand, it is *your* responsibility to get the cards properly stamped in. Should the Maneadero station be closed, you have another shot at it two days later, in Santa Rosalía (at the ferry terminal).

Alternatively, you might try the Mulegé airport (actually closer to Santa Rosalía than to Mulegé).

As the highway wends its way south, you'll pass through many little communities, becoming smaller and sparser as you travel farther south from Ensenada. You'll drive through wine-growing valleys around Santo Tomás and San Vincente, where there are RV facilities should you decide to stop over. But few people choose to spend time here; they push on for the more picturesque parts of Baja.

San Felipe, Gulf-Side

On the Sea of Cortez side of the peninsula, still in the *zona libre* part of Baja, is the town of San Felipe. It can be reached by paved highways either from Ensenada or Mexicali.

Why San Felipe? Those RVers who customarily winter in Tucson or Yuma have discovered that by driving a few hours south, they find all the advantages of Arizona or California desert environs, yet they enjoy the extra excitement of visiting a foreign country. Many RVers consider San Felipe a great alternative to winter sojourns in places like Tucson, Yuma, McAllen, or Palm Springs. The town has all necessary conveniences and is full of friendly people, both Mexican and RVers. The bonus over Yuma or Phoenix is the panorama of mountain and seashore. Fishing is wonderful, with sea bass and red snappers hungry for your bait. In Yuma you might haul a sluggish catfish from the muddy Colorado, and in Phoenix, the catch of the day comes from a supermarket deepfreeze.

Becoming a Tradition

The majority of the people we interviewed here return repeatedly. One couple, who drive their Ford cab-over camper to San Felipe each winter, says: "We used to stay in Arizona, near Parker Dam. But we enjoy San Felipe a lot more. Everything costs about the same here as in Arizona, but then, we don't travel to save money."

RV people in San Felipe have formed several social organizations, just as they would do if they were back home. Among others, there is a chapter of Alcoholics Anonymous and an organization called *Las Amigas*, which is a ladies club, meeting every Friday for luncheons.

Many well-equipped parks, most perched on the edge of the Sea of Cortez, cater to the several thousand trailers, campers and motorhomes that visit every winter. Everything you need is here, including visiting mechanics who will maintain and repair your rig right in the park.

Trailer space rentals vary from almost free north of town to moderately expensive in town and points south. Monthly rentals in a nice park generally run about $240 a month or $10 to $15 a day, some with palm-thatch palapas for welcome shade. One park offers ingenious two-story palapas; your vehicle parks in the shade with a covered patio beside it, with stairs leading up to a deck covered with palm-thatch. Here you take breakfast while watching the sunrise over the water's horizon, or sip cool drinks while enjoying colorful sunsets over the peaks of the Sierra San Pedro Martir to the west

About five to seven miles before you get to town, there are five small RV parks which aren't listed in any guide. There are no hookups, but many have thatch palapas for shade, and some have water. There are miles of deserted beaches here for strolling and clamming. Boats can be launched at San Felipe, but sometime it's difficult because of low tides and shifting sands. You can hire a four-wheel-drive truck to get you in and out, though.

Thirty years ago, San Felipe consisted of two unpaved streets, two bars, a gas station, a motel and a couple of RV parks. The beach was deserted save for some abandoned shrimp boats lying on their broken sides, slowly rotting away. About 500 local people lived there. Dirt streets were littered with broken beer bottles and trash, the highway with skeletons of old cars and junk.

What a difference today! When you first enter town, you are greeted by a tasteful set of arches and desert landscaping. The main streets are now clean and paved. Today, San Felipe has *nine* bars, ten RV parks, eight motels (some rather elegant) and a whole array of restaurants. The town even boasts of three banks!

Party Town

A previous drawback to San Felipe was the unruly crowd of bikers and dunebuggy enthusiasts who descended upon the town like a plague of mechanical locusts. They loved to drink beer and race their unmuffled engines along the beach and the main street. Happily, rigid police enforcement clipped the "party-town" image to a great extent. Conspicuous signs posted along the *malecón* (the beach-front promenade) announce that public beer drinking will result in arrest.

Around 14,000 Mexicans live here today, with about 3,000 Americans and Canadians who bring RVs for temporary housing.

At times, there are as many as 5,000 gringos in the area. A few heat-proof northerners stick it out all year, but not many. Pleasant fall, winter and spring make up for fierce summer weather by providing gloriously sunny days, perfect for enjoying the outdoors. You can be pretty sure it won't rain on your picnic here, because sometimes a year can go by without a drop. When it does rain, as anywhere in Baja, the desert suddenly bursts into a symphony of lush greenery and brilliant flowers. This is an unforgettable experience for those lucky enough be there when it happens.

To the average gringo who brings his rig here, San Felipe doesn't seem very Mexican. All neighbors come from the United States or Canada. Nobody really needs to speak Spanish; many never try. Some prefer it this way. Nevertheless, they are in a foreign country, and the opportunity to pick up some Spanish and make Mexican friends is there, should they care to participate.

Baja California Sur

The peninsula is broken into two political entities, north and south, with the territory of *Baja California Sur* only recently elevated to statehood. Technically, the state boundary line follows the 28th Parallel, just north of Guerrero Negro. But when RVers refer to "Baja Sur" they usually think of the part south of civilization, that is, anywhere below San Quintín. Below there, the landscape changes from scattered farmlands to pure desert wilderness. The highway dips into deep canyons of eroded badlands, rich in fossils and dinosaur bones, then up and over granite summits studded with bojuum trees, thorny cardón and saguaro cacti. From here, all the way to the tip of Baja, it seems that every half-hour of driving makes the landscape change completely— a treat for the eyes.

The pavement follows the old trail that was blazed by Spanish padres, two and a half centuries ago. El Rosario, El Progresso, Cataviña, and so on, each settlement along the road stands at or near the site of an ancient mission. Most of the mission buildings crumbled long ago under two hundred years of neglect—the villages only recently making a comeback because of the new highway.

The desert landscape around Cataviña is one of the most picturesque anywhere. Native *Washington* palms grace a rocky wash, and RVs can camp just about anywhere they please, as long as it's away from the commercial facilities here. From here the road runs down the center of the peninsula with the closest paved route to the sea at Bahía de Los Angeles junction.

Bahía de Los Angeles

Sixty-eight kilometers along a nicely-paved road brings you to a very popular destination for RVs and fishermen: Bahía de Los Angeles. With a backdrop of rugged mountains to the west and a large island, *Isla Angel de la Guardia,* to the east, Bahía is wonderful for quiet camping and fishing.

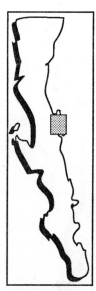

The island does a good job of protecting the beach from *chubascos* (unpredictable storms), making it an attractive place for boating. Many feel confident to venture out even in inflatable kayaks or motorized rubber boats when the water is calm. (Winds can be a problem here, though.) Others haul larger boats, for this is the next put-in place on the gulf south of San Felipe, and boasts two good cement ramps. Fishing is great, clams and oysters plentiful.

Three small RV parks line the beach, with several small grocery stores within walking distance. Overnight charges are $3 to $4 a night including cement pads and electricity. A real bargain, considering the ambiance. RV folks here enjoy their traditional lobster dinners at "Guillermo's," converging en masse, making weekend reservations advisable. By the way, electricity goes off about 10 p.m.

The water supply in Bahía de Los Angeles is quite inadequate; it comes from a pump sunk in a dry lake bed and the system verges on the unreliable. But the scarce water supply is good news for us RVers who love isolation and solitude, because there probably won't be any high-rises going up in the near future—if ever. Do everybody a favor and try to make it there with full water tanks so as not to put pressure on the town's supply. But don't worry about running out, because a water delivery man drives his truck around weekly to fill tanks for about $1.50. He draws water from a spring high on a mountain, and it tastes fine.

Mission Towns

Back on the main highway, and driving south, you pass through some fascinating towns: Santa Rosalía, San Ignacio and Mulegé, with Loreto farther on south. All but Santa Rosalía were also old mission settlements. Back when it was "13 Colonies" instead of the "United States," industrious Jesuit missionaries planted date palms, oranges, lemons, figs and grapes. When the King of Spain suddenly expelled the Jesuits in the late 1700's, they abandoned their orchards and vineyards along with the missions. Finding optimum moisture in the high water table, citrus trees, date palms and grape vines grew wild, forming a lush, jungle-like oasis.

For old-highway travelers—before pavement—these towns were a true sight for parched eyes after days of fighting desert dust and dry heat. Today, it's still a wonderful experience, to crest a hill and suddenly behold a lush green jungle before you. Both towns deserve a leisurely pause; both have nice RV facilities, with good drinking water.

In Mulegé, a slow-moving, tropical river runs through town, emptying into the sea two kilometers away. The river is fringed with bamboo, tall trees and massive date palms. A couple of trailer parks face the river and have docks for fishing boats. Two good ramps are available for boat launching. Since we're still on the Sea of Cortez and a long way from Pacific breezes, summers here are hot.

Visiting Santa Rosalía (between Mulegé and San Ignacio) is a special treat; it's like stepping back in time 100 years. The French mining company that worked nearby copper mines, built the town in the latter 1880's. It was a "company town" with homes and commercial buildings patterned after southern France of that day, looking like nothing you'll see anywhere else in Mexico. Santa Rosalía's arid climate preserves the old buildings remarkably. The pre-fabricated sheet-iron church is particularly worth a visit: it was designed and built by the same Eiffel who built the Paris Eiffel Tower. Apparently this church was built for display at the St. Louis world's fair, and somehow ended up being dismantled and re-constructed in Santa Rosalía. This may be the only one left in the world; were it not for the extremely dry climate, this one would have long ago rusted away. It still looks brand new.

Several respondents recommended the trailer park at San Lucas Cove, about nine miles south of Santa Rosalía. "The cove is protected and it was easy to pull our 12-foot boat up a bit to secure it for the night. The beach is about the

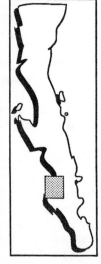

cleanest I have ever seen, and there were no flies," says Faye Holmes (Mexico West). Then a few more miles to the south is San Bruno, and a few more miles after that Punto Chivato. These are great camping places, with some of the prettiest beaches in all of Baja, where fishermen offer you first choice of their catch or try to barter scallops for T-shirts. Shrimpers anchor here to rest during the day (they do their work after dark) and you can sometimes talk them into selling some wonderfully fresh shrimp. According to Walter Mueller (Vagabundos del Mar), there are often 25 trailers on the beach at San Bruno, paying about $1 a night. An interesting side trip is to San Marcos island, just off-shore, where there is a lime plant in operation.

Bahía de Concepción

Several important boondocking beaches are found south of Mulegé on Bahía de Concepción. Perhaps "boondocking" isn't the right term, because sometimes 50 to 100 RVs bunch up together, almost as tightly as in a conventional trailer park. Offshore, a peninsula more than 25 miles long forms a narrow bay, and, like the island off Bahía de Los Angeles, this protects the beach from choppy waves. Camping is just about anywhere you please, wherever you can get down to one of the coves. Some beaches charge $2 or $3 a day, others are free.

Fishing, clamming and swimming are the order of the day. Butter clams can be gathered by the bucketful simply by running your hands through the sand, right next to the shore. (Tip: they are just an inch or less beneath the surface of the pebbly sand. Gently sift for them.) A grocery truck comes through frequently (sometimes once or twice a day), and the living is easy. Many people stay the entire winter, setting up camp complete with palm thatched ramadas and elaborate patios which invite spontaneous social get-togethers.

Loreto, Baja's Oldest Town

To the south is Loreto, the last place to launch a boat until you reach La Paz. Several regular RV facilities handle the RV and boating crowd, and good launching facilities are here. Like the favorite beaches farther north, Loreto is also protected by an offshore island (Isla del Carmen).

This place has been a fishing mecca for years. Before the highway, many fishermen flew in and stayed in primitive accom-

modations, with burlap cots for beds. Today, a steady stream of
RVs, dragging boats behind them, make the trek each winter.
From what I hear, the fishing is still excellent, although when I
was there last, it was raining and fish weren't biting. A local
fisherman explained that fish in Baja don't bite when it's raining
because they lose their appetite when they get wet. Or something
like that.

Loreto, the oldest town in Baja, was originally a mission and
then first capital of Baja. A series of hurricanes destroyed most
older buildings, so things are more or less recent. Some fine
boondocking beaches are found to the south, places where fishing
for yellowtail and collecting clams and scallops are tops.

Puerto San Carlos

A place seldom listed in guidebooks, but highly praised by
Baja travelers is Puerto San Carlos. West of Ciudad Constitución,

off Highway 22, a paved road runs through hilly
desert terrain to Magdelana Bay. A good place to
park is 3-1/2 miles south of town, right on the
beach. Walter Mueller claims: "You can take a
five-gallon bucket and follow the tide out, picking
up clams as fast as you can bend over for them."
If you love clams—steamed, frittered, fried or
made into a rich chowder—you will be in heaven
at Puerto San Carlos.

This is a spot for boondocking, since there
weren't any formal trailer parks, the last I heard.
But one couple reported that they found almost 50
campers and trailers parked on the sand there at
one time. Fern Holmes says, "We camped at the
edge of town, near a *cantina*. The town itself is
small, but gasoline and food are available. The
view of the water from our location was lovely.
Mangroves line the shore..."[*]

La Paz and Points South

After a singularly uninteresting stretch of farming country
and agricultural towns, from Ciudad Insurgentes to Santa Rita the
highway finally heads toward La Paz, the capital of Baja Sur. La
Paz has six RV parks with a total of 411 spaces. Most have good
water, but make sure which faucets are drinking water before you
fill your tanks. Some parks have well water for washing and
watering plants and just one or two spigots of city drinking water.

* *Mexico West* July, 1988

Respondents praised La Paz parks, claiming that not only are they topnotch, but the personnel are extremely helpful. "We came in with a blown tire," said one report. "The owner of the park said, *'No hay problema!'* And before we knew what was happening, we had two men replacing the hard-to-find radial tire, which they had to run into town to locate. 'No charge for the labor, just for the tire!' said the owner. We tipped the workers, and they were delighted." Another man describes one La Paz park as: "...without a doubt, the best in all Mexico...first class."

Hint: Try to get to La Paz during Mardi Gras or *Carnival* (pronounced "car-ni-VAL"). A recent innovation, this *carnival* is growing into one of the finest in all of Mexico. The main street along the bay converts into a mile-long celebration of outdoor restaurants, food stands, souvenir stalls, games and happy people thronging along the avenue. Several loud bands provide music for street dancing. But the marvel is an incredibly long and jolly parade with imaginative, well-made floats of all descriptions, interspersed with hilarious clowns and jesters. The 1989 parade was headed by a float from the Mount Shasta (California) Rotary Club! (I assume that either La Paz is a "sister city," or else the float took a wrong turn on the way to downtown Mount Shasta.) One lady, who was staying in our RV park, took her two children to the parade and later remarked, "I've never seen so many happy, yet polite, people in one place in all my life!"

South of La Paz, via a mostly-paved road, is Bahía de Los Muertos, and just above it, Bahía de La Ventana. There are several boondocking beaches here, and a great place for catching tuna, wahoo and dorado, as well as marlin and sailfish. Last I heard, there is room for eight to ten RV's at Los Muertos, looking out over the bay, with a "dry" camp possibly underway.

Bahía de Palmas

About halfway between La Paz and Cabo San Lucas, on your way south, is a sparsely-settled but growing North American colony spread along the Bahía de Palmas, also known as the "East Cape Area." Some rather fancy homes are here as well as some ordinary places. Some interesting RV parks, not far from the highway's pavement are found in Los Barriles and Buena Vista: four parks, three of them on the beach (Verdugos, Playa de Oro and La Capilla). There are 110 spaces in Los Barriles, and 43 in Buena Vista. Nothing is crowded, and if you're looking for isolated

beaches, beautiful ocean, peace and quiet, then you've found it. Boat launching here is possible, but not always easy because of the sand characteristics. By now, there may be a cement ramp, I don't know.

Los Barriles and Buena Vista are the larger communities along the bay, but neither is large enough to be called a village. From here on south runs a dirt and gravel road that follows the coast through some really spectacular ocean scenery, all the way to San José del Cabo. Few people live here, yet you'll find scattered RVs boondocking along the way, taking advantage of the view and isolation. From April through July and August, this is the place to come for fishing. Striped bass, blue and black marlin fishing is reputed to be the best in the world.

From here on south are numerous RV locations, both paid and free. Some snowbirds regularly lease or rent lots for their campers, then equip them with septic tanks and solar water desalinators.* In this sandy soil, sewage disposal is easy. Simply dig a pit, make a box of sturdy planks to keep it from filling with sand, then cover it over, leaving an entrance for your sewer line. Since you seldom need building permits or inspections, you can do it yourself, or seek the help of a couple of $12 a day laborers. Naturally, you won't place the septic tank near or uphill from a well. But you won't be drinking well water anywhere near the beach, since it's probably contaminated with salt water.

To get to most of these beaches, you'll have to brave a some-times-graded road. Just take it easy, and most any kind of rig can make it. My objection to these isolated beaches is that I would feel lonely. I need neighbors to talk to, to tell jokes, stories and tall tales. Other people love these beaches because there *aren't* neighbors like me there to bore them to desperation with bad jokes and long-winded stories!

Just south of Los Barriles, along the paved highway, is one of the most interesting towns in Baja Sur, a place called Santiago. It sits in a wide canyon watered by year-around volcanic springs, unaffected by drought or low rainfall. The result is a lush oasis of trees, vegetation and flowers. Streets are lined with flowering trees which flaunt blossoms so brilliantly red that they look sur-realistic. The Palomar Hotel there has one of the best chefs in Baja, famous for his soups. Even though there aren't any RV accom-modations, it's worth the detour to see the town and perhaps lunch at the hotel.

---

* According to Neal Allen (*Mexico West*, July, 1988) a solar-powered water maker produces 12 gallons of drinking water a day. I failed to get the distributor to send me any detailed information.

Todos Santos

Another interesting place and a location that is due a big boom in RV facilities is Todos Santos. Directly west from Bahía de Palmas, Todos Santos is on the Pacific side of the peninsula and is reached by an excellent new highway from La Paz. (If you're going directly to Cabo, this is the highway to follow—even though it looks like a secondary road on most maps.) Todos Santos is an area that obviously doesn't suffer from water shortage, because there are numerous orchards and vineyards in the area. It isn't much of a tourist center, which may be a plus, yet it has attracted a few American families as permanent residents. Farming and avocado production are the main industry here. "Quaint and unspoiled" is how one respondent describes it. Seafood restaurants here are famous.

The attraction in Todos Santos is the beaches. Some claim they are the prettiest in Baja. Before the new highway (1985), few people had the chance to visit these beaches, and even today they're relatively isolated and undeveloped.

Los Cabos

At the lower end of the Baja Peninsula are the towns of Cabo San Lucas and San José del Cabo, known collectively as *Los Cabos*. A three-day drive from the border clearly doesn't faze RVers, for this is a very popular destination. All trailer parks report that winters generally mean a full house.

San José del Cabo is a wonderfully pretty and clean town. North Americans are moving here with surprising frequency, and like Cabo San Lucas, prices are shooting sky high (for Mexico). There is only one RV park, situated on the south edge of town, with 100 spaces. The rates are about the same as other places in Los Cabos, about $240 a month for long stays. The American manager warned that if you want to stay for the winter, you need to get there about the first of November to make sure you have a spot. All the other parks in the area report the same. She asked me to remind readers that any rates quoted by this book or *any* book are never chiseled in granite. They can and do change from month to month. Apparently she has been upset by travelers raising hell because her rates aren't the same as some three-year-old guidebook reported.[*]

At La Playa, a small village on the beach near San José del Cabo, several RVs sit year-around on lots leased from villagers. Some are covered by ramadas to keep the sun from melting the

---

[*] Recently, the Brisas Trailer Park changed management, from Ele Holmes and her son, to the "ejido" that actually owns the land and leased it to Ele.

occupants in the summer. Some rigs are fenced with sturdy wire mesh, set on substantial cement pads and look quite permanent.

Cabo San Lucas, a few miles south, has six parks with a total of 295 spaces. That's not many, considering the number of people who make the trek each winter. One park, the San Vicente, is pirmarily for retirees and full-time living. Openings happen from time to time, so it might pay to check if you are looking for a permanent spot. Next door is the Vagabundos del Mar's spiffy new park, both under the same management.

While San José del Cabo is my favorite larger town in Baja, Cabo San Lucas has never thrilled me. I must be missing something, though, because enough people find it so exciting that it's one of the fastest-growing retirement areas in all of Mexico.

Baja vs. the Mainland

We've dedicated a large portion of this book to Baja California. As I said earlier, this is because it's the one most popular destination for RVers in all of Mexico. Does that mean it's the best place to visit? Not necessarily.

I have mixed feelings about Baja. On the one hand, I probably know it more intimately than any other single part of Mexico. That's partly because I've traveled so much of it by jeep at 10 miles an hour. You get to know the country pretty well that way. There is a certain mystery about the desert, a marvelous harmony about the way plants, animals and the environment work together; and the desert solitude is conducive to quiet, philosophical introspection.

Yet, there is something about mainland Mexico that evokes entirely different feelings. I love its tropical, balmy weather, lush green vegetation and warm ocean surf. Its lofty mountains and cool highland villages exude a magical charm that makes Baja's towns seem almost squalid in comparison. Since I speak Spanish, I can enter into the mainland's everyday activities in a way seldom possible in Baja, where most of the people I talk to every day are from the United States or Canada.

Choosing between Baja and the mainland is trying to choose between two good things. Each one different but wonderful in its own way. However, if asked to make a recommendation to a first-time RV traveler in Mexico, I suppose I'd recommend Baja as a starting point because of the large numbers of Americans and English-speaking people there. That's providing you don't have to travel from the East Coast to get there. Should you live in the eastern part of the continent, don't feel bad about skipping Baja (for a while, at least), because you have access to a Mexico that's just as exciting. In its own way, even better.

Chapter Eight

Catching the Ferry

For an ideal way to see the Baja California peninsula, drive one way, then catch a ferry boat to the mainland for a change of scenery on the way back. (Or vice-versa.) Actually, these are *ships* rather than boats. They are standard ocean-going vessels. Some ferries boast several decks with staterooms, movies and restaurants; a couple even have dance floors, complete with bands. All ships don't have all these facilities, however, and lately, it's difficult to know which ships are going to be in service. But it's guaranteed to be an adventure. Getting reservations can also be an adventure, as we shall see later on.

The ferry between Puerto Vallarta and Cabo San Lucas was my favorite: a 21-hour cruise. The restaurant food was excellent, the cabins almost luxurious and the ride very smooth. The last I heard that run has been discontinued, temporarily, at least. Other crossings range from comfortable to spartan, but can be fun.

My last trip across the Sea of Cortez (Feb. 1989) was from Topolobampo (Los Mochis) to La Paz, on the smallest ship and worst of the fleet. It was a plain, two-deck affair with no cabins or facilities other than a salon of reclining chairs similar to those found on Greyhound buses in this country. The food was grim, to say the least. The crossing took eight hours, from ten in the morning until six in the evening. They say that crossing in the other direction is *really* agony because it sails late at night. You must try to sleep in these uncomfortable-looking chairs, and the restrooms become impossible after the first couple of hundred customers. At least, the direction we traveled (toward Baja) was in daylight hours. So far, I've traveled on three different Baja ferries, but this had the worst facilities of all.

Wait a minute! This doesn't sound like much fun, does it? To my surprise, this turned out to be the *best* ferry crossing of all—*because* I was driving an RV! Let me explain: it seems that this small ship first stores heavy trucks in the hold, for ballast, then puts RVs up on the *main* deck. Most other ferries put all vehicles below and passengers are barred from going below until arrival.

But we were parked on deck, right next to the rail. In effect, we had our own private cabin (with a clean bathroom) and a marvelous view! We mixed cocktails, opened cold fruit juices and entertained some other Americans whom we met while waiting for the ship to load. I cooked one of my famous clam spaghettis and we dined lavishly—sipping California chardonay and sampling Mexican cheeses—while other passengers trudged drearily past the cafeteria's steam table, fending off starvation with a dubious-looking brown stew. For us, that eight-hour voyage seemed all too short!

Economics of Ferry Crossings

The shocking thing about ferry crossings is the cost. This last trip cost each of us the same amount as we paid for a cocktail the evening before: $1.73 apiece. The fare for our motorhome was $23, the price of a first-class dinner for two in a nice Mexican restaurant. It was the best transportation bargain I've ever encountered!

The ferry system has been losing money for years, with the government putting up a 90 percent subsidy. Tiring of this, the government put the ferry system up for sale in December, 1988. There is a strong rumor afoot that the Japanese are going to purchase the ferry system from the Mexicans. If this comes about, we can expect improvements in both facilities and service, plus substantial increases in fares. This would be both a blessing and a tragedy. A blessing, because it might eliminate the waits for reservations and make crossing more comfortable, but a tragedy because of the hardship the extra fares will cause Mexican travelers. Tourists can easily afford higher rates—they are embarrassingly low now—but Mexicans would find it impossible to travel back and forth if they have to pay much more. Most of the Mexican travelers I talked to on my last trip were on their way to Baja to find jobs in the booming economy there. If they have to pay high fares, they might not be able to go. Baja would be even more isolated from the mainstream of Mexico.

Ferry Crossings

There are eight ships in all plying the Sea of Cortez routes. In addition to the La Paz-Topolobampo Ferry, there is another one sailing the La Paz-Mazatlán route, plus one from Santa Rosalía to Guaymas. Hopefully, someday the Cabo San Lucas-Puerto Vallarta run will start up once more. The Santa Rosalía-Guaymas ferry is Swedish-built, and has comfortable staterooms for the over-night crossing, as does the La Paz-Mazatlán route.

At Santa Rosalía, you will need to use all of your bag of tricks to get on board, because this is a popular crossing for commercial vehicles who journey to Tijuana and points in-between. Remember that trucks are supposed to get first priority. Many RVs boondock in the ferry parking lot, waiting their turn, so you won't lack for company. This is a great place to do the "piggy-back" trick on a flat-bed truck. The truckers are delighted at the chance to earn some extra money by carting an RV on board. (Details later on.) You can then book a stateroom and get a good night's rest before hitting Guaymas the next morning.

A word about schedules: they change so often that it's almost a waste of time trying to print them in a book. Sometimes it's hard to guess which ferry will show up to take you aboard. My only advice is to call ahead and get the current departure hours, and then be there early, maybe get in line the night before and be ready. With an RV, that's no problem.

How to get aboard

If you are crossing from the mainland, you already have your car papers because you can't get into that part of Mexico without them. But if you are crossing from the Baja side, you'll need to get car papers. Try not to leave the border until you get them; the reservation agent won't even talk to you without them. If you *didn't* get them at the border, be sure to do so in Santa Rosalía (at the ferry terminal) or in La Paz. The *Registro Federal de Vehículos* is on Calle Belisario Domínguez near the intersection of Calle 5 de Febrero. Vehicle papers are free, although a tip is appreciated.

If and when the Cabo San Lucas ferry starts sailing again, make sure you get your car permit and tourist card in *La Paz*, because if you don't have them when you get to Cabo San Lucas, you can't get on the ferry. You'll have to drive three hours back to La Paz to get your vehicle permits.

If for some reason you neglected to get a tourist card by this time, or if the card was never stamped at a Mexican immigration station, then go to the immigration office at Paseo Alvaro Obregón and Calle Muelle in La Paz (also at the Mulegé airport or the ferry terminal in Santa Rosalía). You can't cross to the mainland without it, and you aren't legally in Mexico until this is done. It's easy to make this mistake, since a tourist permit isn't required to cross the border, and the immigration station south of Ensenada is generally closed.

Next, you need to pick up your reservations and tickets. If you haven't already phoned in for them, you might be looking at a wait. Have someone who speaks Spanish call for you if possible, although most employees speak at least some English. Trouble is, the phones are busy so much of the time that you need patience. Travel agencies are the best bet for getting reservations, although you'll pay a little more. The official numbers in Mexico City are 584-8140 and 584-8051; in La Paz, (526) 822-0109, 822-5677 or Telex 525-05; in Mazatlán, 253-78; in Santa Rosalía, (526) 852-0013 or 852-0014; Cabo San Lucas (if they ever start running again) (526) 843-0079.

Even if you've phoned in your reservations, there's still a chance you might have to wait since the ferry's main purpose is commercial transport. Trucks are supposed to get priority. I've seen campers and motorhomes bumped off the passenger list at the last moment to allow a cargo truck to board. One man complained bitterly that "they scratched my name off the list and put some guy named *Bimbo* in my place!" I looked up just in time to see a bread truck rumbling up the gangplank. On the side were painted the words *Pan Bimbo* (the "Wonder Bread" of Mexico).

Another problem is RV caravans. When 20 or 30 of these guys muscle into line, you can again be left behind. With caravan numbers increasing every year, this can pose a big problem in the future for freelance RV travelers. On the other hand, they have to go all together, or not at all, so you can get your breaks that way.

Reservation Philosophy

Some people spend days waiting for reservations while others roll right on board. (I've never had to wait.) I've loaded my vehicle while others waited despondently in line, hoping for space on the next crossing. How to do it? *Play the game.*

To understand the game, you must understand something of the philosophy and psychology of business relations in Mexico. Business dealings are conducted on a different level than in the United States. There is more of a personal relationship between employee and customer in Mexico, as opposed to the strict, logical, step-by-step procedures we follow. In our system, reservations are made on a cold, first-come-first-served manner. People are faceless numbers to our clerks. Mexicans view our business dealings as extremely cold and impersonal. That's our system.

But in Mexico, there *is* no system. The clerk hands out reservations as he or she sees fit. If the applicant is a friend, or seems like a nice person and really needs to get on the boat, why not slip him on the list? If the applicant is nice and also holds a $20 bill in his hand (only as a last resort) to demonstrate his intense need to cross the Sea of Cortez, of course he gets reservations. *"We'll just cross this Pan Bimbo truck off the list!"* However, if the applicant is a jerk, no matter how much money he offers, chances are that the bread truck will make it instead. Moral: smile once in a while!

It doesn't do any good to complain or to try to change the system. (I have to keep saying that, because Americans somehow think that by complaining, things will shape up.) The reservation clerk is like the Mexican cop in some ways: underpaid and overworked. He figures that any tip he receives is money earned by doing favors for nice people. To you it might seem patently unfair, but to the underpaid employee, the system is only just. Don't get me wrong: I'm not suggesting that every employee can be bought off. Some wouldn't think of it. Furthermore, if the ship is full, there is nothing that can be done and the clerk may not be in a position to help in the first place. But if there are a couple of last minute cancellations, and if you are a nice person, you'll probably get on board even without a tip. (Please don't go offering money, unless you see that it's hopeless otherwise. You make it tough on the next person.)

Learn to play the game. If you can't speak Spanish, it helps a lot if you have someone who speaks it call to make your reservations. Someone with a pleasant voice, preferably. When the reservations are confirmed, be sure to thank the clerk profusely, and ask his name. When you arrive at the ferry dock, ask for this person and remind him that you spoke to him on the telephone. That should do it. Another *Pan Bimbo* truck scratched off the list.

If you haven't made reservations from the 'States and want to make the trip, the easiest way is to find a travel agent who has an "in" with the reservation clerks. These agents have a personal business relationship with the clerks; they can get you aboard when no one else can. The commission is sometimes about 50 percent of the ticket price, but well worth the hassle of standing around a ticket office vainly trying to get the attention of the harassed reservations clerk.

Travel Agents

Going from Baja to the mainland, you can try several travel agencies in La Paz: at Viajes Lybsa, contact Lourdes Anguiano (706) 822-6011; Servicios Turisticas Briones, 822-6837; Viajes de la Peña, 822-1544; and Viajes Palmiras, 822-4030. They can make reservations for Topolobampo or Mazatlán. From the mainland, you can try the travel agency in the Hotel Santa Rita: Viajes Flamingo, Apdo 1034, Los Mochis, Sin., Mex. Telephone 2-16-13. If they can't make reservations from Mazatlán to La Paz, they will know someone who can. On my last trip they booked me with no problems. I drove on past people who had been told that the ferry was booked solid for the next six weeks. (The lady at the agency refused a tip, seemed embarrassed that my friend offered one.) For additional help in La Paz, call the Tourism Secretariat at 822-7975 and 822-1199.

Playing Piggyback

If you find yourself up against the reservation window, and the clerk tells you that the ferry is booked up until the end of next month, and there is no way in the world of your getting aboard, and he can't put you on the waiting list—don't give up! Your next step is to look for a trucker who speaks English. I've found Mexican truckers to be wonderfully helpful. If anybody at the terminal knows who to approach for a boarding pass, it's a trucker. And, if he can't get you aboard, he can certainly find any number of flatbed or stakebed trucks with drivers who would love the chance to load your rig aboard their truck and take it across for you. They know where to find loading ramps near the ferry and on the other side. You simply drive aboard the truck, chain your wheels down, and book your stateroom. I'm always surprised at the number of RVs waiting at the dock while empty flatbeds rumble aboard.

Should the Japanese actually buy the ferry system, there's a good chance the system will change. I suspect that Japanese philosophy of making reservations may be quite different from the Mexican philosophy. Too bad. Just when I had the system down pat!

Aboard Ship

Understand, these are no luxury liners. There are no padded lounge chairs, no striped umbrellas and waiters attending to your needs. And, should you fail to get cabin accommodations, you will have to sleep in "salon" class, which means rather uncomfortable reclining chairs. The bad news is that often they sell more tickets for salon class than there are seats, in which case, you had better get on early to avoid sleeping on a steel deck.

With the exception of the one ferry I took, all vehicles will be locked below deck and you won't be able to get to yours until the trip is over. It's a good idea to be prepared, carrying everything you need with you. A jug of drinking water, maybe a picnic lunch or snacks, air mattress, sleeping bags (if at night), toiletry items, a jacket and reading material are highly desirable things to have with you topside.

Schedules

Schedules change depending upon the condition of the ships and other logistical details. Fares listed are those as of the time of writing, and will probably go up soon. Prices quoted here are for automobiles; motorhomes, campers and trailers cost more, depending upon length.

Santa Rosalía-Guaymas: leaves Sunday, Tuesday, Friday and Saturday, late evening for a seven-hour trip. Price per person: 2-person cabin with private bath, 18,000 pesos; 4-person cabin, 8,000 (no bath); salon class, 4,000 pesos; car, 27,000 pesos.

La Paz-Topolobampo: leaves six days a week (the day off keeps changing) for an eight-hour trip. Leaves in morning from Topo and in evening from La Paz. Price per person: 2-person cabin with private bath; 16,000 pesos; 4-person cabin, 7,000 pesos (no bath); salon, 4,000 pesos; car, 25,000 pesos.

La Paz-Mazatlán: daily for 17-hour trip. Departs in afternoon. Price per person: 2-person cabin with private bath, 26,000 pesos; 4-person cabin, 12,000 pesos; salon, 6,500 pesos; car, 50,000 pesos.

Chapter Nine

Mexico's Mainland

Much of northern Mexico is desert. Except for the eastern gulf coast area, rainfall is meager and water supplies scarce. Wherever irrigation is possible, the desert flourishes lush and green, while across the road it can look like the Mojave desert in August. Northern cities tend to be far apart, towns and villages dusty and listless. For many travelers, this is the most uninteresting part of Mexico. Large areas are seemingly uninhabitable; cactus, sagebrush and thorny shrubs extend for miles with no visible life except for an occasional morose, sharp-boned cow, staring enviously as you speed past on your way to somewhere else.

Not everyone finds the desert as depressing as cows do. We've already discussed Baja California, a magnet for RVs *because of* its total desert environment. Well, along Mexico's mainland west coast you'll encounter beaches and mountain panoramas just as inviting as Baja's. Due to the new four-lane highway that's pushing its way south, the north-west coast may someday approach Baja's popularity as an RV destination.

Let's take a look at just a few locations.

El Golfo de Santa Clara

The closest mainland RV facilities are 40 miles south of the Arizona border, at a village known as El Golfo de Santa Clara. There are three rustic RV camps here, no hookups, but popular with fishermen and RV visitors. Incidentally, my claim to immortality rests on the beaches of El Golfo. Twenty-five years ago, before there was a highway, I chanced to meet a developer who wanted to build a resort on an isolated beach south of the village. He was convinced that once the highway was finished, El Golfo de Santa Clara would become "another Acapulco."

The next morning we loaded his crew into my four-wheel-drive truck and we drove down the beach to survey the property. The developer waxed enthusiastic as he described the high-rise hotel and time-share condos he planned to erect on this beach. (I couldn't quite see this place as "another Acapulco," but I politely kept my mouth shut.) The problem with El Golfo de Santa Clara is that it's located near the top end of the gulf, and tremendous tides sweep past like water sloshing in the shallow end of your bathtub. The ups and downs are as much as 22 feet! Often at low tide, there is nothing but muddy sea bottom as far as the eye can see. (Mud, because it's close to the mouth of the Colorado River.)

But I said nothing. In an impulse brought on by *cerveza*, euphoria and gratitude for my help, the developer decided to name the beach after me! It became *Johnny's Beach*, or *Playa de Juanito*. He named his resort: *Las Aventuras de Juanito* (Johnny's Adventures).[1] Unfortunately, my friend ran out of money before his dream high-rise condos could become reality. He did manage to complete a few anemic motel units and an open-air restaurant before he realized that "another Acapulco" was a bit optimistic. But the restaurant is still called "Johnny's Place," and the beach is still *Playa de Juanito*. My name may live forever on the Sea of Cortez, even though at times my namesake is but a strip of sand separated from the sea by several kilometers of sticky mud. You can usually boondock there—above the tideline—if you like. There are also some trailer spots not far from the restaurant, with palapas for shade.

Above the town is a high plateau with petrified wood that washed down millions of years ago when the Colorado river once emptied its flood waters along this plain. We're not talking tiny scraps of petrified wood; I've found logs of beautifully gnarled cypress too heavy for two men to lift. However, as more collectors scrounge, fewer good pieces are to be found.

Puerto Peñasco

Next is the town of Puerto Peñasco, about 70 miles from the U.S. border town of Lukeville, Arizona. I've talked with people who have driven the beach from El Golfo to Peñasco by dune buggy or truck, but I've also heard rumors of a kind of "quick-

---

1. When villagers asked why I would brave rough, desert trails just to visit a God-forsaken place like El Golfo, I tried to explain by saying: "For adventure." You see, it's difficult to explain the concept "hobby" to people who work 10 hours a day, seven days a week. Hence the name "Johnny's Adventures."

sand" (pockets of mud lightly covered by dry sand) along that beach. I wouldn't try it without a good 4-wheel-drive.

Puerto Peñasco and its neighbor, Choya Bay, are well-liked by Arizona RV travelers since they are convenient to Tucson and Phoenix and fishing is great. This is one of the most important shrimping ports on the gulf. Shrimp caught in the upper gulf can be enormous, almost the size of Maine lobsters, but sadly, these shrimp are too expensive for the U.S. market. Most are shipped to Japan, where people can afford such luxuries. Sometimes you can manage to scam a kilo or two if you can strike up an acquaintance with a shrimper crewman.

The large number of full RV hookups here is an indication of popularity: 265 spaces. Choya Bay is seven miles away, on the north side of the bay. It started as a fishermen's hangout, but now it's filled with trailers, campers and beach cottages. CB radios substitute for telephones here, and RV people are particularly friendly and open.

The colossal tides that hit El Golfo also affect Puerto Peñasco (without the mud). The cutoff point seems to be around the Midriff Islands, starting at Kino Bay (to the south). The extraordinary low tides here turn out to be a boon for those interested in malacology (study of mollusks), for scientists and collectors can venture far out into the sea floor in search of crustaceans. (I don't care to study them particularly, but I love to eat 'em.)

Bahía Kino

Driving down the new four-lane highway to Hermosillo is a snap today, compared to the hassle it used to be. The highway is wide and its surface hasn't had time to deteriorate. It will some day, but I'll take a rough divided highway over a smooth two-laner any time.

The next place south where you can head toward the seashore is at Hermosillo. A pretty good highway heads west to Bahía Kino, a pleasant road traversing rich farming country. Where irrigation hasn't touched the desert, you can see how stark the entire area used to be.

When people speak of Kino Bay, or *Bahía Kino*, they usually mean "New Kino." The old, original village of Kino is about seven miles away, at the south end of the bay. It's a rustic place with dirt streets, although there are a couple of good RV facilities (see RV directory). Here is where you look for a mechanic should your rig crave maintenance. You can watch carvers working ironwood and purchase some fine artwork at half the price elsewhere.

The new town is as different from the old as day from night.

Extending along the beach for miles, New Kino is mostly one street wide with a few side streets jutting away from the beach. The main street is paved, wide enough for bicycles and traffic at the same time, with sparse traffic. This is one place I'd trust bicycle transport without hesitation.

Bahía Kino is one of the most peaceful towns I've seen in Mexico. A good indication of how peaceful is the absence of bars on windows or high walls surrounding most houses. Many homes look expensive, owned either by wealthy farmers from Hermosillo or well-to-do American retirees, and undoubtedly left vacant for part of each year. Anywhere else, they'd be protected with steel gratings and walls topped with broken glass.

There are five RV facilities here, all nice, either on the beach or just across the road. Almost everyone we met on our last trip there were "old-timers" who had been coming to Kino for years. "We used to stay in Yuma for the winter," said one couple from Colorado. "We came here five years ago and haven't been back to Yuma since."

If you travel in the summer, you can be assured of plenty of space, because most "snowbirds" go home for June, July and August. Be prepared for summer heat, although it's easier to take that kind of dry heat than steaming hot Midwest summers.

Seri Indians and Wood Carvings

The town of Kino Bay is protected by Tiburón Island looming large in the distance. This was the ancestral home of the Seri Indian tribe. Removed to the mainland a few years ago by the government, the Seris today lead a nomadic life, making a living through fishing and carving ironwood into polished sculptures. Their main village is about 25 miles north of Kino, and well worth a visit. The gravel road going there is usually kept in good condition, although some washboard crops out here and there.

There are no formal RV facilities at the village. It's boondocking only. When you set up camp on the beach, you will immediately be visited by Indians trying to interest you in ironwood carvings, finely woven baskets or beads. They love to barter and prefer trading for clothing or cooking pots rather than money. They are good bargainers, from what I understand, and usually end up with the better end of the deal.

Ferne Holmes told of parking her RV on the beach at the village, and the next morning finding the camper encircled by Seri Indians. "One very handsome woman, with a small girl clinging to her long skirt, seemed to be in charge. They were selling beautifully crafted necklaces made of shells, dyed shark vertebrae, seeds and unfired clay beads. A child peeked shyly out from behind her mother's skirt and smiled. When I offered her a box of cookies, she refused to take them, so I gave them to her mother, saying: *'regalo,'* (gift). Two days later, just before we left, the woman ran up to our truck and pressed a lovely, delicate shell necklace into my hands. When I reached for money, she shook her head and said quietly, 'No . . . *Regalo.'* What a wonderful way to end our visit to Kino Bay."

San Carlos Bay

A most popular place, and the mecca for many, many RV fans is San Carlos Bay, 256 miles south from Nogales, Arizona. *Bahía San Carlos* has seen an astounding boom in recent years. When I first camped there, over 30 years ago, it was sagebrush and empty beach save for one motel and one private club. Today, it's a small city, with a bank, supermarkets, restaurants, drug stores, a full-fledged country club, everything you might expect. Just so you don't forget that you are in Mexico, there are even a few Mexicans living there. They think of everything at San Carlos.

With a backdrop of rugged mountains and gentle beach at your doorstep, it's small wonder that RV fans love this area. The same people come back year after year, holding reunions with friends of last season. "We've met the same people here every year for the last ten winters," reported one couple.

Two marinas accommodate sports fishermen. One marina is next to one of the largest trailer parks there, and they will store your boat there for the off season should you decide not to haul it home. This is an RV world. Some of Mexico's nicest trailer parks are found here, complete with all amenities, some even have washers and dryers that work! One park has over 300 spaces. One respondent reports a boondock area right on the beach, just north of an abandoned, never-finished hotel. "It's close to good eating places, post office, grocery, etc. There's room for 50-60 RVs and police come and check two or three times a day."

Summers in northern Mexico do get warm. Like conventional travelers, most RVers move to cooler climates as temperatures climb. Not all. Some simply switch on the air-conditioning and enjoy San Carlos in the summer as well. At least one RV park sells permanent spaces and buyers can leave their rigs year around. Some have built fancy-looking homes of stucco and glass on their lots to replace the RV. I saw one advertised for sale at over $50,000. "Why build a home in an RV park?" I asked. "Because I get 24-hour security, and I don't worry about my place when I'm not here," replied the owner of a home spread over two lots, surrounded by a masonry wall.

Park management and retiree organizations are quite active in San Carlos Bay. They offer Spanish lessons, dancing and art classes for RV residents. They engage in local charities and support an orphanage. Christmas parties for San Carlos kids have become a tradition, with people loading their campers with toys and presents before they leave home. One goal is to provide each kid with enough school supplies to last the year. Another big event is the annual "trick-or-treat" party. Cab drivers bring in kids from as far away as Guaymas to participate. One year they distributed 150 pounds of candy to about 250 Mexican trick-or-treaters.

Alamos and the Lakes

South of Guaymas and Bahía Kino there isn't much in the way of beach camping until you get to Mazatlán. The country in between, however, does have some fishing, hunting and sightseeing attractions. At Oviachic Lake (Obregon) and Mocuzari Lake near Alamos, there are both primitive camps and full hookups. Winters are supposed to see some of the greatest concentrations of white wing, mourning dove and quail anywhere. They say it's not

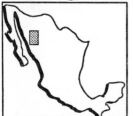

uncommon to see thousands of doves in one field. Unless you've gone to the trouble of getting gun permits, however, you'd best stick with bass fishing. It's reputed to be topnotch.

The town of Alamos is well worth the 35-mile detour off the highway. Tucked away in the foothills of the Sierra Madre, the old Spanish colonial town sits at an altitude of 1500 feet. This is just high enough to make a difference in the summer, keeping temperatures pleasant enough for year-round living.

Once the center of fabulously rich silver mines, Alamos at its peak was one of the most important cities in the Mexican northwest. Wars, revolutions, labor unrest, plus a falling market for silver finally did the town in, leaving it a virtual ghost town. Today, nobody remembers the exact location of the mines. About 40 years ago, a group of artists, writers and affluent retirees "discovered" Alamos and began restoration. They have been notably successful in turning fabulous old homes back into the glories of centuries past. Today, Alamos has been designated an historical monument by the Mexican government. Wealthy mine-owners have been replaced by wealthy North American retirees and artists.

Residents raise money for charity by conducting house tours

and charging tourists for the privilege of seeing some of the marvelous restorations.

Several RV parks accommodate travelers; the town is a regular rendezvous point for caravans. Our favorite park is a three block stroll from the *zócalo* or town center. Many residents of this park stay the whole winter season, enjoying the quiet, elegant atmosphere of colonial Mexico.

Copper Canyon

One desert attraction in Mexico, the Cañon de Cobre, is quite familiar, almost traditional with RV travelers. It resembles our Grand Canyon, only wider and deeper. For years, RV caravans traversed the canyon by railroad flatcar. Motorhomes, campers and trailers are loaded onto rail cars, chained down, then used as living quarters for the long trip between Chihuahua and Los Mochis on the coast. The flatcars are shunted onto sidings so caravan members can leisurely explore trails leading into the canyon, meet the famous Tahaurama Indians and absorb breathtaking views. The air is so pure that it's astonishing. I recall one below-freezing night in January when I looked up into the sky to try and locate a familiar constellation, but to my surprise, all the stars seemed equally bright and so tightly packed together that it was impossible to discern any patterns at all. Unforgettable!

The only other practical way to visit the canyon is to book a seat on the passenger train that winds its way across the sierras. The scenery is truly majestic. The train is brand new and comfortable, and has an excellent dining car. A bonus is that you are permitted to stand in the vestibules and stick your head out the open windows for a better view. The price of tickets makes the trip seem like a gift. To see more of the canyon, you can stay overnight at one of the over-priced hotels at the top. Or, you can continue on to the town of Creel, where more reasonable accommodations are available.

A tip: you can leave your rig in the parking lot behind the Santa Rita Hotel in Los Mochis. The travel agency in the hotel is very helpful in obtaining tickets for the Copper Canyon trip, and also for the ferry boat to La Paz.

Today, there is an alternative for seeing the canyon, at least for RV owners. A road has finally been cut through, connecting Los Mochis with Chihuahua and the rest of Mexico. Although most of the road is graded gravel and slow going, it's said to be good enough that any RV can make it with no problems. I haven't driven the road myself, so don't blame me if the trip bums you out, or if the route doesn't go near the canyon itself. Inquire carefully before exploring this new trail, and take plenty of food supplies for a leisurely trip.

RVs In the Tropics

Because of the relative desolation of northern Mexico, the RV traveler needs to rack up a few miles before he reaches the better-known tourist attractions. Not that some northern towns and villages don't make for interesting visits, it's just that few RVers consider staying long here. They are in a hurry to get into the tropics. If you study the list of RV accommodations you'll note many northern Mexico RV facilities connected with motels, often just a few hookups in the parking lot (sometimes just a space in the parking lot). That tells you that they're used mostly by folks just passing through, people in a hurry to get deeper into Mexico!

Tropical Climates

The Tropic of Cancer is an imaginary line cutting across Mexico just north of Cabo San Lucas on the Baja peninsula and Mazatlán on the west coast, and then between Brownsville and Tampico on the gulf coast. Once you cross this line the climate seems to change dramatically. You are now in the "tropics." North of the line, you'll find dry summers and slightly wet winters. South of the tropic, it's reversed; rain falls in the summer, while

winters are dry. Here, landscapes are greener and vegetation is thicker, just as you might expect in the tropics.

People tend to equate the tropics with unbearable heat and dripping humidity. We think of pith helmets, sunstroke and rivers of sweat. Yes, Mexico's west coast summers can be hot, but not nearly as hot as Illinois or New York summers! Why? The vast expanse of open Pacific keeps temperatures from getting out of control on the west-coast.

Check it out: Acapulco summers are cooler than those in Miami. June highs in Miami average 88 degrees, yet only 84 degrees in Acapulco. That's only part of the story, because Acapulco's humidity is also lower. Or, compare Mazatlán's June temperatures of 81 degrees with New Orleans' 90 degrees, or Phoenix's 101 degree highs. Yet, oddly enough, Mexico's tourism drops off drastically in the summer while U.S. tourists choose to vacation at home in much hotter, muggier places.

Of course, most RV folks travel Mexico in the winter, just like conventional tourists. Those who do venture into tropical Mexico in the summer months enjoy several unexpected benefits. First of all, there is never a thought of reservations, because trailer parks have plenty of openings. Some are downright deserted. Shopping and tourist attractions aren't nearly as crowded, and you can have many beaches all to yourself. Yes, it rains a bit, but a quick tropical shower doesn't chill you to the bone, and evaporation refreshes the air once the shower is over. Often, a low cloud cover shields the sun, preventing Phoenix- or Miami-like temperatures.

Of course, getting to Mexico's west coast involves driving through Texas, Arizona or New Mexico, which can be furnace-like in the summer, and northern Mexico has a similar climate. Once in Mexico, should tropical weather become onerous, you can always move your RV to higher altitudes; in a matter of hours you can change from summer to spring, yet still be in the tropics.

Let's take a look at some lowland tropical RV destinations.

Mazatlán and the Costa de Oro

The famous *Costa de Oro* starts here. This "Gold Coast" runs from Mazatlán south to Puerto Angel and Mexico's newest resort complex, Huatulco. With Mexican roads improving all the time, we can expect to see more and more RVs exploring the Gold Coast.

Mazatlán has become inordinately popular with RV and traditional travelers alike. The weather here equals other beach resorts, the beaches are nice, and importantly for some people, it's closer to the border. Many Americans swear Mazatlán is the best place in all Mexico. Of course, many who hold this view, don't know Mexico all that well.

A problem I have with Mazatlán is that some prices seem elevated and some services depressed, probably because of the strong emphasis on tourism. Taxis are comparatively expensive and bus service is overloaded. During rush hours, so many people crowd the buses that when one more passenger squeezes inside, someone else pops out through a window. The implication for RV travelers is that they can't count on buses to get them back and forth into town during rush hours. This is important, because trailer facilities are all away from downtown and far from the more popular beaches.

There used to be a convenient trailer park at an intersection near the beginning of Mazatlán's *Playa de Oro* (the ritzy beach and hotel section). It was a great location, right across the road from the beach. But, property there is far too valuable for an ordinary RV park; today you must travel a ways to find accommodations.

Most parks are on the north side of town, and all have full hookups, some have pools, groceries, laundries and rec halls.

Last June, I interviewed one park manager on *Calzado*, the main boulevard that follows the beach north. Although all but two of the 120 spaces were empty in June, he assured me that by December, reservations would be prudent. Daily rents were about $10 with a 20 percent discount for a month's stay. At the time, I was on a quick research trip—a fly-and-drive affair—so I didn't have an RV with me. My hotel room in Mazatlán was only $11 (to give you an idea of comparative prices).

There is one place in Mazatlán where you can boondock, according to one source. It's located on the beach, in the parking lot of an old hotel (no longer in operation because it was built too close to the water, in violation of the law). You turn right upon entering town from the main highway, then follow the main road along the beach, about six miles from downtown. It's next to a fish cooperative called "Pescado de Mexico." I've not been there, but my respondent assures me that there are always plenty of RVs around. "The police visit several times a day," he tells me, "and a water vendor comes through selling bottled water for 31 cents a five-gallon jug." Fish, vegetables and lobsters are regularly offered to the boondockers and a dumping station adds to the convenience. He spent three weeks there in spring, 1989.

I don't know of other places near Mazatlán where you can just back up to the beach and boondock, although there's a possibility at some northern villages. If anyone knows of a place, please let me know.

San Blas

Think you'd like to try a sleepy tropical village? A little beach place not totally overrun with tourists, yet enough fellow-Americans around for company? Maybe San Blas will do. It's just a few hours drive south of Mazatlán and about the same north of Puerto Vallarta. San Blas is quiet, a perfect place to set up under a palm tree and do some serious loafing or intense goofing-off. The streets are mostly packed sand or cobblestone. You'll sometimes have to pull over while momma pig herds her feisty little piglets along the street as brazenly as though she paid taxes. Some families live in exotic-looking, thatched-roof houses, and many buildings around the *zócalo* hark back to the days when the King's sailors celebrated shore leave on San Blas streets—in between skirmishes with pirates.

San Blas claims to have been a pirate hangout during the days of the Manila Galleons and the town tries to maintain a "buccaneer" motif. The truth is that the buccaneers mostly dropped anchor at Matanchén Bay, a few kilometers south. Actually, San Blas was founded as a naval base to *chase* the pirates. From here, Capitán Valdez outfitted his expedition to colonize the west coast as far north as Alaska.[2]

Numerous tropical-looking restaurants line the beach serving so-so food, but there are some excellent restaurants in town. On the hill overlooking the village stand mysterious colonial ruins. Roofless buildings of substantial stone, and ancient cannon watch over the ocean, as if guarding against buccaneer ghosts. The king's architect constructed these fine buildings "to last for centuries," but the church, the fort, the governor's mansion and homes of government officials were attacked and burned by rebels during the War for Independence around 1820—never to be rebuilt. The hill is now deserted, save for 78 billion thirsty mosquitoes humming communal prayers that a tourist or two might pay them a visit. Don't try to take an RV up the cobblestone road, because it's extremely steep and slippery with moss.

According to trailer park listings from my combined sources, there should be three parks in San Blas. However, as of summer of 1988, only one was operational. The manager said that although winter sees plenty of RV visitors, there is always room for one more rig. One of the parks listed in the center of town is little more than run-down storage spaces, although I suppose you could camp there if you really wanted to.

Summers here are exceptionally humid (consequently hot), the kind of weather that makes you understand the value of afternoon siestas. Rivers, an estuary and swamps ensure high humidity. Another problem is the "no-see-ums" that come out during certain times of the year. They've never been able to battle the little critters successfully. Ditto mosquitoes. For this reason, you can have the town to yourself during the summer, provided you're liberally supplied with insect repellent. One man told of renting a wonderful three-bedroom house for $125 a month for the summer.

From San Blas to Santa Cruz, all along the beautiful stretch of Matanchén Bay and Playa Los Cocos, there are numerous little trailer parks, some right on the beach. The view of the mountains and Matanchén Bay is marvelous and boondocking opportunities are everywhere. The village of Matanchén hosts several small, family-operated trailer hookups, most with electric connections,

2. The city of Valdez, Alaska, bears this Spanish captain's name.

but few listed in any RV directory. This area is particularly lovely, and unfamiliar to ordinary travelers. The detour is well worth it to enjoy the tropical vegetation and picturesque villages. Santa Cruz is a special jewel. For some reason or other, this part of the coast always seems to be green and lush while the rest of the coast suffers from lack of rainfall during the winter season. Even during the severe drought of 1988, this area looked marvelously tropical and verdant.

Just before you reach Santa Cruz village, is an exceptionally nice RV park on Los Cocos Beach. Across the road are banana groves, adding to the feeling of tropical luxury.

Puerto Vallarta

You'll find no beach boondocking around Puerto Vallarta. It's a tourist's town, catering to those $75-a-day guests who insist upon being right on the water. (Did I hear $100 a day?) They crowd the beaches, the sidewalks, fill restaurants to overflowing, yet tourists love it. They keep coming in droves every year, even in the summer. Why? It's nice, it's exciting, it's Puerto Vallarta.

Naturally, RV travelers also make the trek here in bountiful numbers every winter. But they can't demand RV accommoda-

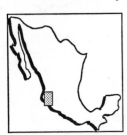

tions on the water, because there aren't any beachfront RV parks in Puerto Vallarta. All facilities are some distance from the beach. The largest ones, and most popular, are on the road to Pitillal, probably a kilometer or so off the main road, away from the ocean. It's nice, with a laundry and a swimming pool plus some shade trees. Bus transportation is fine here; there are so many buses scurrying back and forth that crowding isn't a problem except during rush hours.

Last June, this park hosted less than a dozen RVs, some of which looked as they had been left for the summer. But winter sees a full park. Some people make reservations for *next* year the minute they finish setting up their rigs.

One of the nicest Pacific beach RV parks is about 25 kilometers north of Puerto Vallarta, in the little town of Bucerías. This park has a brick wall, and is open to the beach in the back. Huge trees shade the patios, making it a congenial stay in a quiet, residential neighborhood. It's a long stroll to the "downtown" part of Bucerías, but a pleasant one. I understand that north of here, around Punta Mita and Sayuita, there are RV boondocking spots and places on ejido land that you can rent for the season. Several small towns on the beach to the north are beginning to take off, and RV accommodations are becoming plentiful. Rincón de

Guyabitos, San Franciscito, and other places along this stretch of coast have nice beaches, good RV hookups and growing numbers of North American residents.

Barra de Navidad and Manzanillo

South of Puerto Vallarta, all the way to Manzanillo, is another stretch of interesting road. It follows ocean beaches for a while, then cuts inland, up through pine forests, then down into tropical jungles, then back to the coast again. Less than 20 years ago, most of this was dirt trail, passable only by truck, four-wheel drive or bus. (Buses go anywhere.)

Before the paved road, I once caught the regularly scheduled bus—one a day—from Puerto Vallarta to Barra de Navidad. It was a 13-hour adventure of bouncing over rocky ridges, threading jungle trails, and fording two-foot-deep rivers. Today, the highway is easy blacktop, a three-hour drive. Several lovely places along the way are worth dawdling over; Chamela and Tenacatita, for example. Very tropical, with good RV facilities.

Barra de Navidad is a jewel of a town, with fine beaches, wonderful open-air restaurants specializing in fish and garlic shrimp, plus a scarcity of North American tourists. At this moment, I'm not aware of any trailer parks in Barra, but there are several in the immediate vicinity, just north of town.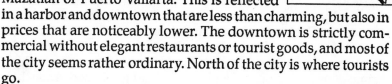

Unlike many Pacific coast resorts, Manzanillo is an active commercial port as well, and is far less spiffy than places like Mazatlán or Puerto Vallarta. This is reflected in a harbor and downtown that are less than charming, but also in prices that are noticeably lower. The downtown is strictly commercial without elegant restaurants or tourist goods, and most of the city seems rather ordinary. North of the city is where tourists go.

Manzanillo draws plenty of sports fishermen. It bills itself as "the sailfish capital of the world." (Seems like we've heard this claim in other resorts!) All in all, the atmosphere here is more informal and relaxed than Acapulco or Puerto Vallarta. My guess as to why it has never enjoyed the tourist boom of other coastal resorts is that the ocean here has nothing to temper the waves. No islands or bay stops the force of the open ocean from crashing ashore. The resulting rip tides and currents can be somewhat deadly, although I have friends who swim there regularly.

There used to be a nice RV park immediately north of town, but recently it went into the business of raising condominiums.

There may be other parks by now, but I'm not aware of them. Check when you get there, because surely someone will take advantage of the need for RV facilities. Tenacatita and Melaque are within easy driving distance, and there are fine parks there.

South of Manzanillo, just before Tecomán, you can turn to the beach town of Pascuales. A friend tells me this is a great boondocking spot. There aren't any facilities, so you park on the beach next to one of the many palapa restaurants. Weekends they feature live music and lots of friendly people. My friend said he and his wife spent six days there in 1987 and four days in 1989.

Playa Azul

Another new road (within the last few years) leaves Manzanillo, heading south along a rugged coastline. This road opened some extremely interesting country heretofore unavailable to anyone but a few Indian families. The highway is an engineering wonder as it follows the winding contours of the ocean on a 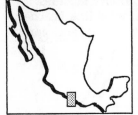 pavement sometimes carved out of sheer cliff above the surf, sometimes alongside gorgeous beaches.

The next logical RV stop along this route is Playa Azul, about halfway between Manzanillo and Acapulco. This is a resort town that caters to Mexican tourists rather than Americans, drawing residents of Morelia and vicinity. I've been there three times, and have yet to meet another gringo, other than RVers. The beach is lined with simple, but exotic-looking bar-restaurants of bamboo and thatch. Fishermen trudge along the beach looking for someone to buy their fresh catch. They fish by casting nets in sweeping arcs from the shore into the surf. It's an interesting technique to watch while sitting in a primitive restaurant, sipping cold beer and munching shrimp *al mojo de ajo* (sauteed in butter and garlic with a touch of ground chili). At night, some restaurants feature bands playing rhythmic, tropical dance music.

The best place to stay is at the Hotel Playa Azul, one-half block from the beach. You stay in the parking lot, which has electrical outlets, is walled-in and guarded, and guests have full use of the facilities. The town looks like a calm place where boondocking on the street is probably okay.

Zihuatanejo

The new road continues on south to Zihuatanejo and Ixtapa, a little more than half-way to Acapulco. Actually, this part of the highway isn't a new route, only paved after years of gravel washboard. You travel through quaint villages and past coconut plantations with copra drying along the roadsides. Don't worry about the military checkpoints here; they are checking for contraband, particularly illegal guns and marijuana. They aren't particularly interested in gringos; they usually wave us on with no more than a quick glance inside the tow vehicle or driver's compartment.

It is commonly said that Zihuatanejo resembles Acapulco of 40 years ago. Trouble is, it's growing so fast that before long it threatens to be more like today's Acapulco. "Zihua," as the locals call it, is changing rapidly from that cozy little village of a few decades ago. The new highway, the air terminal and development of the nearby resort of Ixtapa makes sure of that.

Fortunately, the glamorous resort of nearby Ixtapa draws off enough of the tourist trade to keep Zihuatanejo's prices within reach and its traffic relatively unjammed. As for RV facilities, however, they are scarce to non-existent. On the southern part of the bay, near La Ropa beach, there are a few places, mostly individual locations, where you must obtain permission from property owners. My guess is that increased RV visiting will trigger the development of more parks, but probably not near the beach. La Ropa is scheduled for condo development soon. Too bad.

Acapulco

Until around 1927, the only traffic that could cross the rugged mountains between Acapulco and Mexico City were sure-footed mules. The road was very bad. Even mules made the trip only under extreme coercion, threats and lots of cursing. When a paved road finally snaked its way to the ocean, a few pioneering motorists brought back news of Acapulco's tropical beauty. The beaches were, and are, superlative. It wasn't until the early '40s, when the sturdy DC-3 bi-motored airplanes began flying tourists to those magical beaches, that Acapulco became an international craze. Still, the twisting, narrow highway discouraged RV tourism for many years. (When I was a youth, it took 12 hours of hard driving from Mexico City.) Today, a modern highway—sometimes divided freeway—permits the largest RVs easy, five- or six-hour access from Mexico City. The new highway down the west coast makes it easy from that direction.

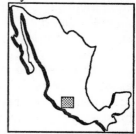

Enchanting Acapulco poses gracefully on a bay of incredibly blue waters. Its beaches are legendary: Condessa, Revolcadero, Hornos, Caleta, Caletita, and more. Shaded by swaying palm trees and blessed with mild breezes, Acapulco quickly became a hangout for the Hollywood crowd, the "beautiful people" and the jet-setters. Hedy Lamar could be seen dining at her restaurant, and John Wayne's tall frame was familiar around town.

If I sound like I'm in love with Acapulco, I am. I first saw it as a teenager, and wept when the time came to leave. It was gloriously beautiful and represented tropical living at its best. Of course, it's changed a bit over the years. What place hasn't?

Acapulco's no longer a small town; there may be as many as a million people living there today. Yet the beaches and natural beauty remain almost the same as in the pristine days of the 1940's and 1950's. The surf still sparkles in the tropical sunlight and the night air is as balmy and tropical as ever. Some things never change, thank goodness.

It might sound ambitious for RVs to travel all the way to Acapulco. But there are at least seven parks on the outskirts of the city, with over 400 hookups between them. Three are in Pie de la Cuesta area, where the old airport used to accommodate the twin-engined DC-3s before the days of jets. Other parks are on the highway approach to Acapulco, and one is listed as being downtown.[3] Local bus service is excellent, with buses passing by every few minutes, so getting into town from the park is no problem.

Should you decide that you deserve a break after herding your RV from the border to Acapulco, you might consider giving your equipment a rest and trying out a hotel. Can't afford it? Curiously, Acapulco has the most expensive accommodations in Mexico, but also among the *least* inexpensive. Why? Because developers have so frantically constructed luxury hotels one next to another, that older hotels—the ones built in the 1950s—often go begging for guests. Twenty dollars can place two people in an air-conditioned room just a block or so from the ocean. If you care to go up on the hillsides, you can enjoy a marvelous view of the entire bay in what used to be a first-class hotel for even less money. Acapulco is a must-see place.

About 50 kilometers south of Acapulco, on the mouth of the Río Nexpa, is a good boondocking location. There always seem to be 15 to 20 trailers and campers here, with Mexican entrepreneurs selling everything from bottled water to fruits and vegetables, clams and scallops. There's no grocery store or ice available, so stock up before you camp.

3. I don't recall seeing this park recently, so be sure and call the number listed in the directory before making too many plans. It could be a condominium by now.

South to Puerto Escondido

The highway turns inland for many miles along the *Costa Chica* or "little coast." (Why it's called this, I have no idea.) Except for a brief moment at Copala, you see no beach until you reach Puerto Escondido. It's a pleasant, eight-hour drive on a lightly-traveled highway. Along the way, you'll run across two very interesting and little-known cultural curiosities.

One is an area where the natives are descendants of African slaves, some brought over to replace Indian workers who were dying of smallpox and other European diseases, while others were escaped slaves in search of freedom.  Slavery was never legal in the Spanish colonies, but it did occur.[4] It's interesting that African slaves were considered too valuable to work in the fields, so they were used as overseers. In effect, they were free men, not slaves. The former isolation of this section of the country kept their descendants in seclusion, thus preserving old-country customs. As you drive through these villages of Cuajihicuilapa, Pinotepa, Chicahua and others, you'll notice distinct African influences. It's claimed that 80,000 Afro-Mestizos live on this 100-mile stretch of coast. Rumor has it that the government is planning a tourist development here soon.

The other curiosity is that you travel through the only place in Mexico where women traditionally go "topless." No, it's not a topless beach or anything like that. Women actually walk along the streets and do daily chores bare bosomed. This custom disturbed the early-day Spanish priests profoundly, so they coerced the ladies into wearing a strange-looking starched blouse of fancy white cotton.

These blouses are still worn today as a traditional costume of the region. Yet the padres were never entirely successful in convincing the women to cover up. Occasionally, you'll see a woman walking along the road, wearing one of their beautifully hand-woven wrap-around, ankle-length skirts, and nothing else. However, the only women I ever saw topless turned out to be quite elderly, with deeply wrinkled faces and white hair. It seems that the younger generation prefers T-shirts or pullover sweaters to go with their Calvin Klein designer jeans. A pity, really. Oh well, on to Puerto Escondido!

Puerto Escondido used to be the well-kept secret of surfers,

4. Blacks were in the colonies quite early. As a matter of fact, six Africans accompanied Cortez on his successful campaign against the Aztecs in 1519.

backpackers and beach campers. But with the development of Puerto Angel and Huatulco farther south, there's no doubt that Puerto Escondido will surrender its conspiratorial secrets. Tourists will someday pack the beaches as they do Puerto Vallarta and Acapulco.

Actually, RV explorers discovered Escondido about the same time as did the surfing crowd. For years, pickup-campers and vans, some with surfboards strapped on top, made their way to Puerto Escondido. The surf is phenomenal here, with huge waves rolling in unencumbered across thousands of miles of Pacific ocean. When the waves finally crash near the shore, they form spectacular, barrel-like rolls. Watching experts body surf inside these tube-like curls of wave and foam is scary and unforgettable at the same time.

In Escondido and in Puerto Angel (to the south) are the only places in Mexico, that I'm aware of, where the police seem to tolerate nude sunbathing on the beaches. In Puerto Escondido the nudist beach is beyond "rock point," a mile or two south of town. Most of the sunbathers are Europeans, who have been going nude in beaches and public pools for years.[5]

Today in Puerto Escondido, one full-service park with 150 spaces sits on a bluff with a view of the ocean, and several dry-camp locations are right on the sand. By the time you get there, there could be more.

The 'New Acapulco'

Every time the Mexican government develops a tourist spot,

it's hailed as "the new Acapulco." Cancún, Ixtapa, and now Huatulco. A curious fact is that Huatulco might be the *original* Acapulco! According to early historical records, the first shipping port and European settlement on the Pacific Coast was founded at a place called *Guatulco*, or *Huatulco*. This was in the early 1500s. Silver-laden galleons sailed up from Peru to discharge cargo at Huatulco, whereupon it was transported to Mexico City by burro-train and eventually to Veracruz for shipment to Spain.

British and Dutch pirates quickly discovered how easy it was to wait until a cargo of silver was unloaded, then swoop into the

---

5. Mexicans seldom go in for nudism; there are strong cultural biases against, and general disapproval of nude sunbathing. This has nothing to do with the Church or religion; after all, the predominantly Catholic countries of Europe are where public sunbathing is most popular.

town, kill and rape, then sail away with the booty. Nice guys. Sir Francis Drake was involved in at least one of these assaults. Understandably, the townspeople grew impatient with this rude treatment, so they looked for a better, easier way to defend the bay. They found it at Acapulco. Immediately, they abandoned Huatulco, leaving no trace of the town for history.[6]

Whether the new Huatulco will ever rival Acapulco remains to be seen. When I was there last, it was no more than a village. Yet today, they tell me that houses, businesses, hotels and other facilities are sprouting like magic. At least two RV parks are supposed to be open now, too new to be listed in any directory I've found.

Nearby Puerto Angel (one of my most favorite places in the world), used to have, at the time of my last visit, some great boondocking locations, although they were reached by a rather bumpy and pockmarked road. The beach at the end of the road was a true tropical paradise. A wonderful place for snorkeling and loafing. Let's hope it isn't shadowed by a 20-story hotel by now. The nudist beach, mentioned earlier is about a quarter of the way around the north end of the bay.

The cove here has quiet water and is a marvelous place for snorkeling. This is where I learned to use a snorkel and I will never forget the brilliantly-colored tropical fish that came up to stare at me through my mask, curiously wondering why I was so drab and so ugly.

South into Chiapas

The road south from Bahía de Huatulco follows the coast to the beach town of Salina Cruz. There are no RV facilities other than a dry-camp park along the spit that goes out to a booster plant for the oil pipeline coming clear across the isthmus from Coatzacoalcos. There's supposed to be a good seafood restaurant here. Salina Cruz has been popular  with backpackers and VW campers for years. It's a great place to kick back and do nothing but enjoy the beach. Informal camping is the order of the day.

The nearby town of Tehuantepec is the major attraction here. I see nothing spectacular about the place; it's just that it's the only

---

6. The exact location of Huatulco has never definitely been pinpointed by historians. After researching the sketchy reports and library references, I'm convinced the town was actually at nearby Puerto Angel. That's a far better harbor, also the trail to Oaxaca—and eventually Mexico City—logically started from here.

town of any size in the region. An odd fashion, something I think that dates back to the time of the Conquistadores, is the wearing of ankle-length skirts by the ladies, usually made of heavy velvet, often black. This time, it's the *younger* gals who consider the old fashions chic. Considering Tehuantepec's heat and humidity, it would make more sense to wear short skirts and go topless.

A couple of RV parks take care of passers-through. Not many people stay for extended periods, there's not that much to keep you occupied.

San Cristóbal de Las Casas

Founded shortly after Capitán Hernando Cortez and his soldiers conquered Mexico, San Cristóbal de Las Casas was the first town in the western hemisphere patterned after a European city

of that time. These were medieval times, mind you. A *zócalo*, or main square, forms the center, a church occupies one end of the square, municipal offices and jail the other.

An extraordinary number of churches checkerboard the town, many over four centuries old! They are open for your inspection, but the weird thing is, they are seldom used. They sit there like fascinating ghosts of Colonial Spain.[7]

The presence of so many churches can be traced back to the town's founder and city planner. A priest named Bartolomé de Las Casas hoped to integrate the local natives into the inevitable Spanish and Catholic culture with as little pain as possible. He petitioned Queen Isabella to respect Indians' human rights, and was largely responsible for persuading the Spanish kings to outlaw slavery in the New World.

San Cristóbal is a national historical monument, and exceptionally worthy of the designation. Cobblestone streets, narrow and mysterious, thread their way past massive homes and buildings centuries old. Indians from surrounding villages tread the streets barefoot, dressed in their tribal garb, not just for festivals, but as every-day apparel. Several tribes are represented: the Tzeltals, Chamulas, Tzotzils, and Zinacantans. The men's costumes are most striking, with some wearing knee-length black skirts,

---

7. Contrary to common belief, the Catholic church is very weak in Mexico. Since it isn't permitted to own property, all churches and everything inside them belong to the government! Many churches have no priests, and are used only on special occasions or by individuals seeking a quiet place for meditation. Read Graham Greene's "Power and the Glory" for a fascinating account of persecution of the Catholic church in this part of Mexico.

others short trousers or bloomer-type pantaloons and bright magenta serapes, all depending on the tribe. Their hats are festooned with various color ribbons which designate the village, clan and marital status of the wearer. In one of the tribes (don't ask which), it's the custom for males to wear sandals, even tiny babies, but for women and girls to go barefoot, no matter how cold (sometimes it freezes in this altitude).

There are three RV parks here. One is next to the hotel Bonampak, and another is a couple of miles south of the center of town. The third is off on a dirt road. It isn't listed in our park directory because I haven't been able to find its name in any of the existing park guides, and don't remember its name. Again, if anyone has info, please pass it along.

One RV couple reports that one of the best RV parking places is right in the center of town: at the municipal parking lot. It's guarded 24 hours a day, and is just below the entrance to the main cathedral. They said: "Cheerful young adults greeted us at the entrance kiosk to the parking lot and welcomed our self-contained mini as a round-the-clock customer. The fee was a mere pittance, so we boondocked there for a week. It proved to be an excellent location from which to participate in the Easter season's many festivities."[8]

Ancient Religious Ceremonies

San Juan Chamula, the ceremonial center of Chamula Indians, is about 15 kilometers from San Cristóbol. If you can, try to visit there, but don't use a camera—not at all. Don't even show one. The Chamulas deeply resent anyone taking pictures. They believe that a photo captures part of their soul. Also, they've seen postcards with other Indians' pictures on them, so they are convinced that you are taking their photos to sell as postcards. I wouldn't like that, either.

The church here is most unusual. From the outside it looks like a regular church, old and somewhat crudely constructed. But inside is totally strange, with little resemblance to a Christian church. There is no furniture, no pews, no altar—just hand-made figurines lining the walls, some carved of wood, some made of unusual materials such as faces made of Quaker oatmeal boxes. Fragrant pine needles spread across the stone floor instead of a carpet. Chamula Indians light pencil-thin candles, set them on the floor and kneel in front of them, their foreheads touching the floor until the candles burn out. I have no idea what any of this means.

I'm not sure if you are allowed to boondock here. Ask for

8. Jim and Ruth Shaw, *Escapees* magazine, Sept./Oct. 1987.

permission at the police station first, and above all, respect the people's customs and their religious beliefs.

Guatemala and Central America

Yes, there are brave people who dare travel south from San Cristóbal de Las Casas into Guatemala, and even on through the Central American republics, as far as Costa Rica. (It's a wonderful country.) But this kind of travel isn't recommended by this book. If you should decide to try it anyway, the safer place to cross into Guatemala is farther west, at Tapachula. Then keep to the route closest to the ocean.

Traveling through Central America isn't all that dangerous, according to some people, but Honduras and San Salvador are frequently in a state of rebellion or war, and there is a chance of being in the wrong place at the incorrect time. Why take a chance? I wouldn't take anyone's word for the safety there. Besides, in order to get to the only safe country (Costa Rica) you must cross five countries' borders, invariably marked by hours of frustrating delays on either side plus rude immigration and customs inspectors. Interestingly, I interviewed a Canadian who drove to Costa Rica in a cab-over camper, and he said the only country that was *easy* to cross was Nicaragua! The customs people asked where he was going. When he replied "Costa Rica," they waved him on with a "have a nice trip," and didn't even look inside his camper! I crossed Nicaragua twice during General Somoza's regime. Going and coming, I was delayed for hours while customs officials questioned me about each of my books (to make sure they weren't "Communistic") and examined belongings item by item, tossing them into a pile on the floor. Thanks, guys.

On the other hand, I've met people in Costa Rica who claim they had a marvelous time driving or pulling their RVs there. I still think it's far easier and safer to fly. By the way, I highly recommend flying to Costa Rica should you have time to spare. You can leave your rig bonded in customs at the Cancún airport (for a very small fee) while you fly to Costa Rica, just a few hours to the south. The bonded lot is fenced and carefully guarded 24-hours a day. The employees there are very congenial, and don't expect (nor will they accept) a tip. As I recall, the bond permit and RV storage cost less than 50 cents a day for the month I visited in Costa Rica. You don't need a visa; you get a 30-day tourist card at the San José airport when you arrive.

South of San Cristóbal, on the Guatemalan border is an interesting national park, *Lagunas de Montebello* that is worth a detour. See the directory for description of facilities there. On the way is the town of Comitán, another fascinating Indian center.

Across the Isthmus

If you've made it as far as San Cristóbal de Las Casas, you might as well continue on across Chiapas to one of the more spectacular RV destinations in all of Mexico: Palenque. From San Cristóbal, the road heads toward Osingo, and then on through some absolutely gorgeous tropical mountains. On the way, you'll see Indians dressed in colorful costumes, living pretty much as their ancestors did long before the arrival of Europeans. Many of them don't speak Spanish. Primitive farms carved from the forest and clinging to hillsides covered with vines and tropical timber make this an unforgettable drive. Part of the road used to be gravel—and may still be—but it was excellent, smooth and capable of 50-mile-an-hour speeds the last time I drove it.

A few miles before you get to Palenque, in the middle of the most picturesque part of the trip, there's a turnoff toward *Agua Azul,* or "Blue Water." Go there; it's worth at least one overnight boondock, even if you've never boondock-ed in Mexico before. "Blue water" is a good description because the water in this river is unbelievably, azure blue, as blue as the bluest sky you've ever seen! I suspect that it's caused by the limestone formation the river flows through, because the only other water that blue is on the Quintana Roo coast, where limestone colors the Caribbean's waters almost the same color.

There may be some commercial RV hookups there by now, but it used to be that you could boondock right next to the river. People simply pulled along side the river's bank, set out their chairs and tables and enjoyed one of the most beautiful camping spots I've ever seen. On my last trip there, I noticed several pickup-campers and motorhomes that looked as if they had been there a while, with elaborate, permanent-looking camps. The blue river is popular with swimmers and fishermen.

Palenque and Villahermosa

For anyone even mildly interested in Mexican archaeology, Palenque holds an enormous fascination. As a graduate anthropologist, I've seen almost every major archaeological site in Mexico and Guatemala, but, in my opinion, Palenque is the most stirring of all. It isn't all that large, not compared to sites like Tikal or Yaxchilán, but it contains more enticing mysteries than any other Mesoamerican ruin.

The nice thing about Palenque is its accessibility. You needn't raft a whitewater river or trek through rain forest to find it. Simply park your rig, buy an admission ticket, and walk right in.

On my first trip there, I was with a river-rafting expedition returning from a 12-day raft voyage down the Usumacinta river. We set up our tents at Nututún campground for a period of recuperation and suddenly found ourselves surrounded by a motorhome caravan. We struck up conversations with these RV folks and found they had driven from all parts of the U.S.A. One couple was on their second trip to Palenque! At the time, that seemed like a long, long way to go, but subsequently, the volume of RV traffic has increased fivefold. Commercial caravans regularly make Palenque a priority stopoff.

Palenque's ruins are set in the foothills of low mountains, heavily forested and lush with tropical growth. Mysterious bas-relief engravings, statues, and enigmatic, oriental-looking arches make this site one of the wonders of the Maya world. In one of the high temples, archaeologists discovered a secret passageway that

led down a steep set of stairs to a spectacular tomb. This is the highlight of the trip for many, the spooky descent into the tomb of a Mayan king, buried over a thousand years ago.

If archaeology grabs your interest at Palenque, you might consider a detour to Villahermosa for a look at another mystery. An outdoor museum in a park setting displays the astonishing artifacts of the very earliest civilization ever found on this continent: the Olmecs.[9] Huge basalt statues and carvings of jaguars and demons have been collected from the area around Ventana and other Olmec sites. A traditional museum displays an excellent collection of artifacts from other parts of Mexico. Villahermosa is worth a visit for these attractions if for nothing else. I can't find a listing for a trailer park in town, but I've seen motorhomes and campers parked on side streets.

Not too far from here is the Graham brothers' ranch and RV park at Aqua Dulce. Buses take you into Villahermosa for the sights. I haven't been here, but I've been told this is one of the best in Mexico. With green lawns, horseback riding, swimming pool, tennis, and full hookups for your RV, you can't ask for much more. It's actually a working ranch in addition to an RV park.

Villahermosa sure isn't a place for summer vacations. Because of drenching humidity, summer here is the hottest I've seen anywhere. Including Houston, Texas! But the inhumanity of Villahermosa is that the sale of cold beer is prohibited after eight o'clock in the evening! Even in summer! Not a drop after eight! Horrors!

9. The Olmec civilization preceded the Mayas by at least a thousand years.

The Yucatán Peninsula

It seems that there are two main reasons for visiting the Yucatán. Most people either want to visit the multitude of Mayan temples and palaces, or they want to soak up sunshine on the Caribbean beaches. In an RV, it's easy to do both.

Almost anywhere you find major archaeological ruins, you will find RV parks. By setting up in Campeche, for example, you have the advantage of visiting a fascinating Colonial city and taking day trips to dozens of famous Mayan ruins. Some of the smaller sites are located in quiet, peaceful rural areas where most RV owners feel comfortable boondocking. Uxmal, the largest of the Mayan cities, has places to park within walking distance of the temples.

My anthropology professor once said that he had traveled over 25,000 miles in the Yucatán, yet he estimated that he had seen only 5 percent of the ruins. Since so much of the peninsula is uninhabited, it's possible to strike out on your own, and discover your own ruins. I did this once, and found it extremely exhilarating. I was camped on the beach north of Playa de Carmen, and decided to take a machete and cut my way through the low, Yucatán forest behind the camp. I hadn't gone 200 yards before I came across the remains of a small temple and several crumbling limestone walls. Compared to Chichén Itzá, these were nothing, but to me it was like finding the lost capital of Atlantis!

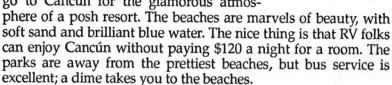

Cancún and Points South

Even Cancún has Maya ruins. You'll find them along the way to Club Med, on the land side of the road. But most people go to Cancún for the glamorous atmosphere of a posh resort. The beaches are marvels of beauty, with soft sand and brilliant blue water. The nice thing is that RV folks can enjoy Cancún without paying $120 a night for a room. The parks are away from the prettiest beaches, but bus service is excellent; a dime takes you to the beaches.

A recent hurricane did considerable damage to this area, but last reports say that things are pretty much back to normal, except that tourism is down. That's good news for RV travelers, because park space should be easier to find and the beaches less crowded. If you want to get away from tourists, yet stay near Cancún, just drive your RV aboard a ferry for the forty-five minute trip to Isla Mujeres. There's a boondocking area on Isla Mujeres, not far from Garafon Beach, a popular place to learn snorkeling.

Frankly, I prefer the beaches south from Cancún. The highway south passes through low jungle—looking so uniform that it gets almost boring—yet all the way to Tulúm, side roads invite you to lovely Caribbean beaches just a kilometer or two away. Long stretches of sand and coral are fringed with coconut palms where farms have been cut from the jungle brush. These beaches are absolutely the prettiest of all Mexico, for my money. The roads leading to the beaches are of a curious type of clay that when dry, resembles smooth cement, and when wet, is slippery but not really muddy.

Just about any road you take ends up at a place to park your RV. Walter Mueller says, "By my count, there are 16 small RV parks along the beach, just between Cancún and Playa del Carmen. You have to watch carefully, because some only have small, hand-painted signs." If not a campground, then you can almost always count on camping next to a family farmhouse in exchange for a fee. That's more fun anyway.

Our most memorable camp was with a Mayan family here, who set up a special table under a palm tree for us and served freshly-caught fish for breakfast. The *plato del día* was whatever the farmer's son caught that morning. Sometimes it was barracuda, sometimes a gorgeously-colored tropical specimen, so pretty that we hated to eat it. But we always cleaned our plates and went for seconds. Some camps (fancy hotels, actually) along this stretch boast gourmet restaurants serving fantastic menus (and prices to match). Our routine was to have breakfast and lunch with our new-found family and hike down the beach and live it up with an elegant dinner, listen to a band, and wander back to our camp in time to get a good night's sleep.

Playa del Carmen has a small RV park set alongside a *cenote*, a natural spring that wells up from the ground with surprising vigor. Several RVs stay the winter, enjoying the convenience of walking to stores and having a beach 50 yards away. The RV camp at Akumal is one of the prettiest commercial parks in this area, with graceful coconut palms and crystal-clear water washing the beach. Tulúm is another famous Mayan site, with mysterious ruins. Many campers here come from Europe, particularly Switzerland, Germany and Sweden. They bring tents rather than RVs.

Overlooked Gems

Chetumal, on the border of Belize, has a couple of highly recommended RV facilities, and is a place often overlooked by RV travelers. About seven miles before you reach Chetumal, there's a delightful tropical bay where you can dry-camp for a couple of dollars a day. Fishing, scuba, snorkeling and so forth are excellent. For less than $4, you can take a bus into Belize.

I have no information about taking RVs into Belize, but I rather doubt that there are any facilities in this country. Check carefully before considering crossing into Belize; I haven't heard many nice things about the country.

A place brought to my attention just recently, ought to be mentioned here. I've not visited there yet, but a trusted friend vouches for it. It's the Largato Lagoon area at the northern tip of the peninsula. Three places, all small "fish camp" villages, are: Río Lagartos, El Cuyo and Chiquita. There are no facilities, but my friend says you'll have no trouble getting food, particularly if you like freshly-caught fish. Last time he was there he brought 10 pounds of apples to give to the fishermen; he made a friends for life. (Apples don't grow in most of Mexico; many people have never tasted one. They're great for gifts.)

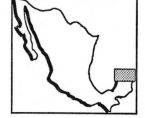

As you trace the coast toward Veracruz, you'll find a string of long islands just off shore, bordering narrow lagoons, just like Lago Lagartos. Follow the road that goes along these bars (using ferries when necessary) and you'll discover many great places to stay on the beach, all the way from Champotón to Villahermosa on Hwy.180. People are exceptionally friendly along here, and the seafood is excellent.

RVing in the Yucatán peninsula could fill a book in itself; there are so many places to visit, so many adventures to be enjoyed. Some people enjoy leisurely traveling through the interior, stopping at villages and parking on the *zócalo*. The Mayan people are so peaceful and so shy that RVers, who wouldn't boondock anywhere else, feel unthreatened here and try it. The local people usually speak Mayan among themselves and polite Spanish to strangers. Mayan children greatly enjoy gifts of bubble pipes, coloring books and school supplies and they seem to have the broadest smiles in all of Mexico!

Gulf Coast

The Gulf of Mexico is totally different from the Caribbean. It seems calmer and lacks the striking blue color that characterizes much of the Caribbean. Yet for many who live in Texas and the Midwest, this coast is the closest part of Mexico, and Gulf water is what they're used to.

Traveling south from Brownsville, you have a long stretch of uninteresting country before you finally reach the gulf at Tampico. A side excursion of about 50 kilometers to La Pesca will break up the trip. This is a friendly fish camp, with a good seafood restaurant. Camping is free and informal. My understanding is that the road south of here to Tampico (along Hwy. 180) is in bad shape because of the way big trucks tear up the roadbed. Therefore detouring through Cuidad Victoria could be easier on your rig. About 60 kilometers out of Victoria is Guerrero Lake, famous for bass fishing. Numerous RV facilities and other enterprises here cater to Texas fishermen.

You finally hit the gulf again at Tampico, but the beach is rather uninspiring, often tainted with oil spills from the many tankers that load here. Better beaches are to be found further south. By the time you arrive in Tampico, you may need to stay overnight; there are several parks listed in the directory at end of this book. But here's an alternative: try the soccer field across from

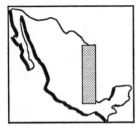

the Posada de Tampico hotel. I'm told that it's permitted to stay overnight if you eat at the hotel's fine restaurant.

From Tuxpan south to Lake Catemaco, we find several scenic towns and villages, most of which have RV facilities of some kind or another. You can tell that RVs don't travel the eastern part of Mexico as much, because of the paucity of RV facilities.

RV facilities are found in Tuxpan and Poza Rica for visitors to the famous archaeological zone of Tajín, or the daredevil *Voladores* at Papantla, in their "flying pole" ceremony (leaping from a pole 90-feet high, and "flying" to the ground in ever-increasing swoops.) Not too far away is Tecolutla, a typical small beach town where it's okay to boondock. No hookups, but lots of friendly people and nice restaurants.

One particularly interesting place is La Antigua, just north of Veracruz. This is where Cortez landed with his soldiers to undertake the conquest of Mexico. The ruins of Cortez' residence is still there. A nice RV park is here, on the river, and parking is permitted overnight on the street. One respondent notes that this is his favorite RV spot in Mexico. All along this highway road are interesting archaeological ruins—remains of pre-European civilizations that were destroyed by Cortez's zealous soldiers, places of mystery and intrigue.

Veracruz

If possible, try to visit Veracruz during its world-famous *Carnival* celebration. You'll probably have to store your rig somewhere, and make hotel reservations a year in advance. It would be a miracle to find an RV parking place at that time. But, whatever you have to do, it's worth it!.

Summer isn't the very best time to visit here, because of the high humidity and ungodly heat. But there is one place I would visit, winter or summer: the town of Lake Catemaco. It's perched in a low mountain range, with just enough altitude to keep things comfortable in the summer. There are two parks here, but I've seen motorhomes and trailers boondocking lakeside, by the city park. If you can't find anything suitable, it's worth a hotel for the night. Try some of the fresh-water shellfish dishes in the restaurants. Nearby San Andrés Tuxtla is in the center of ancient Olmec civilization. San Andrés has an interesting museum that's worth an hour's visit.

Mexico's Interior

Mexico isn't all beaches; there's lots, lots more. The center of the country is mostly high plateau, high enough that temperatures are cool and spring-like year around. Typically, residences have neither furnaces nor air-conditioners. A fireplace does the trick for the few chilly evenings that might come along. In the interior you'll find a wonderful mixture of modern cities, Colonial towns, tiny villages and places purely Mexican Indian.

Guadalajara and Lake Chapala have long been hosts to RV travelers. Many like it here so well they give up RVing and retire permanently in this area. There are more U.S. and Canadian retirees in the Guadalajara region than anywhere else in Mexico—around 30,000 retirees—no one knows exactly how many.

Guadalajara-Chapala is known as the place of "eternal spring." That's not exaggeration. You'll catch a few hot summer days, but these are unusual. Usually, summer or winter, a light sweater or sports coat feels comfortable in the evening, although shirt-sleeves feel okay, too. Even at noon, it's seldom too warm to wear a jacket or sports coat, should you feel more formal.

The altitude here is 5,100 feet, which accounts for the mild temperatures. In turn, the mild temperatures accounts for the high number of retirees.

San Miguel de Allende

This is one of my favorite towns in Mexico. Situated high in the mountains at an altitude of around 7,000 feet, San Miguel is a marvel of cobblestone streets, colonial buildings, with an atmosphere of old Mexico that inspires many artists to perform at their best—and would-be artists to get started. The intellectual atmosphere about San Miguel de Allende and its cultural institutes draws artists, sculptors and writers from all over.

Because it's off the beaten tourist track, it doesn't attract the "ordinary" tourist for an overnight stop before heading on to Cancún or Puerto Vallarta. You must go out of your way to visit San Miguel de Allende. It's a place for long stays, for studying Spanish, art or weaving. It's a place for quiet meditation while you start work on that first novel.

There are a couple of RV parks here. The problem is that they are far from the center of town. It's around the central plaza where the social and cultural life of San Miguel is focused. However, I interviewed two couples who were living in one of the trailer parks; they completely disagreed. "We like it here because it's quiet, rural and peaceful. Besides, we enjoy the long walk to town, and taxis are cheap for the return trip."

The Central Plateau and Other Places

Mexico City isn't the pristine beauty that it was when I lived there as a youth. Traffic is horrendous, smog stains the air, and there are many millions of people crowded together. Still, there is something about the place that will never change. Folks who live there wouldn't trade it for anywhere else in the world. They are like those people who love Manhattan; they see so many good things about living there that they can't see any bad.

Unfortunately, Mexico City isn't a place for RVs. There could be a place or two where you can store an RV, I suppose, but you would have to be braver than Dick Tracy to attempt driving RVs there. Better stay someplace like Cuernavaca and take a bus back to Mexico City for sightseeing. Cuernavaca, incidentally is famous not only for its wonderful weather, but also excellent language schools. There are a couple of trailer parks where you can stay, or the schools will place you with a private family, where you are forced to speak Spanish-only.

There are so many places in mainland Mexico to take your RV that it's impossible to touch more than a few highlights in this book. Guanajuato, Oaxaca, Querétero, and hundreds of other places await your discovery. Hopefully, I've given you enough ideas to get started. The park directory in the back of this book should help.

Chapter Ten

Keeping Healthy

The first thing that comes to mind under the topic of keeping healthy is the often-repeated advice: "Don't drink the water." True, it's important to be vigilant about the water you drink, but in the long run, it's a relatively trivial concern for people who drink water from their own RV water tanks. Instead of constantly worrying whether this hotel or that restaurant has good water, you simply make sure the water supply in your rig is good.

It's true that local water supplies are often contaminated, yet finding good drinking water is seldom a problem. Just draw your water from the same sources as the local people. A common myth is that "natives become immune to bad water." The truth is that nobody can develop an immunity to amoebic dysentery (*entamoeba histocoli*).

The only way to avoid it is to drink uncontaminated water. Every locality has a source of good water, or else no one could live there. If there aren't any good springs, deep wells or high-mountain streams around, then the natives drink water from five-gallon containers of purified water. Failing that, they bring water to a boil. Just bringing it to a quick boil is sufficient; there are no common organisms that can survive temperatures over 150 degrees.

Now, there's a difference between serious amoebic infection and simple diarrhea that one gets from a change in food or water. What happens there is the digestive system encounters new strains of bacteria, and the resident bacteria declare war on the newcomers. The system gets weary of all this fighting and decides to get rid of all the bacteria and start over. This often happens even in the United States when traveling from one section of the country to another. It's not serious, a dose of Pepto Bismol or Lomotil will clear it up in a hurry. Mexicans get the same thing when they travel in the United States. But RVers seldom are bothered by this, because they exercise control over their water and food.

When pulling into a new RV park in Mexico, one of the first questions to ask is: "How is the water here?" You'll soon find out, because if anyone in the park has come down with something, everyone will know. Sometimes, particularly near the ocean, the water isn't contaminated by bacteria or amoebae, but it contains high levels of salt or alkali. There isn't much you can do with this water, because no amount of boiling will make it taste right. In this case, you must make do with your hoard of drinking water until you can replenish it.

A common sight in communities with poor water is a water-tank truck making the rounds. The cost of filling your tanks and jugs is minimal. This isn't just a convenience provided RV parks, but for the entire community. If you can't drink the water, nobody can. Should all else fail, you can usually always find distilled or purified water for $1.50 (or less) for a five-gallon container (plus deposit on the jug).

Good Cooking Practices

Common-sense hygiene involves more than clean water. Mexican housewives intuitively understand the dangers of serving untreated raw fruit and vegetables. They learned from their mothers that food must be prepared certain ways. They wouldn't think about doing it any other way. Taking precautions become second nature, as natural as breathing.

Soaking in treated water makes salad vegetables safe for your table. Some people use a chlorine solution, but I don't care for the taste of chlorine, and it wastes precious water to wash the taste away. Our maid used a small pill with the brand name of *hidroclonazone* (or something like that). She put it into a gallon of water and soaked vegetables for 15 minutes. No chemical taste affected our salads. Purifying tablets, available inexpensively at any drug store or market will do the job. Fruits and vegetables fresh from the market must be stored separately from those already treated. All of this is discussed in the chapter on RV cooking. Properly cooked food is always safe.

Having your own cooking equipment in your rig gives you strict management over food preparation; there is no excuse for getting sick. A common source of sickness among ordinary tourists is that, even though so careful about drinking water and meals, they forget and brush their teeth with tap water. Since we brush our teeth with our own water supply, even that hazard is eliminated.

Ice Cubes and Bulk Ice

Fortunately you won't have to worry about ice coming from your RV freezer because you will have made it with pure water. But you must be careful about commercial ice, particularly if you have an ice box instead of a refrigerator in your rig. Mexico has laws that ice cubes must be made from good water, and although you have no guarantee, chances are the water is good in commercial ice cubes. It would be foolish for a commercial ice-producer or a restaurant to use contaminated water and poison its customers. The cost of pure water is so low that there is no incentive to cheat.

However, bulk ice, the kind you buy in 25-pound chunks isn't controlled, and Mexicans do not expect it to be clean. So, if you have an ice box, remember this and keep melted ice water away from your food. Clean, heavy plastic covering the ice will prevent food from making contact. Don't sterilize your veggies and then put them on ice to keep them fresh. Do it the other way around; wait until you are ready to eat before soaking them in treated water.

Eating in Restaurants

While RV travelers enjoy bringing their own kitchens with them, it would be a shame not to enjoy Mexican cuisine from time to time. Each section of Mexico has its own culinary specialties; it's a delight to sample them and then try to imitate the recipes of your favorite dishes.

When thinking of "Mexican food," many people automatically picture blazing chili peppers and suffering digestive systems. I've never understood why so many Americans think hot sauce is so great. Neither can Mexicans understand this, because most of them dislike too much chili as much as I do. Real "Mexican" cuisine rarely involves chili peppers. Good restaurants would no more dash hot sauce on your food that would good restaurants back home. A top Mexican restaurant doesn't feature "fast-foods" like tacos and enchiladas any more than a first-class restaurant at home would feature hot dogs and hamburgers on its menu. Tacos and enchiladas are items traditionally served from street stands, much like hot dog stands in the U.S. However, they are served in many restaurants simply because tourists expect to find them on the menu.

But, what about eating out in restaurants? Is it safe? For the most part, yes. Restaurants that depend upon return business take care not to make their customers sick. The cook uses the same kind of hygiene in the restaurant as in his or her home. It's only good business.

The clue to trusting a restaurant is if it *depends upon return business.* I have a rule for selecting a restaurant, and as long as I've followed it, I have never gotten sick. The rule is this: *Never eat in a restaurant that doesn't have Mexican customers.* Think about it—there can only be two reasons why local people won't eat in a particular restaurant. Either it is over-priced, or the food isn't good. If local people won't eat there, why should you or I?

All too often, that lovely restaurant—with white tablecloths, sparkling silverware and smartly attired waiters—caters strictly to tourists. The owners don't work in the kitchen, and the low-paid help doesn't really much care whether tourists get sick or not. They know tourists seldom return anyway. Each new meal sees a new set of customers. Should a tourist come down with an illness, there's no way of knowing for sure where it came from because he's eaten at a different establishment every meal. I want to see Mexican businessmen enjoying lunch with their friends. If they have confidence, so do I.

To my way of thinking, the ideal Mexican restaurant is a family-owned affair. Mama works in the kitchen, overseeing the cooks and making sure food is prepared correctly. Maybe the children work there, too, while papa tends the cash register and oversees the customers. They know that keeping people happy and well is the key to continued prosperity.

Many people are shocked to see me stopping at a street stand and ordering food. "My God, don't you know that's dangerous? Aren't you afraid you'll get sick?" Not really. While I don't recommend that everyone try it, I feel safe eating from street stands. The reason is that I apply my rule of eating where local people eat. I've never contracted anything from street stands (of course, it could be just luck). When I see housewives, children, businessmen and workers stopping at these stands for snacks, I have confidence. These stands sell treats that aren't usually available in restaurants, because they are "fast foods." Items like roast tongue, *cabeza*, roast kid, fried cheese and sausages are just a few of the delicious surprises sold at these stands.

Drugstores, Prescriptions and Vitamins

If you take prescription drugs, bring an adequate supply, but don't worry about their availability in Mexico. Most common medications are readily available, and at about 30 percent of their U.S. price. Furthermore, prescriptions aren't required for drugs unless they are addictive.

Some drug stores advertise that it is legal to bring back drugs to the U.S. if bought for your personal use only. I don't know if this is true, but the variety of drugs available without prescription is interesting, to say the least.

For example: I see advertisements for Herpes/Aids remedies (Isoprinosine and Ribavirin) along with the claim that "some studies show these drugs to be beneficial in bolstering the immune system for Herpes and Aids patients." True? Don't ask me. Also advertised are "geriatric products" such as KH3, Zellaforte, Vivioptal and Gero H3. I have no idea what these are supposed to do for the geriatric set. Probably something totally erotic, indecent and scandalous. Should that be the case, maybe I'll buy some on my next trip through Juárez. Then there are drugs we've all heard about but haven't been able to persuade our doctors to prescribe, such as Hairgro-60 (Minoxidil) for growing hair, and Retin-A for smoothing over wrinkles. My doctor claims the Minoxidil might grow hair someplace I don't want it. That could negate the effects of the "geriatric products," so maybe I'll pass on that.

If you take vitamins, it's a good idea to bring an adequate supply. For some reason, vitamins are expensive in Mexico, which is strange, since prescription drugs are so cheap. Vitamin C can cost as much as an antibiotic. They are also not readily obtainable in supermarkets or anywhere except *farmacias*; apparently Mexicans aren't into vitamins as we are.

Many people claim that vitamin B is wonderful for keeping away insects. It seems that heavy doses of this vitamin makes you smell obnoxious to mosquitoes and other beasties. Drinking alcohol is said to lessen the effect of vitamin B, making you smell nice to bugs once more. I guess that's why I'm always scratching bites.

Doctors in Mexico

Mexico has an excellent system of health care. For citizens, medical care is free, a human right. (The United States is one of the few nations in the world, large or small, without a health care system.) For visitors, the costs are downright cheap. Americans who choose to retire or become long-term residents of Mexico may elect to "buy into" the government health program at a cost of $181 a year (currently). This covers all costs, including free prescriptions. If you don't belong to the system, doctors have to charge a nominal fee, but it isn't very high.

The last time I visited a doctor in Mexico (two years ago), he took care of three problems, one of which involved minor office surgery. The total bill amounted to three dollars! Another time, in a small town in Sonora, I felt ill and went to a doctor for a check-up. After a thorough examination, including an electrocardiogram, he prescribed a medication and announced that I would live. Then he said, rather embarrassed, "If you were a Mexican citizen I couldn't charge a fee, but as a foreigner, I must collect something from you." That was okay with me, because I wanted medical care, not something for nothing. When I translated the doctor's fee from pesos into dollars, the bill came to fifty cents! Not having any pesos, I gave him a dollar and told him to keep the change. That was the first and last time I ever tipped my doctor.

When doing research for the CHOOSE MEXICO book, we questioned hundreds of American residents about the availability of competent English-speaking doctors and dentists. According to retirees in every part of the country, there are good doctors and dentists in most cities of any size, and quality hospitals are within reasonable traveling distances. Incidentally, doctors still make house calls in Mexico!

Hospital Care

How good are the hospitals? This is a difficult question to answer. While most of our respondents said they were satisfied with the quality of hospitals, many stated that they would return to the United States for an unusual or serious illness. One woman told of her hysterectomy operation in a Mexican hospital: "The total cost, including ten days recuperation in the hospital was less than round trip air fare to El Paso," she said. "The care was wonderful."

Few Mexican hospital facilities can compare to their U.S. counterparts. They are not as modern, sometimes downright rustic, so naturally they look bad in comparison. Yet, how important is decor? What about the quality of care? Not having had any personal experiences, I have to rely upon hearsay and stories related by other people. The problem is, these stories vary widely. Some have nothing but praise, others nothing but condemnation.

Individual perceptions even of the *same hospital* can be wildly contradictory. In February, 1989 for example, I interviewed a couple who retired in their travel trailer near Ensenada. They joined the medical system in which everything is free. They had superlative things to say about the level of care. Twice the wife was rushed to the Ensenada hospital for emergency care. She had one operation. She praised the hospital highly: "It was bright and cheerful," she said, "and the staff and care were top-notch! I received far better treatment that I could have gotten in Los Angeles, and it was free."

On the other hand, that same month, I read an article in a Baja publication [1] relating an automobile accident victim's experience in the same hospital. It sounded horrible. The hospital was

1. Baja California Magazine, Dec./Jan. 1989, p.9

described as a "great, cold barren building with no heat." The staff was called uncaring and incompetent. The traumatologist who treated the lady was described as a "pompous ass" who presented an outrageous bill for $110 for diagnosis and treatment of two broken ribs, and $45 for the X-rays.

It's hard to believe that both sides were talking about the same hospital! To be fair, I must point out that the story wasn't written by the patient herself, but by a third party (possibly her husband). On the other hand, $110 sounds reasonable for emergency room treatment, and I pay $45 for my dentist just to X-ray my teeth. (I have a friend who spent overnight in a Los Angeles hospital and was handed a bill for over a thousand bucks.)

Another man wrote an article for *Mexico West* praising his treatment in Mexicali for a stroke. He described his arrival at the hospital as "absolutely incredible! Waiting to meet us were the head doctor, some nurses and another doctor. Even the president of Mexico couldn't have expected more attention!"

Note that Medicare isn't good in Mexico. You have to return to the United States for coverage. They may cover some emergency treatment, according to spokesmen for Medicare administration, but I wouldn't count on it.

D. QUINN

Chapter Eleven

Shopping and RV Cooking

Preparing meals in an RV is a challenge. Cooking in Mexico is a double challenge, for you will be using unfamiliar ingredients, and you need to pay attention to cleanliness to a greater degree than at home. Problems for RV travelers are compounded because many trailer parks are located in small villages or else far from the center of town, so most nearby stores are going to be very small, with limited supplies.

You can usually find basics, such as flour, salt, lard and things of that nature, but fresh vegetables, meats and bakery goods can be very spotty. Much depends upon what the villagers are harvesting from their gardens, or what animals are being butchered that week. Small, neighborhood stores aren't served by wholesale grocers with deliveries every day to replenish stock. If they run out of a commodity, they must wait until a truck passes through that happens to have the needed merchandise.

If you have access to larger markets, you'll find shopping delightful, particularly when it comes to fruits and vegetables. Because much of Mexico is tropical and enjoys a year-round growing season, many items like strawberries are available just about always. Bananas, avocados, tomatoes and produce like that are picked when they are ripe and ready for the Mexican market, not green and expected to ripen on the way to the United States. It makes all the difference in the world when you taste them. By the way, there are probably a hundred varieties of avocados in Mexico, the place of their origin. In the U.S.A. we only have two or three—for some reason it's prohibited to bring in other varieties—so we have no idea how tasty an avocado can be. Hint: the best kind are small, black and shriveled-looking. They taste like they're made with walnuts and butter!

When planning shopping excursions into small towns, remember that most stores observe siesta. This means they close from 12 or 1:00 o'clock until 3:00 or 4:00 in the afternoon. If you don't allow for this, you could have an annoying wait. Sometimes the only places open are restaurants during the siesta, and sometimes not even restaurants.

Menu Planning

One piece of advice was passed on by a savvy lady with lots of experience in RV travel in Mexico: "Don't plan your weekly menu and then go shopping. Do it the other way around; plan your menu as you shop." There's no point in planning a shrimp paella if the local store doesn't have shrimp that day.

Personally, I prefer it that way. It's fun browsing through a store, imagining what kind of meals can be concocted using fresh cilantro, chicken and thin spaghetti. Or, if those ingredients aren't available, how can sweet basil, Swiss chard and side pork (or whatever) be worked into the menu? Sometimes a store will offer tasty porterhouse steaks, and the next day the only meats available are frozen chunks of unappetizing beef. Sometimes nothing is available. But if someone in the neighborhood has just butchered a hog, you might be lucky enough to garner a choice length of loin. Cut into thick filets, butterflied and then fried in peanut oil, they're absolutely delicious! Barbecue them over a low sagebrush fire for a great dinner.

When a farmer plans on butchering a hog or a steer, he notifies the stores around the village and takes "reservations" on preferred cuts. If you are going to be around for a while, you might ask what meat will be available and put in your order.

Chicken is almost always available in small stores, but inexplicably, is more expensive than beef or pork. Sometimes meats are fresh, sometimes not. Check it out first. One lady told of ordering a chicken and waiting while the storekeeper ran one down and butchered it. That's fresh chicken! Lamb is seldom found in smaller markets. Instead, young goat (cabrito) is sold. It tastes not at all like lamb, but is delicious roasted. (I've never had the nerve to roast one; I always order it in a restaurant and feel guilty.)

Vegetables depend solely on the season. When local gardens are yielding carrots or tomatoes at their prime, better plan your menus around carrots and tomatoes. Next week it might be Swiss chard and potatoes. Take advantage of the moment and buy whatever looks fresh.

Shortages

Smaller stores are notorious for being out of whatever you need. Sometimes it's paper goods. Other times matches or cooking oil. One lady, remembering her last trip to Mexico when she couldn't find paper towels, loaded up the cupboards with 20 rolls of towels. She figured to use some of them as gifts to other RV campers. When she arrived, she discovered that the shelves were bountiful with paper towels, priced lower than she paid at home. But this time there were no matches. Naturally, she forgot to stock up on them. You never know.

By shopping judiciously before you cross the border, you can pack enough staples into your rig to get you by in the face of unexpected shortages. Some RV cooks recommend bringing enough of your favorite brand of cooking oil or shortening because, even if available, the quality of Mexican oils can vary widely. They also suggest bringing several boxes of old-fashioned kitchen matches (the strike-anywhere kind). They're much superior to Mexican matches, and they make great gifts to gringos and Mexicans alike. At the end of the chapter is a check-list of items for your kitchen.

Supermarkets and Native Markets

Sometimes a small town will have a *supermercado*. Usually they really aren't "supermarkets" as we picture them. They are closer to our convenience stores. The term really means a store where you wait on yourself rather than asking a clerk for every item. Small supermercados will have a fairly comprehensive collection of your needs, but vegetables and meats are still very seasonal. Milk is usually available at these stores, but not milk as we know it. Because of the lack of refrigeration, Mexico uses the method of irradiating milk and packaging it in cartons which don't have to be chilled. The cartons will keep on the pantry shelf for several months. It tastes great, and it's a wonderful way of preserving a valuable food resource. It's too bad we don't have irradiated milk in the United States. Milk producers here fiercely resist the idea, but it's readily available all over Europe.

Another type of market is the *Conasupo*. This is a government-franchised store that is often found where the town is too small to support a large market. Prices are usually lower here, although the variety is sometimes limited.

Real supermarkets are found in just about any large town. Some of these offer astounding varieties of food and merchandise. Acapulco has an enormous store that stocks quality food of every description. It has a terrific deli section, complete with gourmet take-out foods that rival any fine restaurant I've seen anywhere. Wonderful pastas, chicken courses, shrimp and lobster concoctions, French pastries, regional dishes, just about anything you can imagine—all ready to take out for a gourmet RV meal.

Native Markets

Since most RV campers make a shopping trip once a week, they usually head for the supermarket for the main shopping and patronize neighborhood markets for daily menu supplements. But if you're visiting south of the Tropic of Cancer, you are in for a shopping treat: *el mercado*.

El mercado means "the market," but with a different connotation. A neighborhood or village store is an *abarrote* or *tienda*. A supermarket is a *super*, *supermercado* or (occasionally) *hipermercado*. But when they refer to a *mercado* they usually mean a municipal, cooperative market where local farmers, butchers, artisans and merchants of all kinds gather together to offer their wares under awnings and umbrellas.

Why this should be a tradition found mostly in the tropical part of Mexico is something I don't understand. But you rarely see it in its true form north of the Tropic of Cancer. These open air-markets have long been a prominent feature of Mexican life. They were in existence when the Spanish first visited Mexico over four centuries ago. The format has changed very little.

Every town or city dedicates a certain area (or areas) exclusively to the market. Rows of booths, shaded by awnings, display a bewildering array of produce, foods of all kinds, plus clothing, hardware, parrots, used auto parts, just about anything you can think of. The larger the market, the wider the selection.

Sometimes the markets are outdoors, sometimes under a large, roofed area provided by the municipal government. In smaller towns, the market meets once or twice a week, with merchants setting up their *puestos* on the sidewalks. A whole neighborhood will be transformed into a sprawling marketplace with a festive atmosphere. The vendors travel from town to town, depending upon the market day schedule.

The market is a wonderful place for fresh produce. Women or children spread a cloth on the ground and arrange their wares into little purchase-size pyramids. Pine nuts, chili peppers, avocados, *choyotes*, asparagus—whatever they raise or collect—sit in little piles while their owners squat patiently, chatting amicably with neighbors while waiting for customers.

Melons and other fruits are often sliced open for display. Insist on buying a whole melon; you can slice it when you get back to the RV, confident that it hasn't hosted a housefly convention. Any fruit that can be peeled is perfectly safe to eat on the spot. Fruits and vegetables that need washing should be soaked in a purifying solution.

At the Butcher Shop

Some aspects of the market may not appeal to you, at least until you are used to it. The meat section is often singularly unattractive, with sides of beef hanging in the open, dotted with flies. Most Americans prefer to patronize a regular meat market that has sanitation and refrigeration. Modern meat markets are generally found next to, or nearby the *mercados*.

The best beef is referred to as "Sonora" beef. Whether or not it actually comes from the state of Sonora is dubious, but Sonora beef should be much tenderer than ordinary, range-fed beef. Cattle in Mexico have a tough life, most have to make a living on sparse, desert-like land. They are seldom grain-fed to fatten them up, as we do in the U.S., nor are they fed steroids and antibiotics. That means it takes longer to raise them for market, six months to a year longer. This extra maturity accounts for the rich flavor of Mexican beef. Of course, unless you can buy "Sonora beef," it's going to be tough and stringy. Since RVs seldom have room in the fridge for aging beef, you must find ways of preparing it to compensate for toughness. The flavor of grass-fed beef makes it worth a little extra chewing.

Mexicans don't use hamburger meat as much as we do. I don't know why. Actually, to them, *hamburguesa* isn't hamburger until it's cooked and on a bun. Until then, it's *carne molida* or ground meat. The stuff you see in the supermarket is often very lean, and doesn't taste as we expect; we are used to a percentage of fat in the mixture. It's best to ask them to grind it for you (*Lo muele, por favor*), and ask for *pulpa*, which is a bottom round roast. Have the butcher add a little fat if you like the meat to be more like hamburger you are used to back home. A *pulpa larga* is a rump roast.

Club, or top loin steak is called *chuleta costado*, and porterhouse or T-bone is simply *T-bon*. That's easy enough. Short ribs are *costillas* and a rib roast is *chuleta entera*. The top of the line, filet mignon, is simply *filete* or *filete de res*.

Pork is also quite tasty in Mexico. Instead of being mass-produced on pig farms (or is it hog ranches?) most pigs wander freely about, foraging for themselves. They are a familiar sight in small villages, meandering along the streets with a covey of little piglets as if they haven't a care in the world. (Little do they know.) The result is a lean, red-meat pork, with the consistency of chewy steak. The flavor is great. Be sure to cook it thoroughly, just as you do back home. Overcooking doesn't seem to harm the flavor as much as it does with our pen-raised pork.

Smoked pork chops, *chuletas ahumadas* and bacon, *tocino* didn't used to be very good in Mexico, but they must have done something to the process, because they're excellent nowadays. Pork spare ribs are *costillas de puerco* and are delightfully lean. Mixed with canned sauerkraut, they make a great dinner. A pork loin roast is a *chuleta de puerco entero*. See meat translations below.

Favorite RV Recipes

A wonderful addition to your kitchen is a cookbook by a lady who has traveled extensively in Mexico in her RV over the last 15 years. In her book, *Easy Recipes for the Traveling Cook*, Ferne Holmes gets down to basics: from planning which utensils to pack, to essential foods and condiments necessary for tasty results. She presents new ideas for dishes you never thought you could prepare in the limited space of a tiny RV kitchen, or outdoors on a Coleman stove. Special attention is given to the problem of "making do" with canned meats in a remote area and still achieving gourmet results.

Try to stock a supply of ingredients for easy-to-cook dishes. That way, when you don't feel like running into town for the week's shopping, you can throw something together and postpone things. My favorite fast-food is spaghetti. With canned milk, canned clams, a touch of basil, some flour and jack cheese, it becomes a wonderful clam pasta. If I find an egg and a couple of slices of bacon, it becomes spaghetti *carbonaro*. Ramen noodles, macaroni mixes, canned chili, also make fine emergency meals.

Kitchen Items to Check

Try not to take your entire home kitchen with you. Many things can be purchased in Mexico, of the same quality as at home, and maybe cheaper. But there are certain items that aren't readily available or the quality is lower. Ingredients like peanut oil, salad dressing, vitamins and canned goods are best brought with you. On the next page is a check list of some things you might need. Again, don't bring everything, just what you reasonably will need.

CHECK LIST

- aluminum foil
- baggies
- baking yeast
- bar soap
- barbecue grill
- basil
- biscuit mix
- bug spray
- butter
- canned chicken
- canned chili
- canned clams
- canned milk
- canned tuna
- catsup
- chili powder
- cinnamon
- corned beef

- cornstarch
- dish pan
- flour
- fly swatter
- garbage bags
- good can opener
- horseradish
- instant potatoes
- liquid soap
- mayonnaise
- mustard
- non-dairy creamer
- olive oil
- oregano
- pancake mix
- paper plates
- peanut butter

- peanut oil
- pet food
- plastic bucket
- plastic containers
- plastic wrap
- powdered garlic
- salad oil
- sauerkraut
- scouring pads
- soup mixes
- soy sauce
- tea bags
- tenderizer
- vinegar
- wax paper
- wood matches
- worcestershire

MEATS

English	Spanish	English	Spanish
beef	carne de rez	roast	trozo, rosbíf
blade steaks	rebanada de paleta	rump roast	pulpa larga
bottom round	pulpa	sausage	chorizo
chicken	pollo	sliced	rebanada
chuck steak	shuck stek	smoked pork	
club steak	chuleta costado	chops	chuletas ahumadas
eye of round	pulpa cuete	Sonora beef	res de sonora
filet mignon	filete, lomo	spare ribs	costillas de puerco
goat (kid)	cabrito	T-bone	T-bone
ground beef	carne molida	tenderloin	lomo, filete
ham	jamón	tip roast	pulpa bola
	or, pierna ahumada	tongue	lengua
kidneys	riñones	top round	pulpa negra
pork	carne de chancho	tripe	menudo
	or, carne de puerco	turkey	guajalote
pork chops	chuleta de puerco	veal	ternero
rabbit	conejo	venison	venado

VEGETABLES

almonds	*almendras*	grapes	*uvas*
apples	*manzanas*	lettuce	*lechuga*
apricots	*chauacanes*	lima beans	*habas verdes*
artichokes	*alcachofas*	olives	*aceitunas*
asparagus	*espárrago*	onions	*cebolla*
avocado	*aguacate*	oranges	*naranjas*
banana	*plátano, plata*	peanuts	*cacahuates*
basil	*albahaca*	peas	*chícaros*
beans	*frijoles*	pineapple	*piña*
beets	*betabeles*	plums	*ciruelas*
broccoli	*brócoli*	popcorn	*palomitos*
cabbage	*col*	potatoes	*papas*
cantaloupe	*melón*	radishes	*rábanos*
carrots	*zanahorias*	rice	*arroz*
cauliflower	*coliflor*	sauerkraut	*col agria*
celery	*apio*	squash	*calabaza*
corn on cob	*elotes*	strawberries	*fresas*
cucumber	*pepino*	sweet potatos	*camotes*
dates	*dátiles*	swiss chard	*acelgas*
eggplant	*berenjena*	tangerines	*mandarinas*
figs	*higos*	tomatoes	*jitomates*
garlic	*ajo*	watermelon	*sandia*
grapefruit	*grepfrut, toronja*	zucchini	*calabacitas*

SEAFOOD

mackerel	*sierra*	salmon	*salmón*
octopus	*pulpo*	shrimp	*camarones*
oysters	*ostiones*	squid	*calamare*
red snapper	*huachinango*	tuna	*albacore*
rock lobster	*langosta*		

AlcoholicBeverages

Mexico's beer ranks with the best in the world. Small wonder, since the top breweries were started by German immigrants. Beer (cerveza) is also downright cheap. Scotch, however, is out of sight. If that's what you prefer to drink, by all means, bring your own before you buy in Mexico. Recommendation: drink *rum* rather than scotch or bourbon! Not just any rum, but *Ron Castillo*, which many consider to be the finest rum made anywhere! It leaves a dry, crisp tingle on your palate, similar to a fine coñac. And best of all, it doesn't taste like rum! It isn't sweet or heavy tasting, like most rums.

Chapter Twelve

Retirement in Mexico?

Forty years ago, my family moved to Mexico City when my father (a veterinarian), accepted a position in a joint U.S.-Mexico program to eradicate cattle hoof-and-mouth disease. In those days, Mexico City was *the* place for Americans to live. It was exciting, elegant. For those with dollars, living costs were wonderfully low and living standards incredibly high. Through intense blue skies floated soft puffy clouds almost every day, and on clear days, snow-capped peaks could be seen in the distance. Mexico City was a paradise for North Americans not only for working, but retirement.

My love affair with Mexico began in those days and will continue forever. When years began slipping away and notions of retirement became more specific, quite naturally, I pictured Mexico as my retirement haven.

Where else? Over the years of visiting and living there, I met many people who had retired in various parts of the republic. I always envied their life-styles. Whenever possible, I took time off work to spend as many months as I could afford, sampling retirement living in different parts of Mexico. I got an early start, when I was in my 40's. This eventually prompted me to begin work on a book, which evolved into CHOOSE MEXICO, a how-to-do-it book on retirement.

My co-author and I went into great detail describing how to find a house or an apartment, the technicalities of hiring a maid or gardener, everything you need to know about retirement in Mexico. We thought we'd covered all angles. The Mexican government thought so too, because when someone inquires at a Mexican consulate about retirement, they are usually told to buy CHOOSE MEXICO. When it hit the book stores, we began to receive queries from readers about *trailer and motorhome* retirement in Mexico.

This took us by surprise, for our ideal Mexico retirement involved gracious living in an old colonial home, lunches in the patio-garden or dinner parties in a spacious dining room with the maid serving after-dinner drinks. Somehow, living in an RV didn't quite fit this picture! Yet, we received so many requests for more information that I decided to investigate further. Since I was doing research on my book RETIREMENT CHOICES, and checking out RV retirement styles in the United States, I enlarged my scope to include RVs in Mexico.

Years ago, the idea of Mexico retirement in a travel trailer or motorhome would have seemed ludicrous. RVs in those days were rare curiosities in Mexico. RV parks were either primitive or non-existent. Road conditions discouraged dragging anything but the lightest rig possible over mountain grades and rough pavement, sometimes even rougher than gravel roads. It's changed a lot over the years.

Today, there are a considerable number of retired folks who take their RVs to Mexico to spend the entire winter. And they do it on a regular basis, so that qualifies as part-time retirement. In fact, while doing research for this book we found the vast majority of RV travelers in Mexico were, in fact, retired. This is understandable, because people who work at regular jobs rarely manage to get time off from work to fritter away a whole winter in Mexico.

Naturally, these RV retiree life styles do not include a gardener, a maid or large dinner parties in the dining room. Their living arrangements are totally different from what Don Merwin and I envisioned when we wrote CHOOSE MEXICO. Different, but perfectly suited to this new style of living.

In the United States and Canada, a growing number of retirees incorporate RVs into their retirement plans. They maintain a base in their home town, and spend part of each year "on the road." While writing the RETIREMENT CHOICES book, we interviewed numerous retirees who regularly close up their homes for the winter. They wisely spend the cold and icy months basking in warm weather and sunshine. Florida, the Texas Rio Grande Valley, Arizona and California attract the bulk of these retirees. Once they find a place they like, they tend to return year after year.

So many RV folks winter regularly around Texas's Rio Grande Valley that they've become a political force to be reckoned with. Known as "Winter Texans" these RV retirees register to vote as soon as they arrive for the season and often determine the outcome of local elections. (Texas law permits this.)

Other winter immigrants aren't retired, they are construction workers or farmers escaping their non-productive winter months.

They've been dodging winters for years; it's comparatively recently that more retirees have discovered the joys of RV retirement, enjoying winters economically in pleasantly warm climates.

For many people, the economic aspects of retirement are crucial. There used to be a saying around the Rio Grande that northern farmers arrived with a pair of overalls and a five-dollar bill and returned in the spring without changing either. Today, there is an air of affluence among RV travelers; they are a welcome economic bonanza for local economies. Nevertheless, it is comparatively inexpensive living.

Since RV living in Mexico isn't any more expensive than in the U.S. (often even *less* expensive), many retirees look across the border to investigate possibilities there. They are going to Mexico in ever-increasing numbers. Since Baja and Mexico's west coast draw the most RV travelers, that is where you'll find most retirees. Many parks fill to capacity in winter, but when summer weather rolls around, most retirees roll back home to enjoy the best part of the year there. Good arrangement.

Winter Retirement

As an example of one retirement style that includes Mexico, let's look at the itinerary of Carl and Barbara. They have a house in Monterey, California and they own a small travel trailer. About the first of November, they rent their house to graduate students from a local university and then head for Bahía de Concepción in Baja California. The rent covers all their expenses for the winter.

At Bahía, they have their choice of several different beaches with overnight charges ranging from $4 down to nothing. This last winter, they elected to stay at Coyote Beach, where there is no charge.* "We set up our trailer a little ways away from other people," Carl said. "We weren't being anti-social; we wanted the shade of this large palm tree. The first thing I did was put up a windbreak using war-surplus shelter-halves. Don't try to use plastic, it has to be canvas or nylon. We set out our chairs and I improvised a dining table; we were set for the winter!"

On an unimproved beach like this, there are no showers or toilets. This is where the popular "solar shower" comes in handy. In Baja, where sun shines most every day, it's a matter of minutes before the water in the plastic water container bag is pleasantly warm. (Some people just set a bucket on the roof to soak up the sun's heat.) Utilizing the canvas shelter for privacy, they have

---

* We understand that there is a charge at Coyote as of March of 1989. How long this will last is anybody's guess, because all of the RVs indignantly moved out *en mass* when charges were imposed.

their own shower facilities. "About once a week, we went into Mulegé and treated ourselves to a real shower at the hotel," Barbara added. "For a dollar, we enjoyed the luxury of as much hot water and suds as we wanted."

They didn't need to drive into town very often. A well-stocked produce-grocery truck drove by the beach at least once a week. Local fishermen traded scallops and clams for cigarettes (Our friends don't smoke, they just use cigarettes as trading material.) And finally, their RV neighbors always caught more fish than they could possibly eat. This is a seafood-lover's paradise!

To complete their retirement schedule: Carl and Barbara return around the last of February to enjoy spring blossoms in California. Then when summer rolls around, they rent out the house for another three months and head north to Lassen State Park. There they work four hours a day as volunteers, Barbara working at her pre-retirement speciality and Carl at his. Although they receive no pay, they have the use of a nicely furnished house and enjoy weekends traveling around with their trailer. Then, it's back to enjoy the Monterey Peninsula during autumn, the best part of the whole year there. The marvelous part of this story is that the house rental income pays all their living expenses while in Mexico and in the park. This is the type of creative retirement that makes for quality living.

Full-time RV Retirement

Some people are really serious about RV travel. They've given up all semblances of roots. Kay Peterson (of the Escapee's Club) describes these "full-timers" in her book HOME IS WHERE YOU FIND IT. These are folks who have made a complete break with conventional living and have decided to live full time in their rigs. For them, this is an ideal life, a gypsy's existence, following the best seasons and staying wherever fancy dictates. This is a dream many have, but few have the courage to follow their dream.

Many "full-timers" include Mexico on their agenda. They can be found in Kino Bay and San Carlos or along the length of the Baja peninsula. I've run into some in the Yucatan, camping by ancient Mayan ruins, or searching for their own archaeological finds. The Caribbean coast is popular, with some fine boondocking areas and good fishing just a few feet from the beach. Since full-timers have plenty of experience handling their equipment, they think nothing of traveling through some of the more rugged (and pretty) parts of Mexico. Unlike part-timers, who tend to return to the same places every year, full-timers prefer to go to places they haven't yet seen.

Do many people retire *full-time* in RVs in Mexico? Some, but not as many as in the United States. One couple I interviewed, live in Cabo San Lucas. They have their own lot with their 32-foot Coachmen set up under a roofed cabana. It's fenced, with Mexican neighbors on all sides. Lloyd used to work as an electrician, Elaine as a grammar school teacher. As soon as they moved there, Elaine began giving free English lessons to the neighbors while Lloyd made friends by helping a family wire a house they were building next door. "When we take a trip to the mainland, or visit back home in Montana, we don't worry about our things here," Lloyd said. "Our neighbors are like family. They watch our place as closely as they watch their own property."

Thinking of Retirement?

Using your RV as part of your retirement scheme is practical and done by thousands. It's a wonderful way of exploring all possible retirement locations, looking for a situation that would fit your style. You can test the waters, dip and move on to new horizons; that's the wonder of RV living.

But for those people who are looking to "settle down" more or less permanently, it might be better to look for a house or an apartment. The RV can be stored and used for weekend adventures. The reason I feel this way is that I prefer being near the center of things rather than sitting on the outskirts of town. True, its quieter out there in an RV park, but eventually the isolation might get boring once the novelty has worn thin, and, you would be missing out on many cultural and social events that happen around the town's center.

Should you seriously think of full-time retirement, I urge you to pick up our book *CHOOSE MEXICO* for complete details on how it's done. In the meantime, look at the following section on how to do it legally.

Legalities of Mexico Retirement

Few people would think seriously of Mexican retirement if they had to forfeit their U.S. citizenship in the process. Of course, it isn't necessary. You can become a legal resident without affecting your citizenship in any way.

The options open range from six-month tourist cards to *Inmigrado* status which gives you all the rights of Mexican citizen except the right to vote. The tourist card gives you the right to travel and live with few restrictions, and the *Inmigrado* card adds the privilege of working and owning property without going through a lease maneuver.

Here is a brief summary of the options open to someone who wants to spend more than half a year in Mexico:

Tourist Card

Good for six months, free, easily obtainable upon proof of U.S. or Canadian citizenship. The disadvantage is that it must be renewed every six months by a trip to the border. If you have an RV or other vehicle, you must take that with you, or else have it bonded. A tourist card doesn't permit you to bring in household goods, appliances, etc. (What you bring in your RV isn't counted, because it's considered part of the vehicle.) Also, you *cannot* work. (This doesn't apply in the case of a writer, artist, or photographer doing work in Mexico to be sold outside the country.)

Multiple Entry Tourist Card

Same as above except that you can enter and leave at will, without having to go through the motions of getting a new card every time you enter Mexico. This is very popular with folks with trailers near the border who want to return home often. You'll need passport-size photos when you make application.

Visitante Rentista

For people who don't want to bother returning to the border every six months. Good for two years, but must be renewed every six months. It requires a fixed income which must be deposited in a Mexican bank every month. (That's to make sure you aren't destitute or working.) You will, like a tourist, be prohibited from owning a business or holding a job. At the end of two years you must leave the country, re-enter, and start over. You have to be 55 or older to obtain this status.

Inmigrante Rentista

This is especially for retirees. It conveys several rights and exempts you from some taxes. You can also bring in household furnishings and car tax free. You may buy real estate for your residence as long as it isn't located within 62 miles of the border or 31 miles of the coast. Even in these "forbidden zones" it is now possible, under a new law, to obtain use of land for your residence. This involves long-term trust agreements, and a lawyer or bank in Mexico can furnish you with the details.

Inmigrado Status

This is for people who decide to make it permanent. In-migrado status gives you all the rights of a Mexican citizen except the right to vote. You can work, own a business, or buy and sell property. The restriction against owning property near the ocean or the border still holds, however. To obtain this card, you must either spend five years as an Inmigrante Rentista or invest a large amount of money in a business. It requires a lot of red tape, but many feel it's worth it.

Buying Property

First of all, it is illegal for any foreigner to own land in Mexico within 50 kilometers of the coast, or within 100 kilometers of the border. The reason for these laws is to prevent gringos from coming down to Mexico and buying up the entire country. However, there are ways to control property as if you owned it.

In 1973 the government, recognizing the desirability of North Americans retiring and living in Mexico, passed the "Foreign Investment Act." This provides for a *fidecomiso* (trust), to be held by a Mexican bank, in the interest of the buyer. This trust is good for 30 years. During that time, you can build on it or sell it, just as if you owned it outright. But, at the end of the 30-year term, the property was supposed to be sold to a Mexican or Mexican corporation.

In May of 1989, the laws were liberalized, permitting an additional 30 years to be tacked on to the leases, and permitting foreigners to own resort property outright. Previously, they were limited to 49 percent ownership, with 51 percent belonging to Mexican citizens. Needless to say: before buying anything, be sure and have good legal advice.

Trying it Out

My recommendation would be to first go on a tourist card good for six months. You can usually apply for and receive a slight extension of the card, but most people simply return to the border once every six months and obtain a new card. My mother did that for five years before she decided to apply for *inmigrado* papers. She enjoyed taking the train to El Paso twice a year for a shopping spree. I know one couple who lived in San Cristóbal de Las Casas for 17 years who renewed their tourist permits with an overnight trip to Guatemala every six months.

The big advantage of trying retirement in an RV is: if you decide it isn't for you, you can easily pack up and go home.

Chapter Thirteen

Buying Insurance

If you've read other sections of this book, you know the emphasis I place on having proper insurance. Some information in this chapter has been presented elsewhere in this book, but it's worth gathering together in one place for your information. Having proper insurance is even more important than having insurance at home, because laws are different in Mexico and you might find yourself caught up in a Kafka-like nightmare because of a minor fender bender. Regardless of what your policy may indicate, your U.S. policy isn't recognized in Mexico very far south of the border. That's the law.

So, get property-damage and liability insurance without fail. Since Mexican courts don't award ridiculously high damage claims, most people feel comfortable buying just the minimum liability coverage. As pointed out earlier, personal damages are limited by law, and are based on the minimum wage rates.

What about collision? Fire? Theft? Even though your insurance might appear to cover collision on your vehicle, it doesn't. There's no way that an adjuster can enter Mexico to assess damages and make payment. It's not permitted past the border towns. To compound the problem, should your vehicle be totaled, it's up to you to either take the vehicle back (you entered with one, you must leave with one), or get the proper papers to either store it in a garage or donate it to a junk yard. (You need papers for both.) No U.S. insurance company is going to drag a total wreck back for examination.

Therefore, if your rig is worth more than the cost of repairs, don't fight it. Get collision insurance. On the other hand, since repairs are cheap in Mexico, you might take a chance on just liability insurance if you have an older vehicle. Sometimes I travel in a 1972 VW camper. The amount I'd pay for collision insurance would go a long way toward repairing any damage I might sustain. Other times, when I take my small motorhome (worth about $10,000) I buy collision and fire-theft insurance in addition to liability.

Boat and Trailer Insurance

What if you're towing a boat or a trailer? Make sure that the towed vehicle is *also* covered for liability. Too often an insurance policy is specifically invalidated if you are hauling an uninsured trailer. Check on it, and if in doubt, get a policy on the boat trailer, too. Some long-term group policies (sold through travel clubs) automatically insure you against liability for anything you happen to be towing at the time of an accident.

Suppose you're going to be sitting in a park for several months? Do you need to have insurance? Well obviously you won't need liability or property damage. Fire and theft, you might want, depending upon how you feel about fire. Theft of the whole rig isn't too likely. Why? Given the scarcity of Mexican RV owners in Mexico, a Mexican thief would stand out like the proverbial sore thumb, and would have a difficult time getting rid of his booty. No market. An American thief wouldn't chance taking it across the border. As far as I am aware, theft of an entire RV isn't common, but theft insurance is part of the fire coverage package anyway.

Many folks who are planning on long stays don't bother with anything more than day by day coverage to get them to their camp destination. In the more popular spots, there are insurance brokers, sometimes right in the park, who can sell short-term insurance for your return trip.

Some companies offer special fire and theft coverage for people who don't plan on moving around once they get to Mexico. But if you're going to be there for some time, a season perhaps, then buying the year-long full coverage group policy from a travel club makes a lot of sense. That way, if you feel like unhooking and doing some touring, you won't have to worry about hustling around for insurance when you're ready to go.

Group Insurance

Available through some travel clubs, this is the most inexpensive way to buy insurance for anyone who is planning on staying over three weeks, or who might return to Mexico more than once in a year. Examples of prices are: Full coverage for a year on a vehicle worth $10,000, $150. Liability only: $100 or less. These are good for multiple entries. By the way, I'm not an insurance agent, and the rates quoted here are only approximate. If they are higher or lower when you go to get your insurance, you are welcome to curse at me. By the way, it's my understanding that the group policies aren't valid when on an organized caravan. The caravan outfitters will give you information on insurance.

Group policies are sold for a full year, starting from the first of a quarter. Usually they start on one of the following dates: January 1, April 1, July 1, or Oct. 1. This means if you don't get around to ordering your insurance until the middle of March, the coverage starts from Jan. 1, and will expire on the next Dec. 31.

Another type of group policy covers the driver, no matter what car or vehicle he is driving. And this can be bought for the actual time you are traveling in Mexico by notifying the insurance company when you plan on crossing the border and then when you return. You are billed later.

Most group policies are restricted as to the parts of Mexico where they are valid. Should you travel outside the insured zones, make arrangements for extension of coverage. As an example, for a vehicle worth about $20,000, it would cost around $50 a month to travel elsewhere. If you were driving a rig worth less than $10,000, the additional premium would be about $40 a month. Still cheap for long-term travels.

Additional Coverage

Besides being covered for liability and collision, many RV drivers feel comfortable with some extended coverages. Here are a few suggestions:

Legal Services—provides for payment of fines, legal fees and bonds resulting from accidents in Mexico. The insurance company reimburses any fines connected with an accident, provides bonds so you can go on your way while the investigation progresses and if necessary, will fly a lawyer to your side to cut through the red tape. For my money, the $13 or so it costs to purchase this option is well worth it. This will pay even if you are in the wrong. When you have a lawyer on your side in addition to the insurance company, you are covering one more gap.

Personal effects—Fire and theft coverage on personal articles in your auto or RV. Ordinary policies don't cover anything but total loss.

Excess liability—This option increases basic auto liabilities to a total of $200,000. Some people feel better, although many say it's not necessary to insure so high.

Tour Aid

Common road service, such as provided by AAA and other U.S. insurance companies, isn't valid in Mexico. To take up the slack, special road insurance is provided for the security and well-being of RV travelers by several insurance brokers. Both

Gateway and Lewis & Lewis carry it. The cost of a policy has recently been lowered from $50 a year to $25 (which is an indication of good experience with RVs).

This policy, "Tour Aid," covers emergency services—Reimbursement for towing and emergency road repairs, parts, service, and guarantee of hospital costs in Mexico. Should you need cash in an emergency, an instant loan of $300 is available. Another interesting service is making sure you have repair parts in case of a vehicle breakdown. John Rebel (Gateway Insurance) told of a motorhome that lost its oil pump in Cancún, and no parts were to be found. The necessary replacements were sent by air; the RV owner had to pay for the parts and any customs, but the delivery was free. "Of course, should it be something big, like an entire engine," John added, "we couldn't do that. But we can get most parts to our clients, if they are not available in Mexico."

Texas Travelers Insurance

For people who live in the eastern part of the continent, the closest place to enter Mexico is through south Texas. The Vagabundos del Mar recently expanded its insurance coverage to cover the eastern Mexican states of Nuevo Leon, Tamaulipas and Veracruz. This is a group policy, only available through Club Vagabundos. For those "Winter Texans" who spend a lot of time along the Rio Grande, this might be an attractive bargain.

These policies are good for one year, and there is no need to report when entering or leaving Mexico. You can cross the border as often as you wish, and you keep the actual policy with you. The transactions can be done by mail, which means you won't have to wait at the border for insurance. Your boat or trailer is also covered for liability as long as it is connected to your vehicle.

Current Rates: collision, fire, total theft, glass, liability, $25,000 property damage, $30/60,000 bodily injury, $2,000/10,000 medical payments, for a vehicle under $5,000 valuation: $105. Under $15,000: $165. Under $30,000: $210.

Boat Insurance

Many RV travelers are also boat lovers. Launching a boat makes the trip a wholly different experience. Mexican waters are renowned for fishing, and it would be a shame not to drag the old scow down for the winter. But, you'll probably want insurance.

There are several forms of boat insurance. The most limited is coverage only while being towed. To be covered, you add the value of the boat and trailer to the value of the tow vehicle. Make sure the policy mentions the boat *and* trailer. Some policies are invalid if towing an uninsured boat trailer. I understand this is a common disclaimer in the United States, as well.

Don't think that your U.S. company will cover your boat, because they have no way of helping you in Mexico. Some policies appear to cover you for damage, but since U.S. insurance adjusters aren't permitted to work in Mexico, you're again left on your own.

Another form of insurance is while the craft is afloat. You can insure it for liability, property damage and bodily injury. But, Mexican liability insurance won't cover passengers, whether it's a boat, auto or airplane.

Finally, you can insure your boat and motors for damage to the hull or total theft. These policies are good only in Mexico. As far as I know, U.S. insurance companies won't insure boats in Mexican waters.

U.S. Auto Policies

For those who stay in Mexico most of the year and just travel to the U.S.A. every six months to renew their tourist cards, there is another insurance problem. "Shall we keep up our U.S. insurance, even though we use it just a few days each year?" That's expensive. The alternative is to take a chance by breaking the laws and violating common sense by driving in the United States without insurance.

A solution to the problem is to buy U.S. insurance by the day, just as tourists in Mexico buy their Mexican insurance by the day. The policy, sold by international Gateway brokers (Bonita, California) and underwritten by a Pennsylvania company, can run from five to 365 days. Example: Bodily injury of $50,000/100,000, Property damage of $25,000 and medical of $2,000 would cost $106 for a 15-day policy. Full coverage would add about 50 cents a day extra for $10,000 coverage.

Insurance Brokers

Below is a list of sources for insurance. The list is far from exhaustive; there are hundreds, maybe a thousand places to buy insurance. As you approach the border, you'll find them all over. Grocery stores, pharmacies, liquor stores, just about anywhere you look, you'll find Mexican auto insurance for sale. Don't worry about it; the prices should all be about the same. There are several Mexican insurance companies, but rates are set by the Mexican government. I've listed the brokers below, not as endorsements, but simply because I've either dealt with them, or I've interviewed them, or I've heard good things about them.

Anserve Insurance Service—739 Fifth Ave. Suite 29, San Diego, CA 92101. Phone 800-654-7504, or California only 800-262-1994. $56.00 including tax for a year policy that's good for up to 60 days a year. Any combination of days, in or out of Mexico as you please. No club membership required.

Club Mex—Tony Burton, Hidalgo 75 Lake Chapala (between Chapala and Ajijic). Newly opened office selling discount insurance to people in Guadalajara area, with savings of up to 40%.

Gateway Insurance—3450 Bonita Road., Suite 103, Chula Vista, CA. 92002—(800) 423-2646. Connected with Mexico West. John Rebel is the broker, a man who has lived and worked in Mexico for many years, and very knowledgeable about insurance and Mexico travel.

Lewis and Lewis Insurance Agency—8929 Wilshire Blvd., Suite 220, Beverly Hills CA 90211. Phone (213) 657-1112. Sells through various travel clubs. Has several options for non-club members. Perhaps the first agency to begin selling discount insurance.

Mexico West—P.O. Box 1646, Bonita, CA 92002. Phone: (619) 585-3033, Shirley Miller. Club group discounts and other benefits. Helpful people. Membership price: $35.

Stanley "Hambone" Lieberman—P.O. Box 300 San Carlos, Son., Mex. Phone: (622) 6-02-74. You must belong to Club Deportivo of San Carlos. A $100 lifetime membership in the club and then fairly cheap insurance. His office is in San Carlos (Sonora) and his CB handle is "Hambone." Group insurance good only on West Coast of Mexico.

Vagabundos del Mar—P.O. Box 824, Isleton, CA 95641. Phone (707) 374-5511. Club group discounts. Membership price: $35. Also sells insurance for East Coast of Mexico. Social aspects of the club are worth the price of membership.

Chapter Fourteen

Getting Involved

Mexicans don't seem as friendly as Americans. They don't come up and slap you on the back, or laugh heartily at jokes. When they shake hands, it's usually with a weak, unenthusiastic hand. Is it that Mexicans are shy? Or is it that they don't like us? If they do like us, why don't they show it?

The answer is that Mexicans have different ways of showing friendliness than do North Americans. Their entire cultural personality differs radically from ours. It starts with childhood. Whereas American children are praised and encouraged for being aggressive, competitive and outgoing, Mexican children are reprimanded. To "show off" is embarrassing for parents and family. Mexicans grow up with the world-view that to be loud and boisterous is to be thoughtless and impolite. Our kids are forced into Little Leagues and competitive sports from early grades of school, but Mexican kids learn cooperation and family endeavors; sports and competition aren't emphasized. If you notice a group of Mexican children playing together, there is rarely any fighting, bullying of smaller children, or loud, aggressive behavior. They might chase each other about playing tag, laughing vigorously, but rarely scream and shout at the same time, as our kids do.

Australians are very much like Americans; we both have that exuberant "Crocodile Dundee" personality. Mexicans, on the other hand, admire "Ricardo Montalbán" traits. The result is a totally different personality. The ideal Mexican disposition is modest, calm and introspective. The opposite—the aggressive, flashy competitor—becomes a humorous *Cantinflas*-type character: a gum-chewing, back-slapping extrovert (almost a stereotype of the North American personality). Mexican literature and movies are full of these kind of humorous characters.

Don't misunderstand, there's nothing wrong with our warm, outgoing American personality; that's just the way we are. We can't be different, nor would we want to be different. I wouldn't have it any other way. By the same token, Mexican character is molded the way it is, and there will never be any changing it. The interesting thing is that Mexicans recognize the differences and accept them as perfectly normal. The reason they recognize them so well is because they've been exposed to American movies and television all their lives. They see that North Americans act differently. They intuitively understand that our mode of behavior is appropriate for our country.

Social Class

Mexicans have a strong class consciousness that we don't have. For example: When RV folks travel, it doesn't matter how much money someone earns or what their social status is back home; in an RV park, we are all equal. Well, some might have more expensive rigs than others, but we all understand that higher payments tend to equalize things out.

But, to Mexicans, wealth and prestige command respect. This is residual from the early Spanish aristocrats who conquered Mexico in 1521. Mexicans tend to hold in awe anyone from a higher social class, and are uneasy mixing with a different class, higher or lower.

Having explained all this, perhaps you can understand why so many Mexicans seem standoffish or shy when you approach them. First of all, you are obviously extremely wealthy, or else you couldn't afford to be driving that elegant 1975 Winnebago or hauling that fancy-looking 1979 Shasta behind your '77 Ford truck. They feel that you must be in a different social class, probably a higher social class. It doesn't matter if the Mexican is just as wealthy as you, there are no exact counterparts to your respective social classes, so you are still obviously different, making everyone uneasy.

We Americans are famous for hospitality. When we meet strangers we like, we think nothing of inviting them to our home. "How about joining us in our trailer for lunch?" But a Mexican might feel embarrassed and out of place at the invitation. By the same token, you will rarely be invited to a Mexican's home. Not that he doesn't like you, it isn't the custom to invite anyone but family and very close friends. It simply isn't done.

These are partial explanations for the deferent, sometimes embarrassed responses to your overtures of friendship. Another factor is that they've been taught *not* to demonstrate affection the way we do. A polite, formal handshake is the accepted greeting. If you are truly close, then a warm *abrazo* (hug) is expected, but never with semi-strangers. It isn't like many North American circles where casual acquaintances customarily exchange embraces and kisses when meeting or saying goodbye. Or where perfect strangers give hearty, firm handshakes, sometimes with both hands, as if they've known and admired each other for years. If a Mexican did this, he would be considered phony.

Now, obviously, these are stereotypes, and you'll find many Mexicans just as outgoing and aggressively friendly as we are. And, since they expect us to be so outgoing, it's okay to just be ourselves. Trying to be different from what we really are can also come across as phony.

To forge close, intimate relationships in the Mexican community isn't easy. However, you can build lasting friendships if you are sincere and don't start out being "pushy." Mexican custom is that you keep things formal and polite for a time. If later on, you want to invite someone to lunch, and they seem hesitant, you might suggest having lunch at a restaurant rather in your trailer. This puts a different perspective on it.

On the other hand, many Mexicans are very curious about your RV. They've seen hundreds of them rolling along the highways, yet few have ever seen the inside of one. When you ask if they'd like to see inside, their faces light up with pleasure. It's a real adventure for them. But you'll notice that after quickly satisfying their curiosity, they'll step outside.

Volunteer Work

If you're going to be around for a while, an excellent way of participating in the culture is to get involved with volunteer projects sponsored by the North American community. Libraries are good examples of this. By accumulating books for a central library, in Spanish and English, the two communities have a chance to know and respect each other. Providing books and writing materials for rural schools not only helps the children immensely, but encourages the kids to form positive opinions about Americans.

If you don't have the time or inclination to go to the center of town for "American Society" projects, you can easily start your own, right in your trailer park. Almost everyone has been exposed to some English, but few ever get the chance to practice. So, by letting it be known that you are willing to help with English, you can have your own "class" before you know it.

Helping the Needy

Ordinary tourists breeze in and out of Mexico with few if any contacts with local people. There just isn't time enough. But RV travelers have a unique opportunity to tarry along the way and get to know Mexican families. An excellent way of doing this (and helping people at the same time) is to bring a few gifts for needy families.

As you drive through the countryside, you'll often see picturesque little huts of subsistence farmers with the family working at tasks in their yards. As your rig rolls past, perhaps they look up from their chores and stare at the wondrous *casa de ruedas* with curiosity. Just as you wonder who they are, how they live, what they think about the world; these individuals wonder about you. They're curious as to who you are and where you are going. You might think: what a wonderful thing it might be to stop, to visit a while, perhaps see the inside of their house. What a marvelous cultural adventure that would be!

It can be done. The way to do it is through presents. As you might suspect, life isn't easy for some of these families. Almost any kind of gifts can be welcome, if presented in the right way. You can pause in your journey, make contact, and for a moment two cultures can come together. This is one time when they don't seem reluctant to inviting you inside their homes.

As anywhere, gift giving must be tactful and thoughtful. These people don't like to think that they are poverty-stricken, and to their minds, they aren't. They live exactly as their parents and grandparents before them; it seems only right. Everything is relative—many feel that their mode of living is natural—but Americans are unusually rich. If a friend does something nice for you and you want to do something in return, don't offer money, that might be an insult. I bring solar-powered calculators or digital watches as presents for special people. However, if you think the person needs money, you can offer it as a present for his children. That takes the embarrassment out of it.

The Rich Americano

One night in an isolated little coastal village, several fishermen questioned me about life in the United States. "How much money do you earn?" Since my earnings were so much more than theirs, they decided I must be terribly rich. Yet, my humble salary as a newspaper worker hardly qualified me as "rich," so I tried to explain about high living costs, house payments, payments on three cars (which I needed with teen-age drivers and a working wife). My car insurance premiums could have fed a village family for a year. "But why so many automobiles?" they asked. "Because, if my wife didn't have a car, she couldn't get to work," I replied. "And if she didn't work, we couldn't afford three cars and the insurance." I suddenly realized how illogically circular that all sounded. I gave up explaining. I was rich, and that was that.

So, we're rich, and we can afford to hand out presents. Accept it at that. When planning gifts, many people automatically think of booze for the adults and candy for the kids. These are the worst ideas possible. Other gifts make a far more lasting memory and do far more good. A sweater, for example, will not only be useful for months or years, but evokes nice thoughts about *norteamericanos* every time it's put on.

Whenever I canvass neighbors and friends for sweaters, shoes, and children's clothes, I'm surprised at the way we consider practically new clothes as castoffs. They may hang in our closets for months and years, rarely worn. But when given away in Mexico, you can be sure your discarded things will see wear!

Gift Ideas

Naturally, food is great gift idea. Staples like rice, beans, flour and things like that will never go to waste, but these are relatively mundane items. Better go for special treats. Unless a family is on the brink of starvation (rare) I prefer to give luxury items like mayonnaise. Instead of one large jar I give several small jars. Many rural homes have no refrigeration, so small containers can be used up before they spoil. Irradiated milk is also prized. (Sold only in Mexico.) It comes in containers that keep several months in the cupboard. By mixing it with equal parts of water, you have a very fresh-tasting milk. For many lower economic kids, milk is something they rarely taste. Here again, small, half-liter containers are best, because once opened to the air, the milk spoils like ordinary milk.

Paper goods like toilet paper and facial tissues make marvelous gifts as does aluminum foil and plastic wrap. These are luxury goods for many Mexican *campesinos*. Coffee is an indulgence many cannot afford. Instant coffee is considered more elegant than ground coffee, and easier to prepare (few households have coffee pots). Wooden matches, bar soap and dish towels will make a housewife's face break into smiles.

For the husband, ideal gifts are disposable razors (buy a bag for a buck), flashlights or a penknife. They adore Bic disposable lighters because they replace valuable matches when working around the farm. Don't worry about encouraging smoking; the price of cigarettes quickly discourages it. Tee-shirts and sneakers are good for adults and juveniles as well; they love 'em. Especially T-shirts with English writing on them.

How do you give out these gifts? Just stop and start handing them out like Santa Claus in a kindergarten? Some do it this way, and they have a wonderful time. I get slightly embarrassed. I need to slip into gift-giving sideways, casually, as if an afterthought.

My method is to start with children. We take out a soap bubble jar (by the gross, about 38 cents each). We demonstrate for a few seconds, then offer the bottle to the nearest kid. This immediately attracts any other children around, curious, hoping for a gift as well.

Old tennis balls (we've taken a hundred at a time), marbles, little toy cars and trucks, balloons, especially ball-point pens and tablets, are soon clutched in excited little hands. Before long, you can bet the adults come out of the house to see what's going on. At that point, I make some small talk (sign language for those who don't speak much Spanish). Should they appear to be receptive to the idea of gifts, we bring them out, explaining that they are some "extra things" that we aren't using any more.

Rewards of Gift-Giving

I remember one unforgettable evening, my wife and I sitting around a family's hearth, after distributing the last of our gifts. The house was tiny, made of adobe brick and thatched with palm fronds. The hearth was actually an old steel barrel made into a charcoal cook stove. It was New Year's Eve and the lady of the house cooked special tamales, traditional to the occasion, while I strummed a guitar and sang some half-learned Mexican songs and my wife practiced Spanish with the children. This holiday evening was a special, magic circumstance that few ordinary tourists will ever know. The memories are particularly heartwarming because I know that we helped make some people's lives happier, if only for a fleeting period of time.

However warm it may make your heart feel to carry gifts to Mexico, it doesn't necessarily warm the hearts of custom officials. Some feel downright insulted that we consider Mexico a poor country, a place to take worn-out old clothes. In an RV, you have no problem in stashing clothing so it looks like your own things. And I've never heard of any customs hassle on tennis balls, balloons or bubble jars. Just don't mention "charity" when you cross. Chances are slight that they would ask in the first place, though.

If you don't feel like getting involved with a family, you can still do some real good by bringing things for the many orphanages around Mexico. These usually operate on meager budgets; they'll welcome anything you can bring. Again, pens, crayolas and tablets are wonderful. Clothing and food, of course, and just about anything you bring will be appreciated. Check with the owner of the local trailer park for locations of orphanages or other needy institutions.

Chapter Fifteen

Travel Clubs and Caravans

With such a high level of neighborliness among RV travelers in Mexico, it comes as no surprise that they should form impromptu social groups, and eventually, organized clubs. I know of at least four clubs which serve the needs of Mexico RV travelers. Their newsletters keep members up-to-date on what's happening in the world of Mexico travel, and are full of tips on road conditions, current problems and trip suggestions. One of the biggest benefits is reasonable insurance coverage which is available only to club members. For thousands, this alone is worth the price of membership.

The two biggest clubs are *Mexico West* and *Vagabundos del Mar*, both based in California. A third club, based in San Carlos, Sonora, Mexico, *Club Deportivo*, also provides insurance and social contacts for members. The fourth club is *Club Monarca de Acampadores* (Monarch Camping Club) which is based in Guadalajara.

Mexico West Travel Club

This travel club had its origins in 1975 right after the paved highway to La Paz opened, when a newsletter was started for people exploring the new world of adventure opened to RVs. At first bi-monthly, the newsletter became monthly in 1981. The numerous questions directed at Mexico West eventually were handled by a "hotline information" telephone number which presents latest road conditions, peso exchange, fishing reports, gasoline updates and other information pertinent to current travel. The club can also obtain travel visas, fishing licenses and boat permits, all by mail, so if you live on the other side of the country, you needn't come to California to join or to take advantage of membership.

The club was founded by Tom and Shirley Miller. Tom is the author of *The Baja Book,* the definitive book on the peninsula, and Shirley is director of the club and an expert at giving advice and information about Baja travel.

Members calling or writing ahead can receive trip planning, 20 to 50% savings on auto and RV insurance plus 10 to 20% discounts at over 200 hotels, resorts and RV parks in Mexico. Like the Vagabundos del Mar's insurance, the low-cost group insurance is good only in Baja and on the West Coast as far south as Mazatlán. For an extra dollar a day, it covers other parts of Mexico, too.

As members travel more and more on the mainland, the newsletter covers this segment of Mexico travel through articles and reports written by members. Although a good proportion of Mexico West's members (some 6,700) have RVs and boats, it's more of a general purpose travel club than Vagabundos del Mar, the other large club. While the club is service-oriented, there are social aspects, such as fishing derbys and special trips and parties in Baja, and its newsletter is excellent.

Vagabundos del Mar

The club's roots date back to 1966, when a group of boaters "buddied" up for a trip to Mexico's Sea of Cortez. This adventure attracted the attention of other boaters and the idea of a club emerged. As members shared their experience and knowledge of the Baja peninsula with others, the group added more and more members. At first it was an informal association, but after membership grew, they decided to put things on a business-like basis. The club incorporated in 1971 as a non-profit corporation, taking the name *Vagabundos del Mar* from the itinerant Mexicans who roam the Sea of Cortez (portrayed in the book "Sea of Cortez" by Ray Cannon).

Beginning as a special-interest group of boaters and fishermen who coincidentally traveled in RVs, boating is still the major focus of the club. However, many join the club solely for the insurance benefits, and discover that the fun and social activities are the icing on the cake. In addition to their annual convention (*fiesta*), they hold several get-togethers every year in the United States (mostly in California) and organize caravans into Baja. In fact, they have their own RV park in La Paz to better take care of caravans.

Every May the club hosts a famous "Delta Crab Feed" at an RV park on the Sacramento River. I attended this feast in 1989, stuffing myself with huge portions of dungeness crab and salad while washing it down with cold draft beer to the bouncy music of a raucous Dixieland band. It was easy to see why people from all over the west make it a point to attend these social events. I had such a good time that I almost forgot that I was supposed to be interviewing RV travelers.

A newsletter, the *Chubasco*, keeps members informed on the latest developments in Mexico: road conditions, price changes, new trailer parks, caravans, adventure expeditions, anything that might be of interest to Mexico travelers. Whether you join in the social events or not, the price of membership of either club is well worth it for the serious Mexico traveler when you consider the insurance savings, plus discounts given to members by numerous trailer parks, motels, boat rentals and the like.

Monarcas and Club Deportivo

Located in Guadalajara, the Club Monarcas publishes a fine directory of campgrounds, with information and rating provided by members and club officials. They also publish a newsletter, *TravelMex*. The club was founded in 1980 by Carlos Meléndez, a veteran Mexico RV traveler. Dues are $25 a year, which includes the newsletter and the Mexico Camping Directory, as well as other fringe benefits such as discounts, phrase book, etc.

The other club, the *Club Deportivo*, seems to be limited to San Carlos Bay, centered around the country club there and the many RV folk who spend winters in this location north of Guaymas. The club also offers discount insurance to its members. There is a one-time fee of $100 to join Club Deportivo.

People with information about other Mexico travel clubs are cordially invited to send it on to me.

Professional Caravans

There are two ways of RV travel: either by yourself or with a group of friends. Each has its advantages and disadvantages, which are obvious. Traveling in groups or "caravans" is one of the attractions of belonging to a travel club, in that you can usually find friends to make the trip with you should you feel in the mood for company.

For those who don't belong to a club, or who need to make specific plans, the commercial caravan may be the answer. When traveling in a caravan with 20 other couples, you needn't organize your own group of friends. Just as was the case back in the "covered wagon" days, you'll make friends very quickly as you enjoy common goals and destinations.

During the course of research, I interviewed many people traveling on caravans; all seemed to be having a wonderful time.

Almost all were on their first trip to Mexico, choosing the caravan mode to "break the ice." Certainly, a caravan takes away the uncertainties of travel (whether in the U.S. or Mexico). Your campsites are reserved and waiting for you at the end of each day's journey, and an experienced RV/auto mechanic trails behind in the event of a problem. The mechanic's job doesn't stop at rendezvous time, however, since his job is to thoroughly check the vehicles for any potential troubles that may arise. When you make camp, your new-found friends are there to help get settled. Often, a caravan tour provides pre-arranged sightseeing tours with buses and local guides to make everything easy as well as interesting.

To get a perspective from the view of the "wagonmaster" I interviewed Beth Hanson of *Points South RV Tours*.[1]

"Our tours aren't as regimented as you might think," Beth explains. "The RVs drive at their own pace, rather than in a tight convoy. When they leave in the morning (at spaced intervals), the only requirement is that they eventually meet for the evening at the pre-designated campground. They set their own pace, take side trips (within reason), stop and have lunch wherever they choose. They can even leave the tour and rejoin it later if they like. They have almost the same freedom that they have when traveling alone, plus, it's just more enjoyable traveling with a well-run tour. It's also comforting to know that in the event of misfortune, there are always dozens of helping hands."

Points South's itineraries are like many other tour groups in that they offer trips of from 12 to 69 days, to as near as the ever-popular Copper Canyon trip or as far as the Yucatan peninsula. Last year they did 23 tours to Mexico. The Copper Canyon takes the RVs on railroad flat cars, which are then used as observation platforms and living quarters for the trip. The cars are put onto sidings for side trips and sightseeing excursions into the Canyon.

Other RV tour companies (recommended by Monarch Club in Guadalajara) are: Amigo RV Tours from Las Vegas, Caravans Voyagers from El Paso, and Tracks to Adventure, also from El Paso. All are conducted by a wagon-master team and an experienced mechanic.

---

1. See Appendix for address and telephone. This is not to be taken as a specific recommendation for either caravans or Points South Tours, but this company seems to be typical of many tour companies who guide caravans into the more interesting parts of Mexico. As far as I know, they offer quality service at competitive prices.

Chapter Sixteen

Speaking the Language

Do you really need to know Spanish? Not really. You'll enjoy Mexico more, but you certainly won't starve. Most Mexicans who deal with tourists speak at least some English, and sign language goes a long way. Of course, everyone should learn a few words. It's easier to tell the gasoline attendant exactly how much fuel you need, to ask a mechanic to fix your vehicle, and occasionally, you might want directions to the bathroom.

The vocabulary list in the back of the book should help with gas stations and mechanics. If you have a problem pronouncing Spanish, just point to the word or phrase. You'll notice that there's a list in Spanish alphabetical order so the mechanic can look up a word he needs to communicate. This is a feature not found in most guidebooks.

New Doors Open

Since RV travelers will usually park where everybody around them speaks English, there's no big pressure to learn. Many North Americans live in Mexico for years and learn just enough to ask where the bathroom is and to order another round of drinks. Occasionally they enter the wrong bathroom, that's true, but rarely does a waiter misunderstand an order for more drinks. If you plan on hanging around with Americans for all your stay in Mexico, or if you insist on living in expensive hotels and condos, then it really doesn't matter whether you learn Spanish or not.

But, once you do learn to communicate, you suddenly find new doors open to you. Mexico becomes a totally different place. Instead of being limited to American-filled trailer parks and well-known RV resorts, you can go anywhere. With even a smattering of Spanish, you can venture out into the exciting world of Mexico. You might find yourself invited to visit people's homes to join in festivities that before were inaccessible. You will have fun dealing with merchants, talking to people on the streets, and making new friends. You no longer fear hassles with bureaucrats or arguing with policemen and taxi drivers. Spanish is the key.

I often hear people say, "I don't speak Spanish, but I'm sure I'll pick it up after a few weeks." They stand about as much chance of "picking up" Spanish as I have of winning the Pennsylvania Lottery. Since I never buy lottery tickets, that makes their chances pretty slim. Children can learn a language fairly easily, but adults, unfortunately have to work at it. Language is acquired through study and practice, never "picked-up."

Total Physical Response

If you have a chance to take some adult education classes in Spanish, you'll have a head start. Lately, a new direction in language learning has become popular. It's called *Total Physical Response* (TPR) and is being adopted by more and more teachers. By all means look for a program where the teachers use the TPR approach to Spanish classes. TPR was developed by James Asher, a psychologist at San Jose State University (Calif.). According to Dr. Asher's research, a person retains his learning experiences far longer if he is physically involved by *doing* something at the same time he is listening or speaking a foreign language. Asher claims that this is the way children learn, and that adults can learn just as fast as children if they learn the same way! Check around your community to see if any TPR classes are being offered.

Should you find yourself in a location where you plan on staying a while, try to find a Spanish conversation class, even if you already are proficient in Spanish. Besides brushing up your language, you find this an excellent way to meet people. Often, students organize their own social group, with parties and sightseeing trips outside of class. Some of the larger trailer parks offer Spanish classes, so you don't even have to commute.

"Castilian" Spanish

"I studied Spanish in high school," I hear people say, "but it was *Castilian* Spanish, and here they speak *Mexican* Spanish. I can't understand a thing they're saying." This is a particularly lame excuse. Spanish spoken in Mexico is excellent, with a neutral accent and few of the differences that often distinguish isolated accents in Spain or South America. The bulk of the original European settlers in Mexico came from Valencia (in the south of Spain) and they brought this neutral accent with them. Indeed, linguists will tell you that there is *less* difference between Spanish spoken around Madrid (so-called Castilian) and that spoken in Mexico than there is between English spoken in Nashville and that spoken in Milwaukee. It takes a fluent Spanish-speaker to tell whether a speaker comes from Madrid or from Mazatlán, so please don't use that excuse any longer!

Why We Can't Understand

Our high school and college Spanish doesn't work in actual practice because we learned it incorrectly. We studied it from books. We memorized grammar and learned to read and write printed words. We thought we were learning the Spanish language, but we weren't! The problem is this: letters, words and grammar are *not* language. Why not? Language is *a system of sounds plus the meanings these sounds carry*. Letters and words just *represent* the sounds. Grammatical rules simply *describe* what happens when people talk. You might be able to recognize all of the written words in the book, you may be able to parse verbs all day long and memorize all the grammatical rules ever discovered, but if you can't understand the sound system, then you *don't know the language*. It's as simple as that.

What happens in school is: first we learn to read and write Spanish words. Then, when we hear spoken sounds, we mentally convert these sounds into letters and then divide them into Spanish words. Next, we mentally translate these Spanish words into English words, and finally attach meanings to the translated words, all the while trying to remember whether the endings of the verbs were in the pluperfect or imperfect subjunctive tense. In the meanwhile, the speaker has used a half a yard of rapid-fire sounds you didn't have time to catch. In school, unless you were lucky enough to have native speakers for practice, you didn't learn *language,* only words, sentences and grammar.

It does little good to ask a question in Spanish—perfectly pronounced and grammatically correct—just as you learned in the university—if you can't understand the answer when it comes back at you in Spanish. Next thing you know, you've made that wrong turn again.

Then comes the excuse that "Mexicans talk too fast." Listen to the way *we* talk. We speak just as fast and run everything together as Mexicans do. We don't pause at the end of each word either, not like we did in our high school Spanish classes. Again, spoken language and written language are two different things. I speak from experience, because I used to teach English to foreigners for San Jose Unified School District. Rather successfully. I didn't use a text in my classes. We didn't *study* English. We *spoke* English.

If you are serious about learning Spanish, look for a good conversation class, taught by a native Spanish speaker if possible (preferably one using TPR methods). Another excellent way of getting a head start is buying a set of cassette tapes for home study. This is really helpful if you already have a background in Spanish, but lack listening and thinking practice in the language.

Not just any tape will do, however, because some systems perpetuate the emphasis on grammar and learning individual words. Find a system that gives listening practice at the normal speed of a native speaker. Some learning systems are good only for putting the listener to sleep with verb conjugations and vocabulary lists.

One of the best systems available is also one of the least expensive for what you get. It is put out by the U.S. Government and appears to be sold at the cost of production. These tapes can be ordered from: National AudioVisual Center, Customer Services PF, 8700 Edgeworth Drive, Capitol Heights, MD 20743-3701. Credit card orders can be done by phone (800) 638-1300. Ask for a catalog. The Foreign Service Institute of the State Department produced these tapes; they're used to train diplomats and military personnel. The emphasis is on listening and repeating and thinking in Spanish. Although there is a grammar section in each chapter, the essential element is sound. You learn grammar the same way a child learns it, by listening and by intuitive analysis.

It's Not in the Dictionary!

Although Spanish is a remarkably uniform language around the world, there are certain differences from locality to locality and from country to country. This is true of English, as well, but we are not always aware of it. For example, there are many words in the United States that vary depending upon where in the country a speaker lives. A *frying pan* becomes a *skillet* or a *spider*, depending on where you were raised. A *davenport* becomes a *sofa* or a *couch*, or sometimes a *chesterfield*. A Spanish-speaker may become confused if he knows the word "sofa," and you throw "davenport" at him. So you see, this problem of lexical differences isn't restricted to Spanish. If you've ever been totally confused by an Aussie or a Scotsman, you'll understand.

So, it isn't surprising that some words you will encounter in Mexico cannot be found in your dictionary, particularly not a dictionary printed in Madrid or Buenos Aires. The solution to this problem is to read as many newspapers and locally printed books as you can and to buy a dictionary printed in Mexico. Keep a notebook in which you write down every new word you encounter. Try to find ten words every day to mark into your book, then review these words several times a day; you'll be amazed at how your vocabulary expands. And, try to memorize the sound and meanings rather than the actual spelling of the words.

Early settlers in Mexico found many unfamiliar foods and cultural items with no Spanish equivalents. They simply adapted the existing Indian words. For example, the Spaniards called the unfamiliar turkey a *pavo* because it reminded them of a *pavo real*, a peacock. But Mexicans prefer the Aztec word *guajalote*. If you listen carefully, that's exactly what turkeys go around saying: "*Guajalote! Guajalote!*" It doesn't mean much to us, since turkeys aren't very good at making conversation, but animal behaviorists have discovered that *guajalote* actually translates into "Thanksgiving! Caramba!"

Many words are influenced by Mexico's proximity to the United States. For example: most dictionaries claim that the word for grapefruit is *toronja*. But you might confuse a waiter, because most Mexicans order *grepfrut*. Also, local usage over the years changes the vocabulary, giving different meanings to words that seem to be obvious. Instead of *autobús* for bus, as in many Spanish-speaking countries, the Mexicans often say *camión*, which also means truck. Puerto Ricans will say *gua gua* and South Americans will say *micro*, or *colectivo*, for bus. We've heard people say: "*parque el carro*" for "park the car."

Don't panic if you think it will take you a while to become proficient. There are usually Mexican people around who can speak some English, and who are eager to practice it, so you should get by quite nicely. This is particularly true if you are adept at pantomime and charades. The nice thing about learning Spanish in Mexico is that people are always delighted when they see that you are trying to learn. Unlike the French, who seem insulted if you mispronounce even a tiny nasal whine, the Mexicans are very supportive.

They will tell you: "You speak very well the Spanish," as they congratulate you for your efforts. Of course, if you really *did* "speak very well the Spanish," they wouldn't comment about it. You know when you're close to getting a good accent when people stop telling you how well you speak.

Speaking 'Pidgen' Spanish

Chances are, you will neither have the time nor inclination to really get into learning Spanish. Even if you do, it will take you some time to acquire proficiency. Don't let that stop you. You can get along perfectly well with just a few words committed to memory and a pocket dictionary for the rest.

Once I met a college student who had been traveling Mexico alone for several months. She told me she had no trouble communicating. "I figure these people know a lot more about grammar and sentence construction than I ever will," she explained.

"So, I just give them the nouns and let them supply their own verbs, adjectives and prepositional phrases. For example: at a bus station ticket counter, when I say in Spanish, 'Me, Mazatlán, tomorrow, 2 o'clock,' the guy would have to be an idiot not to know what I wanted."

If she had difficulty pronouncing a noun, she didn't hesitate to point to it in the dictionary, or to write it on a note pad. Sometimes verbs are necessary, of course, but you needn't learn all the tense forms of past, future, present, pluperfect, conditional, imperative, etc., etc. That comes later when you really get into fluency. By combining an infinitive with a noun, you've moved onto the next level of communication. If you say to an automobile mechanic, *"Cambiar aceite?"* (Oil change?), he will understand. If he doesn't, you shouldn't trust him to change your oil in the first place; he might fill your engine with tapioca pudding instead of 30-weight oil. If pronunciation is particularly difficult, then have your request written on a slip of paper, just in case. By all means, try to make him understand your words first.

Mexicans won't laugh at you for talking this way. In fact, many of them talk the same way when speaking in a rapid, clipped manner. The formal, textbook way of asking someone to change the oil in your car might be: *"¿Señor, tendría usted el tiempo para cambiar el aceite de mi automóvil?"* ("Might you have the time to change the oil in my automobile, sir?") Nobody talks that way in Mexico or in the 'States. Better: *"Cambiar aceite?"* ("Oil change?")

The one vocabulary inventory you should stock up on is numbers. Learn to understand them by having someone read series of numbers aloud while you write them down. (A method of Total Physical Response learning, putting meaning to sounds while physically responding.) Then, when you tell the gas station attendant, *"Treinta mil pesos, Nova,"* there can be no mistaking that you want 30,000 pesos worth of regular in your tank.

Spanish-English, English-Spanish

To supplement your pocket dictionary, I've included a list of common words that have to do with auto maintenance and repair that won't be in your pocket dictionary. I've also added a feature that might be helpful: a *Spanish-English* translation. If your mechanic has a problem communicating with you, he can look up the Spanish word, point to it so you can understand.

Chapter Seventeen

Questions and Answers

■ *Is insurance required in Mexico?*

No. Is isn't required, but if you plan on staying out of jail you might think about getting some. The minimum you need is liability and property damage. Because Mexican courts don't award enormous sums for punitive damages and pain and suffering you are safe taking the minimum coverage, but by all means, get it. Too often the foreigner is considered in the wrong no matter what, but that won't matter as long as you are covered. If you have insurance, the problem is with the insurance company (unless there is crime involved). Without it, you can be held in jail until you come up with the money to pay damages.

■ *How is the best way to buy insurance?*

Many stores and offices along the border sell insurance, as well as many brokers inside Mexico. Places like Sanborns and AAA can sell insurance by the day, and there is a discount for longer term insurance. The rates are set by law, so they are all about the same. However, for anything over three weeks, you can save by joining a club like Mexico West or Vagabundos del Mar. Their members can get 20% to 50% off the standard rates. Liability only for one year: $100 or less.

■ *Is it safe to travel in Mexico?*

According to the people we've interviewed—folks living in Mexico and people who travel frequently there—Mexico is as safe, if not safer, as traveling in the United States. Reliable statistics are impossible to find, but to the best of our knowledge, the rate of violent crime is extremely low in Mexico.

■ *Is it safe to eat the food? Drink the water?*

Since RV owners will be eating many meals cooked in their own units, obviously, the food will be just as good (or as bad) as back home. Most restaurants observe standard health methods when preparing food. People living in RV parks can clue you in on the better restaurants. Water can be excellent or it can be malevolent, depending upon the location. A quick boil makes it drinkable. Some RV parks have vendors delivering water daily for a very low cost. Purified water in large bottles costs about $1.50 for five-gallons.

■ What permits do I need to travel in Mexico? For my RV or auto?

If you intend to stay over 72 hours in the "free zone" near the border, or if you are going deeper into Mexico, past the free zone, you need a Tourist Visa Form (commonly known as *tourist card*). You will need either a passport, a birth certificate, military discharge, or sometimes, a voters' registration to apply for the card. Vehicle permits are given when the vehicle is inspected and a windshield sticker issued (either at or near the border). In Baja California, no car permit is required. Boat permits are required.

■ Must I be able to speak Spanish?

Most people who deal with tourists speak some English, and many know a little, although too shy to use it. Carry a pocket dictionary, use sign language and smile a lot; you'll get by. Thousands do it all the time. Mexicans are polite and patient with your efforts at learning Spanish.

■ What kind of electricity does Mexico have?

The same as we have: 110 volt. However, it often varies downward from the 110 volt rating. Most appliances work fine. Be sure to carry adapters to match all possible connections, because some parks haven't gotten around to using the modern fittings.

■ Is it okay to "boondock" in Mexico?

Many people do it amost exclusively. On the other hand, many people won't boondock in the United States. It all depends on how you feel about it. Baja California is a very popular place for boondocking. Any beach there is okay, as long as the land you have to cross isn't private property and the beach not posted. On the mainland, and around larger resort cities, beach boondocking is sometimes frowned upon. Check with local RV people to find out.

■ What kind of gasoline is available?

The government PEMEX stations sell a no-lead (Extra) and a leaded regular (Nova). Both are lower octane than in the U.S., but perform adequately. Sometimes Extra is in short supply, so keep your tank full.

■ How are the RV parks in Mexico.

They aren't as plentiful as in the United States, but most are acceptable. Many are fenced and guarded, all have almost 100% North Americans staying there. Some are downright luxurious.

■ What about bringing a mobile home into Mexico?

Except for some locations close to the border, a 10- or 12-wide unit is highly impractical if not impossible in Mexico. Also, anything over 40 feet long requires special permits. Stick with an RV.

■ How are prices?

Prices in pesos have skyrocketed in recent years. But costs in dollars have stayed very low. Generally, prices have risen slightly in the past couple of years, with some areas of Baja and tourist sections of the mainland taking some steep increases. But most prices are still bargains for folks with dollars in their jeans.

■ Must I change dollars into pesos?

You needn't bother until you arrive in Mexico. Your rate of exchange will be far better. The rate of exchange varies daily, with banks usually giving a fraction better rate. Many businesses will accept dollars, but it's easier to keep track if you don't have to mentally convert to pesos.

■ Can I retire in Mexico? How much will it cost?

Thousands of North Americans have retired in Mexico. Most Mexican families live on less than $200 a month. But North Americans usually need more than that. We figure $400 a month as an absolute minimum, although we've met people who claim they get by well on $300 in their RVs. $400-$800 is a better figure for a couple.

■ How are hunting and fishing in Mexico?

Fishing in Baja and along the West coast varies from pretty good to fabulous. Licenses are usually provided by the people who rent boats or can be purchased in town. Travel clubs (see appendix for addresses) can get your license before you enter Mexico. Fishing is good off the Yucatan peninsula, and also along the Gulf coast. Bringing fishing tackle across the border is no problem.

Hunting, however, is a problem. The government discourages bringing weapons into the country, and the red tape to do so is incredible. About the only type of gun you can import is a shotgun. Best book a package tour with guides and guns provided. Absolutely no handguns!

■ Are there any RV parks with golf courses nearby?

Golf is not a common game in Mexico. In the summer, when it rains enough to keep the courses green, all the golf players are back home in the United States. In the winter, when the tourists are in Mexico, it doesn't rain and it's too expensive to keep up a good course. Whereas Palm Springs has over 60 golf courses, a similar-sized place like Puerto Vallarta has only one. Guadalajara and Lake Chapala have a few. Mexico just isn't golf country.

■ How about tennis in Mexico?

Tennis is popular among the upper classes in Mexico. But there aren't many courts outside of country clubs or hotels. However, many RV parks are connected with hotels or motels, and RV visitors usually have access to the courts. Check the listing in chapter 19 for parks with tennis.

■ Can I get a job in Mexico?

It's possible but not probable unless you have some special talent that Mexican citizens cannot supply or unless you have special *Inmigrado* papers. It is illegal to work in Mexico without a work permit from the Department of Immigration, with its central office in Mexico City and some branch offices elsewhere around the republic. These permits aren't easy to get. The restrictions have relaxed somewhat over the years, particularly in real estate sales and promotion, teaching English, and so forth.

If you are caught working without a permit, you take a big risk. According to the director of immigration in Baja California Sur (Lic. Gabriel Cuervo), "Working without papers in Mexico is a very serious crime and comes with a generous jail sentence of 18 months, or deportation." Another point is that if you do obtain papers, they are good only for the employer specified. Should you decide to change employers, you need to apply for another permit. If you don't, you face the same serious charges as if you didn't have papers in the first place.

Finally, wages are so low in Mexico that you would have to have some kind of special talent that no one else has to demand any kind of decent salary. Real estate and condo salesmen working on commission may do well, however, depending upon their ability and their luck.

None of these rules apply to artists or writers if their works are sold to foreign companies or for sale outside of Mexico.

■ Can we bring our pets with us?

Dogs and cats can be brought into Mexico if they are healthy and have received the required immunizations and you have a veterinarian's certificate to prove it. Although most people don't bother, it's a good idea to get a Dog Permit from the Mexican consulate; the charge is about $15. Vaccinations must be within six months of entry. Birds cannot be brought across the border in either direction. Pets that make a lot of noise must be flattened under your RV's rear wheels before crossing the border.[1]

■ What kind of gifts are appropriate to bring to Mexico?

Any goods that are manufactured in the United States are appropriate. Clothing, food, kitchen matches, throw-away razors, solar calculators, digital watches, pots and pans, tools... anything that can be used around the home or on the farm. For children, bring tennis balls, bubble pipes, balloons, wrapped candies, school supplies, clothing... anything that you might give your children or grandchildren.

Some people frown on giving booze or cigarettes to adults or candy to children. This is strictly a judgement call. An inexpensive bottle of scotch becomes a luxury gift, something to be treasured and doled out in sips for special occasions (taxes push the price of scotch out of reach, even for North Americans). Wine, on the other hand, isn't appreciated as much because few Mexicans drink it (Mexican wine is generally poor quality). As for candy, Walt Mueller tells of a friend who was determined not to ruin the kids' teeth with candy, so he brought pencils to give away instead. The village children happily accepted his gifts and went running away. Later that day, when the friend went to the local *tienda* for supplies, he noticed all his pencils neatly stacked in a jar, priced for sale. The kids shrewdly traded pencils for candy! Ask yourself: when you were a small tyke, which gift would make YOU happier, a pencil or a candy cane?

■ Is scuba and snorkeling equipment readily available in Mexico?

It's available, but not usually when or where you need it. When you stop at an isolated beach, chances are poor of finding anything. Better bring your own. Good quality equipment at

---

1. Actually, I just made that up. A particularly disgusting little terrier with a high-pitched yap-yap once kept me awake all night at the Nututún camp near Palenque. Seriously, since practically all parks welcome animals, you should try to be considerate and keep your pet from becoming a pest. See chapter 5 for details.

home is cheap, and cheap equipment in Mexico is expensive. Besides, rental masks leak and the snorkle tubes aren't long enough.

■ Isn't there any discount insurance available for central and southern Mexico?

Just recently, I've learned of a new company who has arranged for Mexican insurance at discounts for the central part of Mexico. I'm not sure if the coverage is restricted to the Guadalajara-Chapala area or not. The savings are supposed to be 40% and the carrier is one of the largest insurance companies in Mexico. See chapter on insurance for the address.

Monarch, the RV travel club in Guadalajara offers insurance through ANSERV or Allen W. Lloyd. Monarch is currently negotiating for Clubmex coverage (an AAA-type group).

■ Suppose I need special RV-type repairs in Mexico?

Most major cities have experienced RV repair mechanics at your service. There are so many RVs traveling in Mexico today that there are some shops that do no other kind of work, just as in the United States. Major repairs, such as body reconstruction, trailer brakes, hitch and suspensions are no mystery to these mechanics. Monarch's *Mexico Camping Directory* lists dealers and garages that specialize in RV repair.

RV Park Directory

List of Trailer Parks

As far as I can determine, there is no one complete listing of all trailer parks in Mexico. I don't pretend to have visited or inspected more than a fraction of them; neither has anyone else. Therefore, I've compiled information from many different sources. I would appreciate readers sending information about parks or boondock spots we missed, or updates on the ones already listed. Sometimes parks change names and end up with listings under both old and new names. I'd like to hear about this, too. You'll find a higher proportion of park listings for Baja California—for good reason—Baja is the most popular RV destination of all Mexico.

Please, remember that any prices quoted here can be very much out of date, and/or highly inaccurate. I've seen people make fools of themselves by shouting and ranting at a desk clerk or trailer park manager because the rate asked was higher than quoted in their guidebook. One man threatened a trailer park manager, "I'm going to turn you in to the American Automobile Association for charging more than the Guidebook allows!" Understand, neither I nor AAA have anything whatsoever to do with setting the rates. We simply quote the latest information available to us. Just like any business anywhere, an RV park will charge whatever traffic will bear. That's not unfair; that's simply the way business works, in any country. So, if the price is double what we quoted here, just curse at me under your breath and either pay up or go somewhere else.

Ceiling Prices

There are regulations about ceiling prices for most accommodations, but they are often set higher than most places charge anyway. Government enforcement of the price ceilings have always been spotty, so don't worry about it too much. Should you feel you've really been gouged, make a report to the Tourist Hotline (see appendix). You won't get your money back, but it might make you feel better, and there's a chance that action will result.

When fees are quoted, they are for a couple. Extra persons may cost more.

Important: Some Baja California and popular mainland resort locations fill up beginning the middle of November and stay that way through January or February, so you might want to write or phone for reservations if you know exactly when you're going to arrive. You'll be expected to send a non-refundable deposit. However, even with reservations, you can be surprised by a caravan preempting all the empty spaces. Well, that's the good thing about being self-contained and mobile; you can boondock until you find a suitable place to settle in.

If you're making reservations by mail, you'll need to do it *well* in advance, because Mexican mail can be very slow. The service often takes two weeks each way.

Some listings boast of coin-operated laundries. Our experience is that many laundries lack automatic dryers. There's usually a place to hang clothes to dry, but you might prefer to bring a clothesline and clothespins, so you can hang your things next to your rig. Some have washers *and* dryers, but too often one or the other or (both) haven't worked for some time.

Most parks have electricity. It's ostensibly standard 30 amp, 110-120 current, but it varies below these standards depending on the time of day. Some small towns turn off electricity in the evening and sometimes during siesta, when they figure everyone should be napping anyway. So don't be surprised if the lights go out around 10 p.m. and/or if it shuts down at noon and stays off until dusk. Be sure to bring connection adapters to fit the old-fashioned two-prong electrical sockets.

All listings are reported to have at least one shower and flush toilet unless otherwise noted. They may or may not be usable, however. Most claim to have hot water, but be sure to test the shower with your pinky before stepping under the spray. Don't be surprised if the water is icy cold. Don't be surprised if there isn't any water. That's Mexico.

Some parks have phone numbers and addresses listed, and some don't. Some have park fees listed. The reason for this is that the information was assembled from survey returns and six different printed sources, some of which list prices and mailing addresses, some don't. Prices simply give relative costs for different parks, and may not mean much in the first place.

Park Ratings

The question of rating parks is a touchy subject. Trying to derive a consensus of what constitutes a good park and an undesirable one is next to impossible. One person complains that a site is too crowded and recommends a beautiful spot down the beach, whereas another person hates that place because there aren't enough people for a good social life or because there aren't any stores nearby. Where one couple might complain that the restrooms are filthy or non-existent, another won't even notice that, because they are self-contained and never use park bathrooms in the first place.

Often, parks with little to offer in the way of amenities will garner higher ratings because of the natural beauty of the surroundings. The natural beauty may not mean very much to you if you've just driven 300 tough miles and pull into a park at dusk to get some well-earned rest. When you find that the electricity doesn't work and the bathrooms are broken, you might begin to wonder if the people who gave the place a three-star rating weren't on some kind of drugs.

Another problem is that while travelers might generally agree that a park is in good condition and well-managed, by the time you get there, management may have changed, or the park may have been converted into a high-rise condo. (Things like this happen with greater frequency at the quick-growing resort areas.)

In many smaller towns, you'll notice that the only place to stay is at a motel or hotel. Often, this means a corner of the parking lot where you can plug into electricity and use the hotel's bathrooms. This isn't as bad as it sounds, because you usually have access to the swimming pool, tennis courts, restaurant and whatever facilities the place offers, just as the regular guests do. There's customarily a watchman to make sure everything's okay while you enjoy exploring the village or having dinner at the hotel.

The responsibility for recommending RV parking puts far too great a burden on my frail shoulders, so I warn you right now that the system I'm using is very tentative and I refuse to accept any blame should a rating turn out to be ludicrous! As I mentioned earlier, I couldn't possibly visit all of the parks and have to rely on my sources. When you find the ratings off-base, if you have updates on the listed facilities or places omitted, I would appreciate hearing from you. I'll make it a point to include your information in the next editions, and in a revised park guide which I'll make available to contributors at cost. (P.O. Box 2120, Los Gatos, CA 95031)

How the ratings work

Parks which have been rated by correspondents or other park directories are marked with solid stars (★★★); the more stars the higher recommendations. If the parks are very rustic (with no redeeming qualities such as a fabulous location), or if there is no information available, it will be designated by one hollow star (☆). A hollow star carries no recommendation, but that doesn't mean it can't be a wonderful place to stay. I'm depending on reader feedback to make adjustments in the ratings.

BAJA CALIFORNIA

✳ **Rosarito Beach & Vicinity** ⇨ *Just 28 Km. south of Tijuana, convenient to Los Angeles and Southern California. Lots of weekend homes.*

KOA Rosarito—200 spaces ★★★   12 miles south (take San Antonio exit) Fee: $11. On bluff overlooking ocean. Electricity, water, sewer hookups. Dump station. Laundry and rec room. Ice. Nearby restaurant and bar. Mailing address: P.O. Box 2082, Tijuana, B.C., Mexico., B.C. 011-706-686-1412

La Barca—10 spaces ☆   Km. 30 on toll-free road. Bathrooms, restaurant, bar. Hookups?

La Siesta—12 spaces ★★   North end of town. Full hookups.

Martha Trailer Park—44 spaces ★   South end, on beach. Full hookups.

Playa Santa Monica—80 spaces ★★   On beach, free road 13 miles south of Tijuana. Full hookups.

Playa Santa María—50 spaces ★★   South of Rosarito. On beach. Full hookups. Pool, Tennis, jacuzzi, tennis, golf, restaurant, disco, laundry.

Popotla RV Park—177 spaces ★★★   7 miles south on toll-free road at Km. 33. On beach. Full hookups. Pool, restaurant, groceries, laundry, horseback riding. (661) 2-1501.

René's—110 spaces ★   In town. Full hookups. Pool, restaurant. By the month only.

Rosarito Shores Trailer Park—5 spaces ★★   Between highway and beach. Full hookups, club house, pool, tennis, nice park. (661) 2-1125.

Villa Italiana—70 spaces ★   On beach. Full hookups. Restaurant.

✳ **La Salina** ⇨ *25 miles south on free road at Km. 72, 18 miles north of Ensenada*

Outdoor Resorts of Baja—280 spaces ★★★★   On beach. Full hookups, pool, spa, tennis courts, laundry restaurant, grocery store. Very nice. Fee: $20. (706) 686-9255, (800) 356-2252. Formerly known as Baja Seasons Park.

✳ **Ensenada** ⇨ *About an hour's drive south of the border on good toll road. Usually crowded with tourists from Southern California.*

Baja Trails—36 spaces ☆   On ocean north of town. Some full hookups. Good water.

California Trailer Park—50 spaces ★   North of town (Km. 102, on free highway, across from gas station) Full hookups. Laundry, city buses. Phone 8-2037.

☆ Hollow star = No recommendation, or no information available.

★ One or more solid stars indicate positive ratings.

* Baja California
❶ Sea of Cortez Coast
❷ Costa de Oro
❸ Costa Chica
❹ Isthmus of Tehuantepec
❺ Yucatan Peninsula
❻ Central Plateau
❼ Central Highlands
❽ Gulf Coast
❾ Northern Highlands

Locating a Town

Numbers placed by each location match the numbers on the map. This should give you an clue as to what part of the country we're talking about. However, many locations have two or more names in Spanish. For example: El Golfo de Santa Clara can be found on a map by that name, or by Golfo de Santa Clara, El Golfo, or Santa Clara. Catemaco could be named Lago de Catemaco or Lake Catemaco. Lago can become Laguna or Lake. Confusing? Yes it is. But don't give up; you might miss a great camping experience.

About Kilometer Markers

You'll see kilometer markers along most highways. The problem is that you never know if the marker is measuring from the center of the last town, from the last big town, or from the center of Mexico City. When instructions say "turn at Km. 189, the best you can do is to start watching for the Kilometer 189 marker and never mind from where it started measuring.

Campo Playa RV Park—85 spaces ★★   1 miles south near intersection of Blvd. Lázaro Cárdenas and Calle Delante. Fee: $8.00. Full hookups. Near Restaurants. Mailing address: P.O. Box 21, Ensenada, B.C., Mexico. (667)-8-1818.

Corona Beach—32 spaces ★   6 miles south, on beach. Electricity and water hookups. Groceries, horseback riding.

El Faro Beach Trailer Park—50 spaces ★★   South of Ensenada on beach at Km. 15. a few hookups.

Estero Beach Trailer Park—130 spaces ★★★★   Eight miles south (watch for turnoff to right). Fee: $11.00. Full hookups. Dump station. Tennis courts, clubhouse. Posh hotel. Mailing address: P.O. Box 86, Ensenada, 011-706-676-6225.

Granada Cove Trailer Park—35 spaces ★★   North of town at Km 105. On beach. Restaurant, city buses. Phone 8-3681.

King's Coronita Trailer Park—20 spaces ★★   North of town, Km. 107. Full hookups. Boat ramp, city buses. clean. Phone 8-1944.

Playa Saldamando—30 spaces ☆   On beach 10 mi. north of town on old road. (access only from southbound Highway 1-D). Fee: $6.00. No hookups. Mailing address: Playa Saldamando Campground, 3965 College Ave., San Diego, CA 92115. (619) 286-2541.

Rancho Ensenada ☆   South of town, west 2 blocks on Estancia street. A few hookups, bathroom.

Rancho Todos Santos—10 spaces ★   2 Kms. south of town on Estancia street, on beach. Horses, fishing, TV.

San Miguel Village (Villa de San Miguel)—100 spaces ★   8 miles north via Highway 1-D. On Bahía de Todos Santos, south of toll gate. Fee: $6.00. Full hookups. Restaurant. Mailing address: P.O. Box 55, El Sauzal, B.C., Mexico.,

---

✳ **Bufadora/Maneadero** ⇨ *Maneadero is about 15 Km. south of Ensenada. Sometimes an immigration checkpoint. Bufadora farther on, is a popular American RV community.*

La Jolla Beach Camp—180 spaces ★★   At Punta Banda, eight miles from main highway toward La Bufadora. Fee: $4.00. Some electrical, but otherwise no hookups. Disposal station, propane, boat launch, groceries, tennis, rec room. Mailing address: Punta Banda P.O. Box 953, Ensenada, B.C., Mexico

Rancho la Bufadora—200 spaces ★★   16 miles south of Ensenada near Blowhole. P.O. 100 spaces with full hookups. Restaurant, boat ramp, horseback riding. Box 300, Ensenada, B.C.

Villarino Camp—100 spaces ★★   At Punta Banda, eight miles from main highway. Fee: $8.00. Some full hookups. boat ramp, ice, groceries. Mailing address: P.O. box 842, Ensenada, B.C., Mexico.

✳ **Ojos Negros** ⇨ *East of Ensenada. Originally settled by Russian refugees after World War I. Not many left.*

Aguascalientes Hot Springs ★★★   At Km. 26 on road to Ojos Negros, turn south on graded road into beautiful valley. Hot springs, two pools, private baths, restaurant. No hookups. Nice.

Centro Recreativo—37 spaces ☆   18 Km. east of Ensenada, on way to San Felipe. On lake. Electric and water.

✳ **Santo Tomás** ⇨ *South of Ensenada 41 Km. Grape country; has one of the few good wineries in Mexico.*

El Palomar Trailer Park—21 spaces ☆   North side of town, beside motel. Fee. $6.00. Electric and water hookups. Tree-shaded, pool, groceries, ice, gas station. Mailing address: P.O. Box 595, Ensenada, B.C., Mexico. 011-706-678-2355.

✳ **Colonia Guerrero** ⇨ *Also known as Vicente Guerrero. Near ocean.*

Mesón de Don Pepe RV Park—20 spaces ★ South of town. Fee $5.00. Full hookups. Restaurant. Mailing address: P.O. Box 7, Colonia Guerrero, B.C., Mexico.

Posada Don Diego—100 spaces ★★★ South of town, watch for turnoff at Km. 174. 1/4 mi. west. Fees $7. Some full hookups. Disposal station, laundry, ice, restaurant, trailer storage, landscaped. Mailing address: P.O. Box 126, Colonia Guerrero, B.C., Mexico.

✳ **San Quintín** ⇨ *About 200 Km. south of the border. Good fishing, dove hunting. Growing agricultural area.*

Honey's RV Campground—200 spaces ☆ Beach camping 2 miles south of town and turn west on dirt road. Fee: $5.00. No electricity, but some water and sewer hookups. Disposal station.

Cielito Lindo RV Park—65 spaces ★ On beach beyond La Pinta Hotel. Some hookups. Restaurant nearby. P.O. Box 7, San Quintín, B.C.

Campo Lorenzo—20 spaces ☆ North of Molino Viejo, on bay. Full hookups. Mostly perm. residents. Some dry camping.

✳ **El Rosário** ⇨ *Convenient fuel and restaurant stop, about 350 Km. south of the border. Site of old mission.*

Juan Mouett Ranch—11 spaces ☆ 3.5 Km. east (Km. 58). Full hookups.

✳ **Cataviña** ⇨ *Beautiful rock formations and some native Washington palms. Good stopover place in desert setting. Indian cave paintings nearby. Water not always available.*

Parque Natural Desierto—48 spaces ★ Next to La Pinta Hotel. Fee. $4.00. Lovely desert location. Some hookups. Restaurant, bar and gas at hotel.

✳ **Bahía de Los Angeles** ⇨ *On Sea of Cortez side. Protected by large island off-shore. Good fishing, friendly villagers.*

Antero "Papa" Diáz—10 spaces ★ In town, behind Hotel Casa Díaz. Fee: $4. Electric hookups, gas, groceries, boat ramp.

Guillermo's Trailer Park—40 spaces ★ Beachfront, in town. Fee: $4.00. Some hookups. Restaurant boat launch. Groceries nearby.

La Playa Villa Vita RV Park—20 sites ★ Beachfront, in town. Fee $4.00. Electric hookups, disposal station. No showers or toilets. Boat launch, nearby restaurant and groceries.

✳ **Bahía de Los Angeles Junction** ⇨ *Place for gas and overnight. Picturesque desert country.*

Parador Punta Prieta—20 spaces ★ At turn-off point Hwy. 15. Full hookups.

✳ **Guerrero Negro** ⇨ *Salt-producing town. The place to stay while whale-watching at nearby Scammons Lagoon. Some pock-marked pavement here.*

Malarrimo Trailer Park—16 spaces ★ At entrance to town, next to Malarrimo Restaurant (good sea food). Fee $5.00. Water & Electricity.

La Pinta Hotel Trailer Park—60 spaces ★ Next to La Pinta Hotel, north of town. Fee $5.00. Full hookups. Restaurant, laundry and gasoline at hotel.

✳ **San Ignacio** ⇨ *A lovely oasis with old Mission church founded in 1700's. Underground river feeds date palms planted by Spanish padres two centuries ago. A must.*

Las Palmas—20 spaces ☆ On hwy. No hookups. Pool.

Martin Quezada—open camping ☆ On road into town, north of La Pinta Hotel. Open camping under palms. No hookups.

Transpeninsular Trailer Park—20 spaces ☆   North of town, behind gas station. Fee: $4. Electric and water hookups. Sometimes closed.

✴ **Santa Rosalía** ⇨ *Old mining town built by French in last century. Differently picturesque. Ferry to Guaymas departs from here.*

San Lucas Beach—35 spaces ★★   Nine miles south of town at San Lucas Cove, look for turnoff. Fishing, shelling, clamming, snorkeling, shower. No hookups. Restaurant. Highly recommended. Mailing address: P.O. Box 131, Santa Rosalía, B.C.S, Mexico.

San Bruno/Costa Serena—beach camping ★   15 miles south, then west of San Bruno. No hookups. Shower. Clean beach, shrimper's cove, good fishing.

Camp Punta Chivato ★   Turn east on dirt road at Kilometer 156, 14 miles. No hookups. Clean outhouses and shower. Beautiful location. Reservations: Bill Alvarado, (526) 853-0188.

✴ **Mulegé** ⇨ *Another lush oasis started by Jesuit padres centuries ago. On Sea of Cortez (1 Km.) and full services. Good boondocking south of here.*

Playa Sombrerito (public beach)*   Through town about 2 miles, on beach. Fee $2-$3. No facilities.

Jorge's del Río Trailer Park—22 spaces ★   South of town, across bridge. Fee: $8.50. Full hookups, fenced. Mailing address: P.O. Box 3, Mulegé, B.C.S, Mexico.

Huerta Saucedo (Orchard) RV Park—86 spaces ★   South of town, across bridge. Fee $9.00. Full hookups, boat ramp. Shade trees. Reservations: Huerta Saucedo RV Park, Dom. Con. Mulegé, B.C.S., Mexico.

Villa María Isabel Trailer Park—20 spaces ★   Two miles south of town. Fee: $9.00. Electric and water hookups. Pool, shade, bakery on grounds. Reservations: Villa María Isabel, K.134 Carreterra Transpeninsular, Mulegé, B.C.S., Mexico.

Hotel Serenidad Trailer Park—15 spaces ★   Three miles south, at river's mouth, next to hotel. Fee: $7.00.

Playa Santispac (public beach)* ★   13 miles south, first beach turnoff. Fee $3. No facilities. Some *palapas*. Good fishing, clamming.

Posada Concepción—10 spaces ★★   15 miles south. Fee: $8.00. Full hookups (electricity off at 8 pm). Tennis, diving.

Bahía El Coyote (public beach) ☆   18 miles south. Fee: $3. No facilities. Some *palapas*. Great clamming.

El Requesón (public beach) ☆   27 miles south of Mulegé, watch for turnoff east. Fee: $3. No facilities. Pretty location.

✴ **Loreto** ⇨ *Historic fishing village, which is trying to become a top-flight resort city, with first class hotels and other tourist facilities.*

Ejido Loreto RV Park—72 spaces ★   On beach just south of town. Fee: $8.00. Full hookups, laundry, fishing. Mailing address: J. Rodriguez. P.O. Box 68, Loreto, B.C.S, Mexico.

Flying Sportsman—31 spaces ★★   On beach just south of town. Full hookups. Laundry.

Playa Juncalito (public beach) ☆   13 miles south. Fee: $2. No facilities. Excellent for yellow tail, scallops and clams.

Tripui Trailer Park—116 spaces ★★★★   15 miles south. Fee: $17.00. Full hookups, but most spaces rented by year. Very spiffy. Pool, restaurant, laundry, groceries, tennis. Mailing address: P.O. Box 100, Loreto, B.C.S, Mexico. 011-706-833-0399.

---

* Public beaches (*playas públicos*) are open to "boondocking" with a small fee for the people who clean up the beach.

✳ **Cuidad Constitución** ⇨ *Farming city, not much tourist attraction. Full services.*

Campestre La Pila—28 spaces ☆ 2 miles south, watch for turnoff around Km. 209. Fee $5.00. Full hookups, no hot water. Pool, restaurant. Phone 2-0562.

Villa Trailer Park—28 spaces ☆ In town at Allende 24. Full hookups. Phone 2-2082.

✳ **San Carlos** ⇨ *Also known as Puerto San Carlos. About 60 Km. west. Beautiful location on Bahía Magdalena. Respondents seem to love it here.*

Moby Dick—beach camping ☆ Just before town, on beach, West of Constitución. Good clamming. Also more parking 4 Kms. south at end of sand bar.

✳ **La Paz** ⇨ *Pleasant, growing city with all facilities. Nice RV parks. Ferry terminal nearby. Annual Carnival celebration worth seeing.*

Aquamarina RV Park—19 spaces ★★ 2 miles south on bay. Formerly Gran Baja. Fee: $17. Small, but one of the nicest. Full hookups. Laundry, pool, marina, boat ramp, storage. Fishing excursions, scuba diving. Richard and María Adcock, P.O. Box 133, La Paz, B.C.S. (706) 822-3761.

El Cardón—84 spaces ★★ On west edge of town, 2-1/2 miles. Full hookups. Laundry, pool, fishing trips arranged. Nice. P.O. Box 104, La Paz. (706) 822-0078.

El Carrizal—175 spaces ★★★ South of town, .25 mile E. on Hwy. 13. Full hookups. Laundry, pool, shade.

La Paz Trailer Park—96 spaces ★★ 1 mile south of town. Fee: $10.00. Full hookups, laundry, pool, clubhouse groceries, tennis, ice. Good recommendations. (526) 822-8787.

Oasis Los Airpez Trailer Park—29 spaces ★★★ 10 miles north of town. Fee: $10.00. Full hookups, laundry, restaurant, friendly management. Reservations P.O. box 23, La Paz, B.C.S, Mexico (526) 822-0102.

✳ **Pichilingue** ⇨ *Site of ferry terminal for Mazatlán and Topolobampo. Good native restaurants. RVs often park in lot, waiting for ferry reservations.*

Puerto Balandra (public beach)* ☆ Five miles north of ferry terminal, watch for turnoff. Fee: $2. No facilities, some *palapas*.

Playa Tecolote (public beach)* ☆ Six miles north of ferry terminal, watch for turnoff. Fee: $2.00. Nice beach, no facilities.

✳ **Los Barriles/Buena Vista** ⇨ *On beach, between La Paz and Los Cabos. Lightly settled, with growing American influences.*

La Capilla—33 spaces ★ 2 miles south of highway, at Km. 102, west of Buena Vista, on gulf. Full hookups. Boat launching.

Martín Verdugo's Trailer Park—66 spaces ★★ North of Bahía de Palmas, turn half-mile northeast at Km. 110. Fee: $6. Full hookups, laundry, boat ramp, restaurant, ice. Mailing address: P.O. Box 477, La Paz, B.C.S, Mexico.

Playa de Oro RV Park—54 spaces ★★ North of Hotel Palmas de Cortez, Bahía de Palmas. Fee: $7.00. Full hookups, laundry, ice, boat launching (sometimes). U.S. reservations: (818) 336-7494.

Vista del Mar—10 spaces ★ On beach, turn at Km. 108. Full hookups, many full-time sites, may be full.

✳ **San José del Cabo** ⇨ *Clean, neat city, near tip of peninsula. Popular with North American retirees. Some great restaurants.*

Brisa del Mar—100 spaces ★★ Two miles south of town. $10.00. Full hookups. On beach, pool, rec room, laundry, restaurant. Can be full in winter. Recently changed hands from North American to Ejido management. Mailing address: P.O. Box 45, San José del Cabo, B.C.S.

Boondocking— Impromptu parking to the east of town, and along the coast north to Buena Vista and Los Barriles.

✳ **Cabo San Lucas** ⇨ *Resort city at tip of peninsula. Many fancy hotels, fishing boats and tourist facilities. Pacific Ocean helps keep summers bearable.*

El Arco Trailer Park—100 spaces ★★ 2 miles east on Hwy. 1. Full hookups. Restaurant, bar.

Cabo Alegre—12 spaces ★ In town, on Morelos. Full hookups.

Cabo Cielo—21 spaces ★ Four miles north. Full hookups. Near beach. Security. (706) 843-0444.

El Faro Viejo Trailer Park—50 spaces ★ One mile northwest on Calle Matamoros. Full hookups. Laundry, restaurant, ice. Can be full in winter. Mailing address: P.O. Box 64, Cabo San Lucas, B.C.S., Mexico.

El Marlin—17 spaces ☆ In town, facing harbor. Full hookups.

San Vicente RV Park—38 spaces ★★★ 2 miles east of town. Fee: $9.00. Full hookups. Pool, laundry. Mostly year-around folks here. Mailing address: P.O. box 20, Cabo San Lucas, B.C.S, Mexico. (706) 843-0712.

Vagabundos del Mar—95 spaces ★★★★ Next door to San Vicente, 2 miles east of town. Full hookups. Laundry, pool, ramadas, very nice. Reservations: Box 824, Isleton, CA 95641. (707) 374-5511.

✳ **Todos Santos** ⇨ *Lovely area on Pacific side, quaint, unspoiled, non-commercial, beautiful white sand beaches. Lots of beach parking. Popular with boondockers.*

El Molino—20 spaces ★ In town near highway. Full hookups. $8. Laundry. U.S. reservations: (818) 986-7420, Mexico (706) 824-0140..

San Pedrito—70 spaces ★★ 5.5 miles south of town, 2 mi. west. On ocean. Full hookups. $8. Laundry, restaurant. Phone (706) 824-0147.

✳ **El Pescadero/Colonia Plutarco Elias Calles** *Beach Camping.*

Playa Los Cerritos (public beach)* ☆ Six miles south on Hwy. 19. Fee: $2. No facilities. Beautiful, wide beach.

Playa Gasparino (public beach)* ☆ Six miles south on Hwy. 19. Fee: $1. No facilities. Beautiful, remote beach.

Playa Cacho (public beach)* ☆ 13 miles south on Hwy. 19. No facilities. beautiful, remote beach.

✳ **Tecate** ⇨ *Just across border, east of San Diego on Hwy. 94.*

Hacienda Santa Veronica ★★★ 5000-acre ranch owned by matador Alfonso Bustamante, resort has bull ring where guests can see bloodless bullfights. Full hookups, tennis, good restaurant, bar, pool. 20 miles east to El Hongo, turn right at Santa Veronic sign for 7 miles.

Martinez Trailer Park—16 spaces ☆ 40 Revolución, look for signs after crossing border. Laundry, cable TV, water and electricity. Reservations: 706-654-0304.

✳ **El Mayor** ⇨ *Fishing camp on upper gulf side. Very rustic.*

Campo Mosqueda—20 spaces ☆ North of San Felipe, on river. Some elec. hookups. Palapas, restaurant, boat ramp, fishing.

Río El Mayor—10 spaces ☆ On river. Electric and water hookups. Restaurant, boat ramp, fishing.

Sonora ☆ On river. A few electric and water hookups. Toilet. Rental boats, fishing.

✳ **San Felipe** ➪ *About 2 hours drive south of border, convenient to California and Arizona. Growing resort town, popular with RV retirees. Many boondocking areas north and south of town.*

Playa Bonita Trailer Park—40 spaces ★★   One mile north on main street. $12.00. On beach. Full hookups, restaurant. Mailing address: 603 S Del Mar Ave., San Gabriel CA 91776. (818) 282-1337.

Ruben's Trailer Park—54 spaces ★★★   One mile north on main street. Fee $12.00. On beach. Full hookups, covered patios, restaurant. No reservations.

Campo San Felipe Trailer Park—36 spaces ★   Near center of town. $12.00. On beach. Full hookups, patios, restaurant, billiards, ice.

La Jolla Trailer Park—50 spaces ★★   Half-mile west of town, Avenida Manzanillo and Mar Bermejo. Fee: $10. Full hookups, pool, spa, laundry, ice. Mailing address: P.O. Box 978, El Centro, CA 92243. 011-706-577-1212.

Playa de Laura Trailer Park—50 spaces ★★   In town on beach. Fee: $14. Electric and water hookups. Rec room. No reservations.

Club De Pesca Trailer Park—50 spaces ★★★   One mile south on beach. Fee: $12. Electric and water hookups. Rec room, groceries, ice, boat launch and storage, restaurant. P.O. Box 90, San Felipe, B.C., Mexico. 011-706-577-1180.

Mar del Sol RV Park—85 spaces ★★★   One mile south of town on beach. Fee: $17. Full hookups. Laundry, restaurant, groceries, boat launch, tennis, ice, disposal station. Next to Castel hotel, with use of facilities. Reservations (800) 336-5454 (in Calif..)

Faro Beach Trailer Park—150 spaces ★★★   10 miles south of town on paved road. Fee: $16. Full hookups. Attractive, overlooking Sea of Cortez. Beach access, tennis, ice. P.O. Box 107, San Felipe, B.C., Mexico

MAINLAND MEXICO

❻ **Acambay, Mex.** ➪ *Village surrounded by pine-forested mountains. Within driving distance of the capital.*

Parque Recreativo Cruz Colorado—34 spaces ★★   10 Km. north of town on Hwy 55, at Km. 94, west on road to El Agostadero, and 10 Km. to the park. Bathrooms and showers, no full hookups. Lake, fishing, rec room, fenced, nice.

❷ **Acapulco** ➪ *World-celebrated tourist attraction, fabulous beaches, restaurants, discos, night clubs, etc..*

Acapulco Trailer Park—160 spaces ★★★   8 miles north, on Pie de la Cuesta Beach. Fee: $12.00. Full hookups. Laundry, groceries, boat ramp, water skiing. Beach has rough surf. City buses. Mailing address: P.O. Box 1, Acapulco, Guerrero.

Club Tres Marías—7 spaces ★★★   8 miles north, at Pie de la Cuesta, on lagoon. Full hookups. Restaurant, city buses. Boat ramp, water skiing.

Playa Suave Trailer Park—70 spaces ★★★   Downtown, on the Costera Miguel Alemán #275, at Hornitos Beach. 38 spaces with full hookup. May not be there anymore, call first: (748) 2-1163.

El Coloso Trailer Park—150 spaces ★★   Off Hwy. 95 on Hwy. 200, at La Sábana. Full hookups. Rec room, pool. City buses. Phone 28 in La Sábana.

La Roca Trailer Park—20 spaces ★★★   5 Km. east of El Coloso, on road to Puerto Marquez . Full hookups. Pool. City buses. Phone 2-0827.

Quinta Dora Trailer Park—20 spaces ★★   8 miles north on Hwy. 200 at Pie de la Cuesta. Full hookups. Restaurant, boat ramp.

Safari Camping—10 spaces ☆   1.5 Km. from turnoff on Hwy 200 Toward Pie de la Cuesta. On beach, no hookups. Rustic.

Boondocking—Río Nexpa ☆ 50 Km. south of Acapulco, at mouth of river, no facilities. Vendors selling bottled water, fish, supplies. Usually 25 or so RVs parked here.

❽ Acayucán , Veracruz ⇨ *Tropical town with pre-Maya sites nearby.*

Hotel Ritz—4 spaces ☆ Center of town, behind hotel, elec. hookups, one bathroom, restaurant. Near Olmec historical sites.

❽ Agua Dulce, Veracruz ⇨ *Village near famous Olmec site of La Venta. Basalt artifacts now in museum at Villahermosa.*

Rancho Hermanos Graham—200 spaces ★★★★ On Hwy. 180, half-mile past road to Las Chiapas. 70 Full hookups. Pool, tennis, horseback riding, lake, on large ranch. Very nice. Phone 3-0120.

❼ Aguascalientes ⇨ *Large, up-to-date city in Northern Mexico. Famous Bullfight Fair in April.*

Centro Deportivo Ojo Caliente—33 spaces ★★ 1 Km. East on Hwy. 70. No hookups. Olympic pool, hot springs, steam baths, tennis, restaurant. City buses. 6-4098.

Medrano Motel—12 spaces ★★ South side of town. Full hookups. Pool, restaurant, ice, city bus. Phone 5-5500.

❶ Ahome, Sinaloa ⇨ *Quiet village, good fishing*

Johnny's Trailer Park—25 spaces ★ In town. Rustic. Full hookups. Fishermen stay here, near mouth of Río Fuerte.

❻ Ajijic, Jal. *See Chapala*

❶ Alamos, Sonora ⇨ *Colonial monument, exceptionally clean, nice climate, artists and writers colony. Many old mansions of mining barons being restored.*

Acosta Trailer Ranch—30 spaces ★★ 1.2 Km. east, follow signs in town. Fee: $8.00. Full hookups. On fruit farm. Flush and pit toilets. Laundry, pool, restaurant, propane. Mailing address: P.O. Box 67, Alamos, Son. (642)8-02-46.

Dolisa Motel Trailer Park—57 spaces ★★ In town, behind motel. Some full hookups, laundry service. 3 blks. from town center.

El Caracol Trailer Park—65 spaces ★★★ 12.7 Km. west, on highway. Fee: $8.00. Full hookups. Lago ranch. Laundry, pool, horseback riding, restaurant, propane. Credit cds. Mailing address: El Caracol, Navajoa Carreterra, Alamos 85760.

❼ Amazcala, Querétaro. ⇨ *Between Querétaro and San Juan del Río. Old hacienda converted to RV park.*

Amazcala Park—100 spaces ★★ Turn off Hwy 57-D towards Bernal, follow signs for 16 Km. No hookups, some bathrooms. Swimming, sauna, steam baths, rec, hall.

❹ Arriaga, Chiapas ⇨ *Center of coffee and cacao farming, near beaches.*

El Parador Auto-Hotel—7 spaces ★ On Hwy. 200 at river bridge. Some electric and water hookups. Store, pool. Phone 2-0135.

❻ Atlacomulco, Mex. ⇨ *Small town in Mazahua Indian area. Near Mexico City.*

Parque Estatal El Ocotal—50 spaces ☆ East on Hwy. 6 towards Villa del Carbon. Turn north at Km. 13, 1.5 Km. Some water & elec. hookups. Lake, horses, small zoo. Rustic.

Parque Estatal Isla de las Aves ☆ East of Altacomulco, 2 Km. west of dirt road to El Octocal, turn north 5 Km.. No hookups, some toilets. Lake, pretty, but rustic.

⑥ Ayala, Morelia ⇨ *General Zapata's home town. Sugar cane country, excellent climate. Not too far from Cuernavaca.*

El Axocoche ☆ Just east of town. Unmarked camping area, no hookups, some toilets. Small restaurant, guards.

⑤ Bacalar, Quintana Roó ⇨ *Village on beautiful tropical lagoon*

Los Coquitos—20 spaces ☆ South side of lake. No hookups. A few spaces among coconut palms.

❶ Bahía Kino, Sonora ⇨ *Popular RV destination and winter quarters on beach. Quiet town, attracts retirees. Near Seri Indian village. Good fishing.*

Club de Yates—92 spaces ★★★ Turn south toward Old Kino at gas station. Full hookups, near beach. Boat ramp, laundry, restaurant. Nice. 4-6298.

Islandia Marina—80 spaces ★ In Old Kino, on beach. Full hookups some ramadas, boat ramp and storage, mechanic. Phone 2-0080.

Kino Bay Trailer Park—205 spaces ★★★ In New Kino, across from beach. Fee: $10.00. Fee: Covered patios, laundry, groceries, restaurant, city buses. Credit cds. Phone 2-0140. Mailing address: P.O. Box 857, Hermosillo, Son.

Parador Bella Vista 18 spaces ☆ On beach between Posada del Mar & Posada Santa Gemma. @PARK = Posada Santa Gemma—14 spaces ★★ Turn north when Hwy. 16 branches to Km. 11.8. Full hookups. On beach, city buses. Phone 2-0026.

Caverna Del Seri—30 spaces ★ In New Kino, past Kino Bay trailer park. Full hookups, restaurant, nightclub, city buses. Phone 2-0140 in Hermosillo.

⑩ Basaseachic, Chihuahua ⇨ *Tiny village in beautiful setting in Tarahumara Indian country. Highest waterfall in Mexico nearby.*

Campamento Ejidal Basaseachic—50 spaces ☆ Hwy. 16 west from Chihuahua to Tomochic, then 58 Km. dirt road to Baseachic, 3 Km. to camp. No hookups or services (except watchman). Beautiful waterfall in Tarahumara country. Rustic.

❷ Boca de Iguanas *See La Manzanilla*

❷ Bucerías, Nayarit ⇨ *Beach town, north of Puerto Vallarta, quiet, nice, has closest beach RV parking to P.V..*

Bucerías Trailer Court—46 spaces ★★★ 24 Kilometer north of Puerto Vallarta, on beach (watch for signs). around Km. 143.Fee: $12.00. Full hookups. Restaurant, laundry, ice. Mailing address: P.O. Box 39A-Airport, Puerto Vallarta, Jal.

La Martoca Bungalows—5 spaces ★★ 15 miles north of Puerto Vallarta. Full hookups. Beach, pool.

⑩ Caborca, Sonora ⇨ *Town on edge of Altar desert. Growing little city, partly modern and partly old adobes. A logical stopover place.*

Motel Amelia—3 spaces ☆ South on Hwy. 2. possible water and electric hookup. Restaurant, pool.

Motel Posada San Cristóbal—20 spaces ☆ North of town, some full hookups, possibly a bath and shower.

El Sol Trailer Park—13 spaces ★ North of city. Full hookups, bathroom.

❹ Campeche, Camp. ⇨ *Interesting mixture of modern and colonial city, originally walled in for protection from pirates. Some walls still there. Convenient to many Mayan ruins.*

Campeche Trailer Park—30 spaces ☆ 2 miles south, watch for signs. Hard to find. Full hookups. Clean. Restaurant, city buses

Hotel Park—35 spaces ☆   Km. 4. Hwy. 180 toward Merida, on edge of town. Full hookups, one bathroom. City buses. (98) 6-3417.

❺ **Cancún, Quintana Roó** ⇨ *Famous Caribbean beach resort with numerous tourist attractions. RV facilities away from city center.*

Almirante de Gante—50 spaces ★★★   4 Km. north of ferry dock. Water & elec. hookups, bathrooms, restaurant, city buses. Nice.

La Playa—44 spaces ★★   Half-mile from Punta Sam ferry dock. Full hookups. Restaurant, water sports, city buses. Phone 4-2458.

Mecoloco ☆   1.5 miles from Punta Sam ferry dock. No hookups, cold shower.

Rainbow Trailer Park—72 spaces ☆   1 mi. south of airport intersection at Km. 307. Full hookups. Pool. Phone 4-42411 in Merida.

❾ **Capilla del Taxte, Sin.** ⇨ *Village stopover between Mazatlán and Durango. Breath-taking mountain scenery. Near "Devil's Spine" natural wonder.*

Hotel Villa Blanca ★   In spectacular mountain country at Km. 234, Hwy 40. Some spaces beside hotel, no hookups, one bathroom. Hiking trails, good restaurant.

❼ **Caracha, Michoacán.** ⇨ *Tiny village in Michoacán mountains.*

Balneario Caracha—30 spaces ☆   1 Km. before town. No hookups, some bathrooms. An old hacienda, now swimming resort. Horses, pool, restaurant.

❼ **Carapan, Michoacán.** ⇨ *Tarascan Indian area, small town at major highway intersection.*

Hotel La Hacienda ★   At junction of Hwys 15 and 37. A few places with limited hookup. restaurant, groceries. Clean.

❽ **Catemaco, Veracruz** *(see Lago Catemaco)*

❼ **Celaya, Guanajuato** ⇨ *Large town in agricultural area. Site of famous battle between Pancho Villa and Gen. Obregón. Renowned for "cajetas" (carmel goat milk candy).*

Royal Motel—6 spaces ★   In town. Elec. hookups. Pool, city buses.

❼ **Chamela, Jal.** ⇨ *Lovely beach village between Puerto Vallarta and Manzanillo, settled in 1525. Known for giant oysters, sometimes 6" across.*

Chamela Motel—5 spaces ☆   On Hwy. 200. Full hookups. Restaurant, groceries, tennis, pool, city buses. Phone 17-1423 in Guadalajara.

Villa Polinesia—8 spaces ☆   On Hwy. 200. Full hookups. Laundry, palapas. Phone 22-3940 in Guadalajara.

❻ **Chapa de Mota, Mex.** ⇨ *Small mountain town in pine forest, interesting, isolated. Driving distance from Mexico City.*

Campamento Vacacional—44 spaces ★   Hwy. 2 at Km. 65, just south of town. electric hookups, tennis, cock fighting, fenced in. Nice.

❼ **Chapala, Jalisco** ⇨ *On Lake Chapala, popular retirement area, as is nearby Ajijic. Good restaurants and golf course.*

El Manglarcito Trailer Park—25 spaces ★   5 Km. west of Chapala, just south of Hwy 44 by the lake. Elec and water hookups, one bathroom. City buses.

Pal Trailer Park—110 spaces ★★   Between Chapala and Ajijic. Fee: $6.00. Full Hookups. Laundry, pool, rec room., boats. Credit cds. (376) 5-37-64.

---

⑤ Chemuyl, Quintana Roó ⇨ *One of many lovely Caribbean beach locations, white sand and coconut palms.*

Playa de Chemuyul—30 spaces ☆ On beach, 11.5 miles north of Tulúm. One hookup. Restaurant, groceries.

---

⑤ Chetumal, Quintana Roó ⇨ *Fishing, snorkeling, nearby archaeological ruins. On border of Belize and Mexico.*

Sunrise on the Caribbean—26 spaces ★★★ 8.5 miles from west junction bypass (town of Calderitas). On beach Full hookups. Restaurant, groceries, boat ramp, city buses.

Laguna Milagros—10 spaces ☆ 10 kms. west of town, just south of Hwy 186. No hookups, some toilets, lake fishing boats, city buses.

Cenote Azul Trailer Park—40 spaces ★ Off Hwy. 307, 34 Km. north of Chetumal. Elec. and water hookups, tank disposal. Lake nearby.

---

⑤ Chichén-Itzá, Yucatán ⇨ *Near site of world-famous Maya ruins.*

Pirámide Inn—47 spaces ★★ West of town. Full hookups. Pool, restaurant, disco in cave. Phone 5 in Piste.

---

⑩ Chihuahua, Chihuahua ⇨ *Capital of state, large, historic and beautiful city.*

Chemaju—23 spaces ★★ North on Hwy. 45. Some full hookups. Rec room, laundry, city buses. Phone 7-0677.

Nieves Hotel—42 spaces ★★) Just north of town center on Hwy 45. Full hookups. Pool, restaurant, laundry, TV room, city buses.

---

⑥ Cholula, Pue. ⇨ *Enormous Pre-Colombian pyramid with tunnels displaying previous pyramids. Supposedly, there is one church here for every day of the year. Site of University of the Américas.*

Las Américas Trailer Park—60 spaces ★★★ North of town, near Hwy 190. Full hookups, pool, laundry restaurant. City buses. (22) 47-0134.

---

⑦ Chupicuaro, Michoacán ⇨ *Nature park by lake Patzcuaro.*

Chupicuaro Motel—7 spaces. ★ 4 miles from Quirogá on Hwy. 15. Electric hookups.

---

⑩ Ciudad Camargo, Chihuahua ⇨ *Agricultural center. Nearby lake fishing. Hot springs.*

Villa Del Charro—45 spaces ★★ 3.3 miles south. Full hookups. Groceries, pool, tennis, fishing, ice.

Hotel Baca—2 spaces ☆ Hwy 45, Km. 72, just north of town. Just elec. hookups. Pool.

---

⑩ Ciudad Cuauhtemoc, Chihuahua ⇨ *Menonite agricultural area.*

Campo 6-1/2—50 spaces ★ 19 Km. north of town. No hookups, one toilet. Owners are Menonites, and speak little English or Spanish.

Peter's Trailer Park—78 spaces ★★ 8 miles north on Hwy. 28. Full hookups. Groceries. Also Menonite.

---

⑩ Ciudad Delicias, Chic. ⇨ *Agricultural area, some fishing, wineries.*

Motel Río ☆ Downtown, on Hwy 45. A couple of spaces with elec. and water hookup, laundry, TV room.

---

⑤ Ciudad del Carmen, Campeche ⇨ *On narrow island in Gulf. Historic.*

Lino's Motel—10 spaces ☆ In town. Electric hookups. Pool

---

⑩ **Ciudad Jiménez, Chih.** ⇨ *Desert town with irrigation farming.*

Motel Las Pampas ★   At junctions of Hwy 45 and 49, just east of town. A few elec. and water hookups, one bathroom, pool, restaurant, city buses.

---

⑧ **Ciudad Mante** *See Mante*

---

⑧ **Ciudad Valles San Luís Potosí** *(see Valles)*

---

⑧ **Ciudad Victoria, Tamaulipas** ⇨ *Capital of state, good stopover between Laredo and Mexico City. Fine lake fishing nearby.*

El Jardín Motel—16 spaces ★   North end of town where bypass splits from main road. Full hookups, bathroom, city buses.

Victoria Trailer Park—150 spaces. ★★   West off Hwy. 101 & 85 intersection. Fee: $10.00 Full hookups. Rec room. Phone 2-48-24.

---

⑧ **Coatzacoalcos, Veracruz** *(See Agua Dulce)*

---

⑧ **Coatzacoalcos, Veracruz**

Hermanos Graham Trailer Park—175 spaces ★★★★   37 Km. south on Hwy. 180. Fee: $12.00. Full hookups. Restaurant, pool, lake, Fishing, flush & pit toilets.

---

⑧ **Comales, Tamaulipas** ⇨ *Village near border, said to be good fishing.*

El Azucar Motel—7 spaces ★★   North 7 Km. on Hwy 2 to Km. 73, then south on dirt road 14 Km. to lake. Full hookups, restaurant, dance hall, boat ramp, mechanic.

---

⑩ **Creel, Chih.** ⇨ *Small Town in scenic mountains by one end of Copper Canyon. Hot Springs. Tahaurama Indians nearby. Lumber country.*

Complejo Turístico Lago de Arareco ★   7 Km. south on graded road to Batopilas. Several acres of unmarked camping area. No hookups. On lake, restaurant, boats, horses. In famous Tarahumara country.

---

③ **Cuajinicuilapa, Guerrero.** ⇨ *Town on Costa Chica—populated by descendants of African slaves. Posibility of government tourism development.*

Parador Punta Maldonado—10 spaces ☆   South of town on dirt road, at Oaxaca State line. No hookups. Bathrooms.

---

⑨ **Cuencame, Durango** ⇨ *Desert town south of Torreón.*

Motel La Costa—10 spaces ☆   Unmarked spaces with electricity and water. One bathroom. Restaurant.

---

⑥ **Cuernavaca, Morelia** ⇨ *A place of year-around spring. Beautiful, but crowded. Center for language learning; stay with local family and learn Spanish.*

Cuernavaca Trailer Park—100 spaces ★★   Hwy. 57 and Hwy. 160 (watch for signs). Fee: $10.00. Full hookups. Pool, laundry, tennis, exercise room, city buses. Mailing address: Mesalina 3, Colonia Delicias.

San Pablo Trailer Park—70 spaces ★★   13 Km. east on Hwy. 160. Fee: $15.00. Full hookups. Pool, city buses, laundry. Mailing address: Sierra Fría 790, Mexico City, D.F. 72000.

Monasterio Benedictino—60 spaces ★★   In Ahuátepec, on road to Tepotztlán. Elec. and water hookups. Rec room, Restaurant. Phone 3-1355.

❷ Culiacán, Sinaloa ⇨ *Capital of state; modern city, lake fishing nearby. Not much of a tourist attraction, although not unattractive.*

3 Ríos Trailer Park—40 spaces ★★   3 Km. north from Hwy. 15, next to Motel Los 3 Ríos. Fee: $5.00 Full hookups. Pool, restaurant, laundry, city buses. Credit cds. Mailing address: P.O. Box 311, Culiacán, Sin.

❾ Durango, Durango ⇨ *Modern town with mixture of old (founded in 1563). Mild climate and popular "western" movie location.*

Campo Mexico Courts Motel—12 spaces ☆   1 Km. south on 20 de Noviembre. Fee: $6.00. Full hookups. Next to motel, fenced. Pool, restaurant, laundry, city buses. Credit cds. Mailing address: P.O. Box 96, Durango, Dgo. 34000.

❼ El Chique, Zacatecas ⇨ *Tiny village by a lake. Some fishing.*

El Chique Dam ☆   At Km. 207 on Hwy. 54 between Guadalajara and Zacatecas. A few spaces with elec. Pool, boat rentals.

❶ El Golfo de Santa Clara, Sonora ⇨ *Shrimping village, enormous tidal variations. Very rustic accommodations, friendly people. Petrified wood collecting.*

El Conchal—15 spaces ☆   South of town, on beach. No hookups. Fishing.
La Ponderosa—20 spaces ☆   South of town, on beach. No hookups. Fishing.
Las Cabañas ☆   South of town, on beach. No hookups. Fishing.

❼ El Tecuan, Jalisco ⇨ *Beach village, tropical and beautiful. North of Barra de Navidad.*

El Tecuan Hotel ☆   20 miles north of Melaque junction. On beach. Some electric and water hookups. Pool, restaurant. Phone 7-0132 in Melaque.

❹ Escarcega, Campeche ⇨ *Small town where highway forks north to Campeche, east to Chetumal*

Las Gemelas Hotel—4 spaces ☆   Behind gas station, by restaurant. Electric, shower, toilet.

❼ Etzatlán , Jalisco ⇨ *Small town in sugar cane production country. 88 Kms west of Guadalajara.*

Delia's Trailer Park—12 spaces ★★   East of town 1/2 Km. Full hookups. 1 bathroom, horseback riding.

❼ Guadalajara, Jalisco ⇨ *Mexico's 2nd largest city, with thousands of U.S. and Canadian retirees. Climate called "eternal spring."*

Guadalajara Trailer Park—210 sites ★★★★   5 Km. north on Hwy. 54. Fee: $6.00. Full hookups. Laundry, pool, groceries, rec room, library, beauty parlor, insurance, city buses. Mailing address: P.O. Box 1-2062, Guadalajara, Jal. 44100.
Hacienda Trailer Park—98 spaces ★★★★   9.5 Km. north off Hwy. 115. Fee: $7.00. Full hookups. Laundry, rec room, library, pool, nice patios, city buses. Mailing address: P.O. Box 5-494, Guadalajara, Jal. 45000.
Pal Trailer Park—98 spaces ★★★★   7.2 Km. south on Hwy. 15, east of Plaza del Sol. Satellite TV, city buses. Good location. Fee: $7.00. Credit cds. Mailing address: P.O. Box 1-1470, Guadalajara, Jal. 45050.
San Jose del Tajo—225 spaces ★★★   15.5 Km. south on Hwy. 15. Fee: $7.00. Full hookups. Pool, tennis, horses, laundry, groceries, rec room, library, tank disposal. Mailing address: P.O. Box 31-242, Guadalajara, Jal. 45050.

❼ Guanajuato, Gto. ⇨ *Beautiful colonial city, and cultural center. Site of rich silver mines from 1500's.*

Guanajuato Trailer Park—50 spaces ☆ Southeast on shortcut road to San Miguel. No hookups. Tank disposal.

Morril Trailer Park—80 spaces ★ North side of the Panoramic Hwy. with view of city. Watch for signs. Check this one out for a possibly steep road before you pull in. Full hookups, clean.

Motel Embajadoras ☆ Next to Embajadoras Park, near La Olla Dam. A few spaces with elec. City buses, restaurant.

Motel El Laurel—4 spaces ☆ South of town where road to Marfil separates. Elec. hookups, restaurant.

❽ Guayalejo, Tamaulipas ⇨ *Small town, no information available.*

Casa Hogar Alegre ☆ South end of town near bridge. No hookups. Orphanage. Honey for sale.

❶ Guaymas, Sonora ⇨ *Port city, sportsfishing center. Most RV people stay at nearby San Carlos Bay.*

Bahía Trailer Park—80 spaces ★★ On Playitas Peninsula, opposite downtown. Full hookups. On beach. Rec hall, boat ramp, grocery delivery, insurance. Phone 2-3595.

Escalante Trailer Park—104 spaces ☆ On Miramar beach, 6 Kms. west.. Full hookups. Restaurant, ice, city buses. Phone 2-4822.

Las Playitas—114 spaces ☆ On Playitas Peninsula. Full hookups. On Beach. Pool, restaurant, boat ramp, ice, city buses.

❶ Hermosillo, Sonora ⇨ *Modern, prosperous city in center of rich farming country. Turn here to go to Kino Bay.*

Kino Trailer Park—44 spaces ★★ North on Hwy. 15. Full hookups. City bus. Phone 4-1492

Mazocoba Trailer Park—26 spaces ★★ North on Hwy. 15, 1 Km. Full hookups, city buses. Phone 4-3305.

❸ Huatulco, Oaxaca ⇨*Important new development on lovely bay south of Oaxaca. Government is going all out to make this a top resort, and it's growing quickly. A respondent says there are two trailer parks there and possibly more going in. We have no information on these parks other than that they exist.*

❻ Huauchinango, Puebla ⇨ *Foothills of the Sierra Madre. Beautiful location.*

Presa El Tejocotal ☆ Southwest 18 Kms. on Hwy 130. Unmarked spaces, some with electricity.

❼ Irapuato, Guanajuato ⇨ *Commercial city, not much tourist attraction.*

Motel Fresa—4 spaces ☆ North of town on Hwy 15 bypass. Elec. and water hookups.

❹ Isla Aguada, Camp. ⇨ *Quaint, friendly village on Hwy. 180 between Champotón and Villahermosa.*

Campeche—25 spaces ☆ West off Hwy. 180, just before toll bridge. Electric and water hookups. Nice park on beach. Shower, toilet. Fishing.

❼ Ixmiquilpan, Hgo. ⇨ *Center of Otomi Indian area. Historic and picturesque.*

Motel Saisa—3 spaces ☆ Hwy 85 at Km. 159. Near down town. A few spaces with elec & water, restaurant

❺ Isla Mujeres, Quintana Roó Good boondocking facilities halfway between town and south end of island. No facilities. ☆

❷ Ixtapa, Guerrero ⇨ *Spiffy resort, rather new and expensive. Great beaches.*

Playa Linda Hotel—50 spaces ★★★★ At end of scenic drive. Full hookups. On beach. Pool, restaurant, rec hall, laundry, palapas, tennis, ice, watchmen, city buses, baby sitters. Excellent. Phone 4-3381.

❷ Ixtlán del Río, Nayarit ⇨ *Stopping point between Guadalajara and Tepic.*

Las Ruínas Restaurant—6 spaces ☆ On Hwy. 15, west side of town, next to gasoline station. Water and Elec. only. Phone 3-2205.

❽ Izucar de Matamoros ⇨ *South of Puebla in sugar cane growing country.*

Hotel Cristóbal Colon—8 spaces ★★★ Downtown, north of junction. Some full hookups, pool, playground. 243-6-0284.

❶ Kino Bay Sonora *See Bahía Kino*

❽ La Antigua ⇨ *21 Km. north of Veracruz. Original site of Veracruz, settled in 1519 by Cortez. First Christian church on American mainland. Tropical, historical spot.*

Rincón del Piráta—7 spaces ★★ Hwy. 180, at Km. 128, near toll station. On river beach. Elec. hookups, 2 pools, restaurant, boat ramp, fishing. Highly recommended. 293-4-0538.

❷ La Barrita ⇨ *Beautiful tropical village north of Acapulco. Several beaches and lagoons. 52 Kms below Zihuantanejo.*

La Mancha—15 spaces ☆ On beach, in village. Some elec. hookups. Cold showers, restaurant.

❼ La Manzanilla, Jal. ⇨ *On Manzanillo bay, tropical beach location. Good fishing, skin diving and snorkelling. Good seafood.*

Campo Boca de Iguanas—50 spaces ★★★ 4 Km from town, 16.5 Km. above Manzanillo. 2.5 Km. graded road toward sea. Some full hookups. Fishing, snorkeling, beautiful. Phone (36) 21-2387 (in Guadalajara).

Trailer Park Entre Palmeras—55 spaces ★★ Located just before above-listed park. Some full hookups, groceries, ice.

❽ Lago Catemaco, Veracruz ⇨ *Lovely town on lake, in low mountain range. Nice climate, good restaurants serving regional dishes.*

Playa Azul Motel—14 spaces ★★ 2 miles on dirt road, on lake. Electric and water. Pool, boat ramp, Restaurant, laundry, ice. Phone 3-0001.

Solotepec Trailer Park—20 spaces ★ 2 Km. north of town on road to Sonteconapan. No hookups, rustic restaurant.

❽ Lago Guerrero, Tamps. ⇨ *On lake famous for fishing, south of Brownsville. Popular with Texas fishermen.*

Big Bass Trailer Park—48 spaces ★ North end of lake, 9 miles east of Hwy. 101. Full hookups. Boat ramp, boat rentals. Phone (512) 682-8513 McAllen TX.

Charlie Morris Fishing Camp—12 spaces ★★ 40 Km. east on Hwy. 70. Elec. hookups, boat ramp. 131-2-3024.

El Pelicano—10 spaces ★ Mouth of River. Full hookups. Restaurant, boat ramp. Phone 2-1550 in Ciudad Victoria

El Sargento Trailer Park—20 spaces ★★ Off Hwy 101, west of Nuevo Padillo on river. Full hookups. Restaurant, boat ramp and rentals. Phone 2-2655, Ciudad Victoria.

Guerrero Trailer Park—60 spaces ★★ East shore, 12 Km. southwest (look for signs). Full hookups, kitchen, boat ramp.

Hacienda Alta Vista—60 spaces ★★★★ On north end of lake. Full hookups. Pool, restaurant, clubhouse, laundry, boat ramp, rentals. (512) 423-2234, Harlingen, TX

Lago Vista—60 spaces ★★★ North end of lake at Km. 64 of Hwy 101. Full hookups, boat ramp, rentals, restaurant.

Victoria Bass Club—100 spaces ★★ South end of lake. Some electric and water hookups. Restaurant, boat ramp and rentals. Phone 2-3024 in Ciudad Victoria.

❷ Lago Mocuzari, Sonora ⇨ *Near Alamos, beautiful village, good fishing.*

La Cabana Trailer Park—60 spaces ★★★ North off Hwy. 24 at Km. 28, watch for signs. Full hookups, boats, fishing.

❹ Lagunas de Montebello, Chiapas ⇨ *National park near Guatemala border, beautiful lakes, rain forest.*

Albergue Tziscao ★ Watch for signs. 2 spaces with elec., others unmarked. Bathrooms, kitchen boats horses, fishing.

Lake Chapala *See Chapala*

❷ La Peñita, Nayarit ⇨ *See also Rincón de Guayabitos. Village on beach, north of Puerto Vallarta; nice.*

La Peñita Trailer Park—200 spaces ★★ West of town off Hwy. 200, Km. 94. Full hookups. On beach. Pool, laundry, ice.

Russell's Motel—11 spaces ★★ In town. Full hookups. On beach, laundry, ice.

Mary's Trailer Park—17 spaces ★ In town. Full hookups. On beach.

❼ La Piedad, Michoacán ⇨ *City of 100,000, beautiful farming country.*

Cerro Grande Motel ★ On Hwy. 15, on lake. Electric. Pool, restaurant. Phone 2-0710.

❼ Leon de Guanajuato ⇨ *City famous for shoe manufacturing.*

Excelsior Trailer Park—7 spaces ★ At Ciudad Satelite off Hwy. 45. Full hookups, bathrooms, steam baths, pool, laundry, city buses.

❷ Lo de Marcos, Nayarit ⇨ *Beautiful village on beach, north of Puerto Vallarta.*

El Caracol—22 spaces ★★ 8 miles south of Rincón de Guayabitos. Full hookups. On beach.

El Pequeño Paraiso—100 spaces ★ 8 miles south of Rincón de Guayabitos. On beach. Some electric hookups, bathrooms. Seasonal restaurant, ice.

❼ Los Azufres, Michoacán. ⇨ *Hot volcanic pools in large volcanic crater. Lakes, forest, hiking.*

Albergue Los Azufres ★ South at Km. 105 off Hwy 126, 15 Kms. to lodge. Unmarked spaces, no hookups, bathrooms. Hot springs, pools.

Balneario Erendira—25 spaces ★★ Beautiful location in pine forest. Some elec. hookups, toilets. Hot pools and springs.

❶ Los Mochis, Sinaloa ⇨ *Modern city, terminal of Copper Canyon train.*

Barobampo-Marclarck—80 spaces ★★★ North of Los Mochis and San Miguel. Full hookups, pool, store, fishing in river. Nice. Phone 681 2-13-69.

Los Mochis Trailer Park—140 spaces ★★ North on Hwy. 15. Fee: $10.00. Full hookups. Restaurant, laundry, rec room. City buses. Mailing address: P.O. Box 1201, Los Mochis, Sin. (681)2-00-21

Río Fuerte Trailer Resort—58 spaces ★ 18 Km. north on Hwy. 15, on Río Fuerte. Fee: $9.00. Full hookups. Laundry, pool, jacuzzi, tank disposal, rec room, groceries. (681) 5-47-72.

Santa Rita Trailer Park ☆ At traffic circle south entrance to city. Full hookups. Telephone 4-22-40.

⑩ **Magdalena, Sonora** ⇨ *Burial place of Father Kino. South of Nogales.*

Kino Motel—15 spaces ★ Half block off Hwy 15 on Pesqueira St. Full hooku0s, Restaurant, laundry. (632) 2-0998, 2-0983.

El Pollo Loco—6 spaces ☆ 5 Kms. north at Tacicuri. Full hookups, restaurant. Just off main highway. Full hookups. Restaurant. Phone 2-0983.

⑧ **Mante, Tamulipas** ⇨ *Nice stopover city. South of Cuidad Victoria.*

Hotel Mante Trailer Park—10 spaces ★★ 1 Km. north, by hotel. Fee: $10.00.No hookups, no showers. Restaurant, pool (in hotel). Credit cds. Mailing address: Guerrero 500 Ciudad Mante, Tamps. Phone 2-09-90.

❷ **Manzanillo, Colima** ⇨ *Port city, known for good seafood. Good beaches nearby. Trailer park situation was not good at last report (some were closed).*

Don Felipe's—10 spaces ★ On road to Las Hadas, near La Audencia Beach. Full hookups.

Sunset Gardens Trailer Park—77 spaces ★★ Off Hwy. 200 at Km. 9.5. Full hookups, pool, beach, bathrooms, city buses.

❷ **Matachén, Nayarit** *(See San Blas)*

❾ **Matehuela, San Luís Potosí** ⇨ *Near famous ghost town of Catorce Real. Prosperous-looking.*

Las Palmas Trailer Park—35 spaces ★★ On highway, behind Las Palmas motel. Fee: $10.00. Full hookups. Pool, restaurant (in motel). Credit cds. Mailing address: P.O. Box 73, Matehuela, S.L.P. 78700. Phone 2-00-01.

Oasis Motel ★ 3 Kms north, some spaces with elec. hookups. Pool, TV, restaurant.

Motel Rosy—16 spaces ★ On Hwy. at south of town. Electric hookups, restaurant.

❷ **Mazatlán, Sinaloa** ⇨ *Famous beach resort, good beaches and facilities. Sports fishing excellent.*

Boondocking ☆ Supposed to be good free parking at old hotel parking lot by ocean, next to "Pescado de Mexico" fish cooperative, maybe 6 miles north of downtown. Dump station, water vendors, police cooperation.

Isla Venados—50 spaces ★★ North end of golf course. Full hookups. On beach. Phone 2-6666.

La Posta Trailer Park—200 spaces ★★★ North side, near Cameron Glorietta, next to lagoon. Full hookups. Pool, rec halls, laundry, ice, city buses. Phone 3-5310.

Las Palmas—120 spaces ★★ North end at Calzado Camarón Sábalo 333. Full hookups. Pool, groceries, rec hall, laundry, city buses, grocery delivery.. Phone 3-5311.

Las Canoas—60 spaces ★★ 6 Kms. north of Camarón Circle. Full hookups, bathrooms, fishing, groceries, city buses.

Mar Rosa—70 spaces ★★ North end of town, next to Holiday inn. Full hookups. On beach, groceries, city buses.

Maravillas—26 spaces ☆ Far north end, on Cerritos. Full hookups. On beach. Rec hall.

Motel & Trailer Park Camarón—53 spaces ★ At Camarón Circle. Some full hookups, bathroom. City buses.

Ole Trailer Park—100 spaces ★★ Camarón-Sábalo Drive, 2 Kms. north of Camarón Circle. On beach, full hookups, rec room, city buses.

Playa Escondida—200 spaces ★★★ Far north side, 1/2 Km. north of Las Canoas on Sábalo-Cerritos. Full hookups, bathrooms, pool, rec hall, groceries, city buses.

San Bartolo—48 spaces ☆ Far north side Full hookups. On beach. Closed in the summer.

Sábalo Beach Trailer Park—30 spaces ★★ 3.5 Kms north of Camarón Circle, near Camino Real Hotel. Full hookups, beach, laundry, city buses.

---

❷ **Melaque, Jalisco** ⇨ *Beautiful beach village, 5 Kms north of Barra de Navidad.*

Playa Trailer Park—45 spaces ★★ In San Patricio, on beach. Full hookups. Store, ice, city buses. Phone 7-0065.

---

❺ **Merida, Yucatan** ⇨ *Splendid colonial city, near Mayan ruins, great seafood.*

Mayan Paradise—70 spaces ★ Hwy. 261, 5 miles north. Full hookups. Pool, rec hall, laundry, city buses.. Phone 3-2643.

Rainbow Maya Trailer Park—120 spaces ★★ 8 Km. north on Hwy. 261. Fee: $12.00 Full hookups. Laundry, pool, city buses. Mailing address: Merida-Progreso Hwy., Merida, Yuc. 97127.

---

❻ **Mexico City, D.F. (Tepotzotlán)** ⇨ *Nothing in Mexico City proper*

Lago de Guadalupe—65 spaces ★★ Hwy. 57, 10 miles south to Tepotzotlán toll house. Full hookups. Pool, rec hall, lake and nearby golf. Phone 574-5826.

Pepe's Trailer park—80 spaces ★ In Tepotzotlán just south of toll station. Full hookups. Rec hall, store.

---

❷ **Mocuzari, Sonora** *See Lago Mocuzari.*

---

❽ **Monterrey, Nuevo Leon** ⇨ *Large industrial city with nearby sightseeing attractions.*

Balneario Los Rodriguez ★ 5.5 miles east on Hwy. 54 (Mixcoac exit.) No hookups, large parking area. Swimming pools, tennis, amusement park.

California Courts ☆ North on Hwy 85, near university. Some parking without hookups. Restaurant, pool, city buses.

Motel Nueva Castilla Trailer Park—30 spaces ★ 15.5 Km. north on Hwy.. 87, next to motel. Fee: $12.00 Full hookups. Fenced, restaurant, tennis, pool. Mailing address: General Escobedo, Monterrey, N.L. Phone 76-67-70.

Ojo de Agua Pesquería—20 spaces ★ 27 Kms north of Monterrey on Hwy. 54. No hookups, bathrooms, olympic pol, horseback riding.

---

❼ **Morelia, Michoacán** *State capital, and one of prettiest colonial cities in Mexico.*

Campo Real—30 spaces ☆ West on Hwy. 15. A few hookups. Phone 2-3434.

---

❻ **Nevado de Toluca** ⇨ *High in year-round snow country, at Xinantectal volcano.*

Albergue Inde ★ Hwy. 134 from Toluca to Temascaltepec and La Puerta, look for signs, 8 Kms. of graded road. Some electric hookups only. Expect it to be cold, but picturesque.

---

❷ **Novillero, Nayarit** ⇨ *Also called Playa Novillero. Village on long beach peninsula, reached by ferry, south of Mazatlán.*

Bungalos Paraiso—6 spaces ☆ At end of road, turn north 1 Km. On beach, elec. hookups, bathroom.

---

❸ **Oaxcaca** ⇨ *Wonderful colonial city, great climate, near Zapotecan many ruins.*

Motel Loma Bonita—5 spaces ★ 5 Km. west of town at Km. 187. A few full hookups, bathrooms, restaurant (upon request).

Oaxaca Trailer Park—150 spaces ★★★★ 7 blocks north of Hwy. 190 (watch for signs) Fee: $10.00 Full hookups. Fenced, laundry, pool, rec room, city buses, convenient to shopping. Mailing address: P.O. Box 33, Oaxaca, Oax. 68000. Phone 5-27-96.

Rosa Isabel Trailer Park—50 spaces ★★★ Across from Motel Loma Bonita.Full hookups, nice bathrooms, laundry kitchens, rec room.

---

❻ Oaxtepec, Morelia ➪ *Pretty village, hot springs. Montezuma maintained a summer home here.*

Centro Vacacional Oaxtepec—80 spaces ★★★★ Hwy. 169 at Km. 37, turn north. Some elec. and water hookups, 1,000 non-hookup spaces. Huge resort with hot springs, lake, restaurants, tennis, horseback riding, everything, including babysitters. Unusual.

---

❶ Obregón, Sonora *Prosperous agricultural center. Good lake fishing.*

Marina del Rey ☆ At Alvaro Obregón Lake. Full hookups. Restaurant, boat ramp, rentals, fishing.

---

❹ Ocozocuautla, Chiapas ➪ *West of Tuxtla Gutiérrez at interesting park and waterfall.*

Hogar Infantil ★ West side at orphanage, which is operated to obtain funds for children. Full hookups reported.

---

❽ Orizaba, Veracruz ➪ *City near picturesque, snow-covered Orizaba peak. Lots of water from melting snow, which is happily made into beer.*

Hotel D'Alba—5 spaces ★★ Toll highway at Km. 148. Full hookups, bathrooms, pool, fronton court.

---

❻ Pachuca, Hgo. ➪ *Old silver mining town (still producing) in mountain location.*

El Chico Parque Nacional—25 spaces ★ Stopoff point between Laredo and Mexico City. Full hookups. and many boondocking sites. Horseback riding, hiking trails.

---

❹ Palenque, Chiapas ➪ *Tropical town near ultra-famous Mayan ruins. Nice.*

María del Mar—70 spaces ★ On road to ruins. Full hookups. Restaurant, palapas.

Mayabell Trailer Park—44 spaces ★★ 1.5 Km. east of ruins. Fee: $10.00. Full hookups, jungle setting, restaurant.

Nututún—10 spaces ★★★ South of town. Electric and water, lots of undeveloped sites. Good restaurant, river swimming

Tulipanes—20 spaces ★★ Near town entrance, east of fountain. Full hookups, restaurants, laundry..

---

❼ Pátzcuaro, Michoacán. ➪ *Ancient Tarascan Indian capital. Famous tourist attraction.*

El Pozo Trailer park—20 spaces ★★★ 3.5 Km. north on Hwy. 120, on lake. Fee: $5.00. Full hookups. Laundry, horseback riding, fishing. Clean bathrooms, boat ramp. Mailing address: P.O. Box 42, Pátzcuaro, Michoacán. 61600. (454) 2-09-31.

Patzcuaro Motel—9 spaces ☆ One block off hwy. Full hookups. Pool, tennis, city buses. Phone 2-0654.

Posada Don Vasco—40 spaces ★ On L. Cárdenas street past Motel Patzcuaro. Some hookups, pool restaurant tennis, bowling, city buses. Closed in summer. Phone 2-0262.

---

❷ Playa Azul, Michoacán ➪ *Great stopover place between Manzanillo and Zihuatenejo; long beach.*

Hotel Playa Azul—7 spaces ★★★ Nice hotel in center of town. Full hookups under palm trees, walled and guarded. Pool, restaurant bathrooms, block from beach. Phone 24.

❺ Playa del Carmen, Quintana Roó ⇨ *Ferry terminal for Cozumel Island, nice beaches, village.*

La Ruína Camping—7 spaces ★★ 1 block from village square. Electric hookups, bathrooms, laundry. Has Maya ruin on the grounds.

Xcaret Restaurant ★★★ 7 Kms. south of Playa del Carmen. A few spaces, no hookups. Restaurant, swimming, snorkeling, fishing. Another beautiful spot along this stretch of beach.

❷ Playa los Cocos ⇨ *Close to Rincón de Guayabitos, Nay.*

Playa los Cocos—27 spaces ★ Take Miramar exit off Hwy. 200, 29 miles west, then 3 miles north. On beach. Full hookups.

❽ Playa Paraiso, Veracruz ⇨ *Beach village/resort, very tropical, North of Veracruz. Many small, informal camping places along here.*

Motel El Palmar—5 spaces ★★ Hwy. 180 at Km. 75. Elec hookups, pool, restaurant, coconut grove.

Motel Playa Paraiso—56 spaces ★★★ Hwy. 180 at Km. 79. Full hookups plus camping spots. Pool, beach, palm grove, restaurant, TV, laundry.

Trailer Park Neptuno—24 spaces ★★ Hwy. 180, Km. 85. Full hookups, clean bathrooms, on beach, tropical.

❽ Poza Rica, Veracruz ⇨ *In oil-producing country, not far from Tajín, a famous sculptured pyramid and Papantla, where the "Voladores" perform the daredevil "flying pole" ceremony.*

Poza Rica Inn—12 spaces ☆ In town. No hookups, access to motel's facilities.

❻ Puebla, Puebla ⇨ *Beautiful colonial city, full of history and art.*

Trailer Park Las Américas—130 spaces ★★ 16 Km. south on Hwy. 190. Fee: $8.00. Full hookups. Fenced, laundry, rec room, pool, ice. Mailing address: P.O. Box 49, Cholula, Pue. Phone 47-01-34.

Hotel Cuatro Caminos—8 spaces ★★ Hermanos Serdan Ave, near highway to Mexico City. Full hookups. Restaurant, laundry, city buses. clean.

Hotel Spa Agua Azul—5 spaces ★ Next to Agua Azul park. Elec hookup. Pool, mineral baths, restaurant, city buses.

❽ Puente Nacional, Veracruz ⇨ *Beautiful tropical village by old bridge on original road to Mexico City.*

Hotel Balneario ★ Next to bridge. Some spaces with elec. hookups beside hotel. Pool, river fishing. Pretty.

❸ Puerto Escondido, Oax. *Great surfing beaches (sometimes nude bathing). Nice town south of Acapulco.*

Neptuno Restaurant—44 spaces ☆ Main street, by beach. Some elec. hookups, toilets, cold showers, restaurant, fishing boats.

Palmas de Cortés—31 spaces ★★ On beach, in town. Some full hookups. Restaurant, fishing boats, shopping.

Puerto Escondido Trailer Park—150 spaces ★★ 1.5 Km. west off Hwy. 200. Overlooking ocean. Fee: $8.00. Some full hookups. Pool, good water, fishing boats, rec room. Phone 2-00-77.

Puesta del Sol—10 spaces ★ Hwy 200, Km. 144 (east of town). Some full hookups. Restaurant, groceries, good water, horses, cold showers, on good beach.

Restaurant la Cabana ★ In town across from Neptuno. Some elec. hookups, cold showers, restaurant, good water.

❺ Puerto Morelos, Quintana Roó ⇨ *36 Km. south of Cancún, ferry terminal to Cozumel Island.*

Conchita Trailer Park—35 spaces ★ On beautiful beach. Full hookups.
La Ceiba—10 spaces ☆ In town, on beach. No hookups.
Ojo de Agua—35 spaces ★★ On beach, 2 blocks from village square. Full hookups, restaurant.

❶ Puerto Peñasco, Sonora ⇨ *On Sea of Cortez, popular with Arizona and California RVs.*

El Mirador—90 spaces ★★ On beach at end of Matamoros St.. Full hookups. Boat ramp, laundry. Phone 3-2322.
Playa de Oro Trailer Park—200 spaces ★★★ 2 Km. east off Hwy. 8 (look for signs). On beach. Fee: $12.00 Full hookups. Laundry, boat ramp, fishing, trailer storage. Mailing address: P.O. Box 101, Puerto Peñasco, Son. CB radio: Channel 3.
Playa Hermosa Hotel—15 spaces ★★ On beach, in town. Full hookups. Restaurant, fishing boats. Phone 3-2576.
Pithaya Trailer Park—25 spaces ★★ At Hotel Villa Granada, east of town. On beach, full hookups, toilets, no showers.
Sandy Beach—beach parking ☆ Seven miles north of Puerto Peñasco on north side of bay. Nominal fee charged for camping.

❷ Puerto Vallarta, Jalisco *Famous resort town, good beaches, but crowded in winter. See also: Rincón, Bucerías and La Penita.*

Lauries "Tachos" Trailer Park—155 spaces ★★★ 6.3 Km. north, past airport, east 1 Km. toward Pitillal (watch for signs). Fee: $10.00. Full hookups, pool, laundry, store, city buses. Likely to be full in winter. Nice. Mailing address: P.O. Box 315, Puerto Vallarta, Jal. 48300.
Puerto Vallarta Trailer Park—70 spaces ★★★ North side, near Pelicanos. Full hookups. Pool, laundry, city buses, tropical appearance. Phone 2-2828.

❺ Punte Bete, Quintana Roó ⇨ *Starting 2 Km. north of Playa del Carmen, many beautiful beach locations in this area. Tranquil and tropical.*

Capitán Lafitte—6 spaces ★★ East at Km. 296 1.5 Km. to beach. A few elec. hookups, some without. Good restaurant, restrooms, boat rentals.
Marlin Azul—6 spaces ★★ Near Capitán Lafitte's. Some spaces with elec. hookups. Toilet, good restaurant.
Xcalacoco—12 spaces ★★★ 2 Km. north of Playa del Carmen, 1.5 Km. east to beach. Some elec. hookups, clean showers. Boat rental, meals cooked on request. Wonderful place, friendly owners.

❺ Punta Paamul, Quintana Roó ⇨ *Tropical cove 41 Km. north of Tulúm, one of many beautiful beach locations along this stretch.*

Posada Paamul ★ Hwy 307 at Km. 273, then to beach. Some elec. hookups, no water. Restaurants nearby.

❼ Querétaro, Querétaro ⇨ *Famous colonial city, wonderful architecture.*

Azteca Trailer Park—150 spaces ★★ 14.5 Km. north on Hwy. 57, next to Motel Azteca. Fee: $10.00. Full hookups. Pool, restaurant, tennis. Credit cds. Mailing address: P.O. Box 98-C, Querétaro, Qro. 76000.
Flamingo Motel—14 spaces ★★ North side. Full hookups. Restaurant, city buses. Phone 2-0972.

❷ **Queseria, Colima** ➪ *In mountains, 26 Kms north of Colima, by an old hacienda.*

Centro Turístico Carrizalillo ★★   West 13 Kms. to park. Several elec. hookups, some without. On lake, horse rental, groceries, restaurant, one shower.

❷ **Rincón de Guayabitos, Nayarit** ➪ *See also La Peñita. Tropical beach location, one of many along this coast. New resort development.*

Casa Medrano Trailer Park—5 spaces ★   Block north of Número Uno, 1 block from beach. Some full hookups, next to restaurants, palm trees.

Delia's Trailer Park—16 spaces ★★   Across from beach, tropical feeling. Full hookups. Restaurant, groceries, laundry, ice. Also owns park in Etzlan, Jalisco

El Dorado Trailer Park—21 spaces ★★★   East off Hwy. 200 (watch for signs). On beach. Fee: $8.00. Full hookups, clean bathrooms. Pool, boat ramp. Phone (327) 4-01-52.

El Flamingo—20 spaces ★★   On beach. Full hookups, palm trees.

Número Uno—20 spaces ★★   On beach. Full hookups. Food, ice, next to Roberto's restaurant. Phone 25-76-27.

Fiesta Mar Hotel—20 spaces ★   On Avenida Sol Nuevo. Full hookups. Restaurant, laundry, palapas.

Paraiso del Pescador—90 spaces ★★   On beach. Full hookups. Boat ramp, palm trees, nice.

Mary's Trailer Park—13 spaces ★   In La Peñita, next to Motel Russell. Full hookups. Boat Ramp

Trópico Cabana—30 spaces ★★   On beach. Full hookups. Restaurant, palm trees.

Villa Nueva's—25 spaces ★   On beach. Full hookups. Phone 11 in La Peñita.

❻ **Río Frío, Mex.** ➪ *In mountains between Mexico City and Puebla. Snows in winter.*

Parque Llano Grande ☆   At Km. 56 on toll road. No hookups, no showers. Guards.

Parque Río Frío ☆   At Km. 63 on toll road. No hookups, no showers. Guards.

❽ **Sabinas Hidalgo, N.L.** ➪ *Desert town, stopping off place for trip between Laredo and Monterrey.*

Don Luís Motel ☆   North of town. A few spaces by motel, no hookups, restrooms.

Restaurante El Palenque ☆   In town. A few spaces by restaurant, no hookups, restrooms.

❼ **Salamanca, Guanajuato** ➪ *West of Querétaro, south of Irapuato.*

Granja Chury—17 spaces ★★★   East of town, on Celaya highway. Elec. hookups, good bathrooms, pool, restaurant, rec room, small zoo.

❹ **Salina Cruz** ➪ *Laid-back place, beach town for Tehuantepec. Long beaches and good seafood. Very informal.*

Boondocking   Dry camp along spit that goes to booster plant for oil pipe crossing isthmus. Supposed to be nice.

❾ **Saltillo** ➪ *University town, higher elevation and cooler summers. University has summer programs for studying Spanish and Mexican culture.*

Motel Estrella—16 spaces ★★   Hwy. 40, north of town. Full hookups. Pools, restaurant, city buses.

Quinta Colina Trailer Park—12 spaces ★★   1 block south of Periferico Ave., east of V. Carranza. Full hookups, laundry.

➋ San Blas, Nayarit ⇨ *Also, see Santa Cruz Old port town on Banderas bay, reputed to be a pirate hangout. Wonderful colonial ruins on hill behind town. Some parks listed here may be out of business, so check.*

El Dorado—10 spaces ★   3 blocks south of square. Full hookups.

Los Cocos—100 spaces ★★★   Near beach, in palm grove. Full hookups. Rec hall, laundry, restaurant.

Los Flamingos Hotel—11 spaces ☆   In town, next to hotel. No hookups, may be more for RV storage than living.

➊ San Carlos Bay, Sonora ⇨ *Popular cove near Guaymas, many RVs stay the winter here. Full facilities from banks to a country club.*

Casa Móviles (Shangri-La) 334 spaces ★★★   Near end of main street. On beach Full hookups. Pool, Restaurant laundry library, groceries, rec hall, beauty shop. Boat ramp, marina. phone 6-0235.

Tecalal—142 spaces ☆   On main road near next two listings. Across from beach Fee: $10.00. Full hookups. Laundry, Pool, Rec hall.

Teta Kawi Trailer Park—132 spaces ★★★★   On edge of San Carlos. Across from beach. Fee: $10.00. Fee: Laundry, pool, jacuzzi. Mailing address: P.O. Box 671, San Carlos, Son.

Totonara Trailer Park—200 spaces ★★★   On main road. Across from beach. Fee: $10.00 Full hookups. Rec hall, laundry. Phone 6-0323.

➍ San Cristóbal de las Casas, Chiapas ⇨ *Historic, ancient town, high in mountains. Center of indian cultures.*

Bonampak Trailer Park—30 spaces ★★   On Hwy. 190 entrance to town, by Hotel Bonampak. Fee: $6.00. Full hookups. Restaurant, playground. Credit cds. Mailing address: P.O. Box 75 29310. Phone 8-16-21.

Hotel Molina de la Alborada—5 spaces ★   On Periferico highway. Some elec. hookups, restaurant, horses, laundry.

Rancho San Nicolas—25 spaces ★★★   Northeast, at end of Calle Francisco de Leon, watch for signs. Electric and water. Rec hall, horseback riding, laundry.

Muncipal Parking Lot   Many people park in the guarded lot. Attendants happy to take care of your rig for a small fee.

➐ San Isidro Mazatepec, Jal. ⇨ *Village at old hacienda and hot springs. South of Guadalajara about 140 Kms.*

Balneario Río Escondido—18 spaces ★   Some spaces with elec. hookups. Pools, bathrooms, well-maintained.

➐ San Jose Purua, Michoacán. ⇨ *In beautiful Michoacán highlands, in tropical canyon, between Zitacuaro and Ciudad Hidalgo.*

Hotel-Spa San Jose Purua ★★★   5 Kms. south of Hwy. 15. Famous spa with lots of facilities from bowling to tennis and horseback riding. Elec. hookups, many restrooms. Private and family hot tubs and mineral baths.

➐ San Luís Potosí ⇨ *Capital of state and colonial city in transition to modern.*

Cactus Motel Trailer Park—80 spaces ★★   On Hwy. 57 south of traffic circle. Fee: $15.00. Full hookups. Restaurant, night club, pool, rec room, playground, city buses. Use of motel facilities. Mailing address: P.O. Box 393, San Luís Potosí, S.L.P. 78070. Phone 2-01871.

Motel Mesquite—300 spaces ★★★   12 Kms. north on Hwy 57 at Enrique Estrada. Full hookups. Pool, restaurant, laundry. Nice.

Motel Imperial—50 spaces ★★★ Across from Cactus Motel at south entrance of town. Full hookups, pool, restaurant, laundry, city buses.

Nogalia Trailer Park—12 spaces ★★ 12 Kms. east on Hwy 70. Full hookups, some without. Pool. Bull ring!

---

❼ San Miguel de Allende, Guanajuato ⇨ *Colonial town, favorite of artists and writers, haven for retirees.*

Don Ramos—10 spaces ☆ North of town, toward Dolores. Full hookups.

Lago Dorado—65 spaces ★★★★ 3.8 Km. south on Hwy. 49, turn west (follow signs). Fee: $5.00. Electric and water, disposal station. laundry, pool, groceries, rec room. Well-kept. Mailing address: P.O. Box 523, San Miguel de Allende, Guanajuato. 37700. (465) 2-23-01.

Trailer Park La Siesta—70 spaces ★★★ 1 Km. south of center on Hwy. 51, next to La Siesta Motel. Fee: $7.00. Full hookups. Pool, tennis. Mailing address: P.O. Box 72, San Miguel de Allende, Guanajuato. 37750.

Rancho Balneario San Ramón—12 spaces ★ 3 Kms. north on Hwy 51. Full hookups, pool, hot baths. Phone Mexico City 753-5562.

---

❶ Santa Ana, Magdalena, Sonora ⇨ *Stopover point south of Nogales.*

Kennedy Trailer Park—23 spaces ★ 2 miles south of junction. Full hookups. Restaurant, garage. Phone 4-0909.

Punta Vista—12 spaces ☆ 1 Km. south of junction of 2 and 15, just past start of divided highway. Full hookups. New owners. Phone 4-0769

Motel San Francisco ☆ Across from Motel Elba. A few spaces with elec. hookups. Restaurant. Phone 632 4-0322.

Restaurant El Sarape ☆ Hwy. 15, at Km. 164. A few spaces with full hookups, some with elec. Restaurant.

---

❷ Santa María del Oro, Nayarit ⇨ *Lake village near Tepic.*

Bungalows Koala ☆ A few spaces, some with elec, cold shower. Boat ramp, fishing.

Los Tules Trailer Park—14 spaces ★ Right along lakeshore. Full hookups, rustic restaurant.

---

❷ Santa Cruz, Nayarit (near San Blas) ⇨ *Beautiful beach village, tropical, tranquil.*

Playa Amor—40 spaces ★★ On beach. Full hookups. Fenced, with banana groves across street. Nice.

---

❼ Santa María del Río San Luís Potosí ⇨ *Colorful mining town. Hot springs nearby.*

Motel Puesta del Sol ☆ On Hwy. 57 at north end of town. A couple of electric hookup, one bathroom, restaurant.

---

❼ Sierra de San Felipe, Guanajuato ⇨ *Beautiful mountain resort (no village), north of Leon.*

Vergel de la Sierra—8 spaces ★★★ North off Hwy. 37 at Km. 32, follow signs 3 Km. Elec. hookups, near golf course, tennis, fishing, hiking, horses, restaurant. Well-kept.

---

❼ Sayulita, Jalisco ⇨ *One of many beautiful beaches north of Puerto Vallarta. Many North Americans are moving here for retirement.*

Sayulita Beach—20 spaces ★ North of Puerto Vallarta 30 miles, turn on dirt road 1/2 mile. Full hookups.

⑩ **Sonoyta, Sonora** ⇨ *Border crossing south of Saguaro National Monument.*

Nora Motel—11 spaces ☆ Hwy. 2, east of town. Full hookups. Pool (extra charge), restaurant.

⑧ **Sugar Lake, Tamaulipas** ⇨ *South of Brownsville for fishing.*

El Azúcar Motel—7 spaces ☆ On lake. Full hookups. Boat ramps, rentals, gas, ice.

⑧ **Tamazunchale,** ☆ ⇨ *San Luís Potosí. Lushly tropical stopover town on way to Mexico City.*

Quinta Chilla Courts—9 spaces ★★ South side of town. Elec. hookups, restaurant, river swimming. Nice.

⑧ **Tampico, Tamaulipas** *Historic port, important for petroleum.*

Airport Parking Lot Attendants will watch rig for small fee. 24-hour security.
Balneario Rojas—12 spaces ★ From Hwy. 70, turn north east of toll bridge, watch for signs. Elec hookups, restaurant, beach, boat rentals.
Miralta's Trailer Park—65 spaces ☆ 8 miles north. Full hookups. 9-hole golf course, rec hall, laundry.
Posada de Tampico—6 spaces ☆ north of town, near airport on Hwy. 80-180. No hookups, no showers. Restaurant, pool, city buses.

❹ **Tapachula, Chiapas** ⇨ *Clean, modern city near Guatemala border. Ocean nearby. If planning a trip to Guatemala, best enter here.*

Autocinema Trailer Park ☆ Off Diáz Ordaz Blvd.., under a drive-in movie screen! You get to watch the movie for free! Elec. hookups, city buses.

⑥ **Tasquillo, Hidalgo** ⇨ *Pleasant village not far from Mexico City.*

Balneario Tzindejeh—4 spaces ☆ Turn off highway mile north of town. Electric and water. Hot springs, restaurant.

⑥ **Taxco, Guerrero** ⇨ *Picturesque, historic silver mining town built on steep mountain side. Oldest silver mining town in North America. Beautiful must-see.*

Loma Linda Hotel—5 spaces ★★ On highway, close to downtown. Electric and water. Pool, restaurant, good view, city buses.

❷ **Teacapan, Sinaloa** ⇨ *Fishing village on narrow strip of beach, ocean and lagoon.*

Obregón Trailer Park—16 spaces ★ On beach. Full hookups. Restaurant, boat rentals, ice.

❹ **Teapa, Tabasco** ⇨ *Tropical fruit-growing country, heavy rainfall. Famous for hot springs. Near the volcano El Chichonal which erupted in 1982.*

El Azufre ☆ At west end of town, a few spaces (no hookups) at a hot springs resort. Bathrooms, pools, restaurant.

❸ **Tehuacán, Puebla.** ⇨ *Known for mineral water and spas. Archaeologists discovered earliest agriculture here.*

Hotel Hosteria del Camino—10 spaces ☆ 3 Kms. northwest of town center on Hwy. 150. Elec. hookups. Pool, restaurant, city buses. Phone 238 2-3612.
San Bernardino Lagunas ☆ Hwy 150, 15 Kms. north, and 10 Kms. east. A few unmarked spots. Not sure about this one at all.

❹ **Tehuantepec, Oaxaca** ⇨ *Tropical city, not far from ocean. Hot in summer! Nearby hot springs. Famous for its pretty women.*

Calli Hotel ☆   North, off hwy 190. Some electric and water hookups.
Santa Teresa—34 spaces ☆   East off highway near Hotel Calli. Watch for signs. In ruins of old hacienda. No hookups.

❹ **Teopisca, Chiapas** ⇨ *Fertile agricultural area, surrounded by mountains.*

La Amistad—22 spaces ★★   Off Hwy. 190 at KM. 112. Elec. hookups, some full hookups. On lake. Nice.

❷ **Tepic, Nayarit** ⇨ *Quiet city, center of sugar cane production. Huichol and Cora Indians come down from mountains to trade here.*

Apache Motel—15 spaces ★   At south end of town, main highway. Full hookups, pool, city buses.
Kampamento Cora—65 spaces ★★★   3.5 miles south, turn 0.5 miles. Some full hookups. Pool, groceries, laundry, tank disposal.
Linda Vista—20 spaces ☆   On highway 2 miles south. some full hookups.
Motel Los Pinos—27 spaces ★★   2 Kms south of town center on Hwy 200. Full hookups, pool, city buses.

❻ **Tepotzotlán** ⇨ *State of Mexico. North, towards Querétaro. Old village, famous for church built in 1584.*

Pepe's—55 spaces ★★★   In town (look for signs). Full hookups. Landscaping, store, rec hall. Call first: 535-1758 in Mexico City.

❻ **Tepoztlán, Morelia** ⇨ *Famous archaeological zone near this Indian village Tepozteco pyramid on hill overlooking town. Tough climb, but worth it.*

Campamento Camohmila—20 spaces ★★★   2 Kms. east of town. Elec. hookups, 20 bathrooms. Tennis swimming, hiking, games. Run by YMCA!

❼ **Tequisquiapan, Querétaro** ⇨ *Picturesque village turned town. Colonial buildings, hot springs.*

San Francisco Hotel—45 spaces ★★★   4 miles north. Electric and water. Restaurant, mineral baths, golf, ice. Phone 3-0845.
Termas del Rey—33 spaces ★★★   6.5 miles north. Some electric and water. Restaurant, mineral baths, pools. Nice.

❼ **Tlaltizapan, Morelia** ⇨ *Zapata's headquarters during the Revolution.*

Las Estacas—50 spaces ☆   East and north of Tlaltizapan. Unmarked parking spaces, no hookups. Toilets, showers, pools, hot springs, restaurant. Crowded on weekends and holidays.

❾ **Torreón, Coahuila** ⇨ *Northern Mexico site of battles during Revolution. Irrigated farming country.*

Hotel Diana ☆   East of town. One full hookup and a few elec. hookups. Shower, pool, city buses.
Paraiso del Camino—9 spaces ☆   On highway at Reforma and Juárez. Full hookups. Pool, restaurant, city buses.

❺ **Tulúm, Quintana Roó** ⇨ *Beautiful beaches . Famous Mayan site with ruins perched on edge of cliff. Good boondocking here by lagoons, palm groves and beaches.*

Cabanas Tulúm ★★   3.5 miles south of ruins. on beach. No hookups Restaurant, boat rentals, swimming in cenote, pretty..

Playa Xcacel ☆ 10 miles north of Tulúm. On beach. No hookups.
Trailer Park el Paraiso—22 spaces ☆ 2 Kms. south of ruins. No hookups. Toilets, fishing.

---

❽ Tuxpan, Veracruz. ⇨ *Oil country, tropical, beaches, lagoons, beautiful. Tarpon fishing tournament held in June. Good local seafood restaurants.*

María Barbara Trailer Park—250 spaces ★★★ 1.6 Km. west of river bridge, on beach. Fee: $10.00. Some full hookups. Laundry, boat ramp and dock, groceries, disposal station. Phone 4-21-21.

---

❹ Tuxtla Gutiérrez, Chiapas ⇨ *Modern city set in pretty, tropical country. Archaeological ruins nearby. Coffee and tobacco grown here*

La Hacienda—20 spaces ★★★ West of town at Dominguez and Periferico. Full hookups. Pool, TV, groceries, city buses. Well-managed.

---

❼ Uruapan, Mich. ⇨ *Lovely area, near famous volcano Paracutín (now dormant) which sprang from a cornfield in 1943.. Famous for lacquerware and wood products..*

La Joyita—7 spaces ★★ South off hwy near shopping center. Full hookups, city buses.
Motel Pie de la Sierra ☆ North of town on Hwy 37. Unmarked spaces, no hookups. Pool, restaurant.

---

❹ Uxmal, Yucatán. ⇨ *Astounding archaeological ruins of the Puuc Maya civilization. Immense and famous. Takes at least two days to see them all.*

Rancho Uxmal—20 spaces ☆ 3 miles from archaeological site. Electric, restaurant.
San Miguel Trailer Park ☆ Hwy. 261, 2 Kms. south of Muna. A few elec. hookups, bathrooms.

---

❼ Valle de Bravo, Michoacán. ⇨

Don Antonio Trailer Park—10 spaces ☆ In town, near police station. Some full hookups.

---

❽ Valles, San Luís Potosí ⇨ *Pretty city near mountains, west of Tampico.*

El Bañito Trailer Park—60 spaces ★★★ 11.5 Km. south on Hwy. 85. Fee: $8.00 Full hookups. Laundry, restaurant, hot springs, rec room. Mailing address: El Bañito Trailer Park, Ciudad Valles, S.L.P. 79050.
Hotel Valles Trailer Park—27 spaces ★★★ 1 Km. north on Hwy. 85. Fee: $10.00. Full hookups. Pool, use of Hotel facilities. Phone 2-00-50. Mailing address: Hotel Valles,, Ciudad Valles, S.L.P. 79050.

---

❽ Veracruz ⇨ *Important seaport and tourist attraction. World-famous carnival celebration. Mexico's oldest city, founded by Cortez in 1519.*

Fiesta Trailer Park—37 spaces ★★ 8 Km. south on Hwy. 180, across from gulf. Fee: $8.00 Full hookups. Fenced, fishing, city buses.
Parador Los Arcos—105 spaces ★★★ 8 Km. south on Hwy. 180, across from gulf. Fee: $8.00. Swimming, fishing, tennis, rec room. Phone 37-40-75.
Villa del Mar Hotel—11 spaces ☆ 1 mile past center on Blvd.. Camacho. Across from beach. Full hookups. Pool, restaurant, tennis.

---

❼ Villa Corona, Jalisco. ⇨ *Saltwater lake here, plus numerous hot springs.*

Agua Caliente Resort—62 spaces ★★★ Off hwy, 9 miles west of junction. Full hookups. Restaurant, laundry, tennis, hot springs, 4 swimming pools plus private pools.
Chimulco—50 spaces ★★★ Off hwy, 8.5 miles west of junction. Full hookups. Restaurant, laundry, tennis, hot springs, 3 swimming pools, boat ramp.

❺ Yucatán Peninsula Boondocking. *See also Cancún, Campeche, Chetumal, Tulúm, Chichén Itzá, Playa del Carmen, Escárcega.*

Lago Lagarta ☆ Topmost tip of peninsula on long spit of land. Boondocking at Río Lagartos, El Cuyo and Chiquila. Fish camps almost unpopulated in summer, friendly people.
Celestún to Sisal ☆ Northwest corner of peninsula, not far from Merida. Long spit of land enclosing lagoon. Boondocking, lots of places to park. With good fishing on lagoon and gulf side.
Isla del Carmen ☆ Villahermosa to Champotón ☆
Boondocking along Hwy 180 on peninsula and island, connecting with ferries. Lots of nice camping places, good seafood.

❾ Zacatecas ⇨ *State capital. Beautiful city carved from canyon. Interesting architecture and historical significance. Site of battles between Pancho Villa and Federal troops.*

Del Bosque Motel—6 spaces ☆ In town. Steep road. Electric and water, city buses.
El Convento—4 spaces ★ East of town. Full hookups. Pool, restaurant, city buses..
Morelos—20 spaces ★ west of town 11 miles, at junction. Full hookups. Restaurant.
Trailer Park el Molino ★ 16 Km. west, behind gas station. Full hookups, restaurant.

❻ Zimapan, Hidalgo ⇨ *Quiet old mining town surrounded by pine forests.*

Fundición Hotel ☆ South end of town. A few elec. hookups, restaurant, pool, laundry.
Posada Del Rey—8 spaces ★ On north end of town. elec. hookups, Restaurant, pool, tennis,.

❼ Zinapecuaro, Michoacán ⇨ *Hot springs and colonial buildings.*

Balneario Atzimba—60 spaces ★★ Half-mile west. No hookups. Restaurant, hot springs, swimming pools and bathrooms.

Names and Addresses

- **AIM—Adventures in Mexico Newsletter.** AIM, Apdo. Postal 31-70, Guadalajara, 45050, Jalisco, Mexico. Newsletter about retirement in Mexico. Sample copy $2.

- **Air-Evac 24-hour air ambulance.** Houston (713) 880-9767; Imperial Valley (619) 292-5557; Los Angeles (213) 849-2014; Phoenix (800) 854-2569; San Diego (619) 278-3822 — Intensive care, nurses and physicians.

- **Club Deportivo (San Carlos, Sonora)** P.O. Box 300, San Carlos, Guaymas, Sonora — Organization of North Americans who travel to and live in San Carlos Bay.

- **Columbus Travel Copper Canyon Tours.** 6017 Callaghan Rd., San Antono, TX 78228. (512) 523-1400, (800) 225-2829. RV tours through the canyon.

- **Copper Canyon, personally escorted tour: Hector Colmenero.** Reforma 1600-2 Chihuahua, Chih., Mexico. Telephone 16-016-89, or Telex 349688 — Recommended by veteran Mexico traveler who doesn't like to go by rail.

- **Copper Canyon Lodge (Sierra Madre Hiking Lodge Co.** 1130 E. Big Beaver, Troy, MI 48083. (313) 689-4180 — Tours into Copper Canyon, staying at a lodge in the village of Batopilas. Operated by Suzanne McWilliams.

- **Escapees, or S.K.P.** Route #5, Box 310, Livingston, TX 77351 — RV club with lots of full-timer members. Members travel extensively in Mexico, and club newsletter a good place to locate others to caravan with.

- **Gateway Insurance.** (619) 422-3022 or (800) 423-2646 — Insurance, tourist permits.

- **Good Sam Club.** Box 501, Agoura, CA 91301. 800-423-5061 — An offshoot of *Trailer Life Magazine*, the Good Sam Club organizes one caravan a year into Mexico. Sells insurance for RVs in the United States, but not Mexico.

- **Loners on Wheels, Inc.** 808 Lester Street, Poplar Bluff, MO 63901 — RV club for singles. Members form caravans for RV traveling in Mexico.

- **Mexican Department of Fisheries.** 1138 India St., San Diego, CA 92101. (619) 233-6956 — Call first to see what is required.

- **Mexico West Travel Club.** 3450 Bonita Road, Suite 107, Chula Vista, CA 92010 (619) 585-3033 — Newsletter, insurance, car and boat permits, road information.

- **Mexican Hunting Association.** 3302 Josie, Ave., Long Beach, CA 90808. (213) 421-1619 — Can get hunting and gun permits.

- **Peter Johnson Baja Deliveries.** (206) 285-2807 — Hauls trailers or drives motorhomes to Baja for setup on your lot or brings it home if you don't feel like driving.

- **Raul Martinez Yacht Documentation.** 12601 Venice Blvd., Los Angeles, CA 90066. (213) 398-5797 — Boat and yacht documents.

- **Romero's Mexico Service.** 1600 W. Coast Highway, Newport Beach, Ca 92663, (714) 548-3481 or 548-8931 — Boat and yacht documentation papers. Fishing licenses, hunting licenses, gun permits, dog permits, etc.

- **South Point RV Tours** 20644 Roscoe Blvd., Canoga Park, CA 91306. (800) 421-1394 — Caravan tours to Mexico.

- **Stanley "Hambone" Lieberman Insurance.** P.O. Box 300, San Carlos, Guaymas, Sonora. CB handle: Hambone — Group insurance, and daily insurance for return trips to U.S.

- **Travelmex Newsletter. Club Monarca.** Apdo Postal 31-750, Guadalajara, Jalisco, Mexico. Phone: 001-523-622-8925 — Travel club for mainland campers and RV travelers.

Mexico Tourist Offices

Listed below are addresses and phone numbers of local tourist offices. In case of problems or complaints, or if you need assistance, don't hesitate to contact a representative.

- **Acapulco:** Costera Miguel Alemán 187 — 4-63-04, 4-50-44.
- **Aguascalientes:** Madero y Plaza Principal, Hotel Francia — 5-11-55
- **Campeche:** Av. Ruiz Cortines 7 16 de Septiembre — 6-60-68.
- **Chetumal:** Av. Alvaro Obregon 457 Poniente — 2-09-42, 2-15-81
- **Ciudád Juárez:** Av. Juárez y 5 de Mayo Altos — 2-00-86, 2-15-74.
- **Colima:** Francisco I. Madero 59 Altos — 2-01-81, 2-45-60.
- **Cuernavaca:** Av. Morelos Sur 802, Las Palmas — 14-37-94, 14-38-60
- **Cuidad Victoria:** Matamoros y Ocho — 21057
- **Culiacan:** Palacio de Governio — 4-23-45, 4-06-25
- **Durango:** Hidalgo 408 Sur — 1-21-39, 1-11-07.
- **Guadalajara:** Morelos 102, Plaza Tapatia — 14-01-23, 14-01-56.
- **Guanajuato:** Av. Juárez 7 5 de Mayo Altos — 2-00-86, 2-15-74.
- **Hermosillo:** Blvd. Kino 1000 — 4-73-99, 4-83-97
- **Jalapa:** Primo Virdad 25 7 Zaragoza — 7-03-30, 7-37-96
- **La Paz:** Paseo A. Obregon y 16 de Septiembre. — 2-11-99, 2-11-90.
- **Merida:** Av. Itzaes 7 Calle 59 — 1-59-89, 3-96-87
- **Monterrey:** Emilio Carranza 730 Sur, 2ndo Piso — 40-15-55, 42-34-88
- **Morelia:** El Nigromante 79, Palacio Clavijero — 2-98-16, 4-13-42
- **Oaxaca:** 5 de Mayo 200 — 6-38-10, 6-01-23
- **Pachuca:** Palacio de Gobierno, 2o Piso — 3-14-02, 3-14-19.
- **Puebla:** Av. 5 de Oriente 3 — 46-09-28, 45-12-85
- **Queretaro:** Pasteur 6 y Cinco de Mayo — 2-32-00, 2-91-00
- **Saltillo:** Blvd. Francisco Coss y Manuel Acuna — 4-31-75.
- **San Luis Potosi:** Jardín Hidalgo 20 — 2-31-43, 4-29-94
- **Tepic:** Exconvento de la Cruz — 3-07-24
- **Tijuana:** Via Oriente 1, Canalización Rio Tijuana. — 3-10-13 or 3-20-23.
- **Tlaxcala:** Plaza de la Constitución 21 — 2-00-27, 2-25-24
- **Toluca:** Morelos 102, Plaza Tapatia — 14-01-23, 14-01-56
- **Tuxtla Guiterrez:** Av. 14 de Septiembre 1499 — 2-07-32, 2-77-73.
- **Zacatecas:** Blvd. Lopez Mateos 108 — 2-01-70, 2-41-70

Bibliography

Asher, James J. *Learning Another Language Through Actions*. Los Gatos, CA: Sky Oaks Productions, 1988.

Holmes, Ferne, *Traveling Cook*. Phoenix: Golden West Publishers, 1987.

Howells and Merwin, *Choose Mexico*. San Francisco: Gateway Books, 1988.

Howells, John, *Choose Latin America*. San Francisco: Gateway Books, 1986.

Howells, John, *Retirement Choices*. San Francisco: Gateway Books, 1987.

Miller, Tom, and Hoffman, Carol. *The Baja Book III*. Huntington Beach, CA: Baja Trail Publications, 1987.

Wayne, Scott. *Baja California, A Travel Survival Kit.*. Berkeley, CA: Lonely Planet Publications, 1988.

Williams, Jack. *The Magnificent Peninsula*. Sausalito, CA: H. J. Williams, 1987.

Periodicals and Magazines

Atención San Miguel, weekly in San Miguel Allende. Apdo. 119, San Miguel de Allende, Gto., Mexico.

Colony Reporter weekly paper in Guadalajara. Lopez Cotilla 2057, Guadalajara, 44140, Jal., Mexico.

Mexico Journal, weekly magazine. Balderas 68, Centro, Mexico City 06050, D.F., Mexico.

Travelmex, monthly newsletter. Apdo Postal 31-750, Guadalajara, Jal., Mexico.

Baja California, bi-monthly magazine. P.O. Box 148, La Paz, B.C.S., Mexico.

Baja Times, Rosarito Beach, monthly. P.O. Box 755, San Ysidro, CA 92073.

Chubasco, bi-monthly publication of Vagabundos del Mar. P.O. Box 824, Isleton, CA 95641.

Ensenada News and Views, weekly for Ensenada. Blvd. Costero 22800, Ensenada, B.C.N., Mexico.

Mexico West, monthly publication of Mexico West travel club. P.O. Box 1646, Bonita, CA 92002.

Vocabulary

Ordinarily, I object to travel books that pad out the thickness by printing page after page of vocabulary. A small dictionary will give you most of the words you need, and you can carry it around in your pocket. However, there are many words not in an ordinary dictionary. For example, when you're trying to explain what a problem to an automobile mechanic, just try to locate the word for *head gasket* in your pocket dictionary. Can't be done.

Therefore, I've compiled this word-list of terms which could be of use when dealing with problems specific to motoring and RV travel. If you have a problem speaking or pronouncing the words, simply show the mechanic the words on this page.

Included is a unique feature: an additional set of translations, this time from Spanish to English in alphabetical order. If you don't understand what the mechanic is saying, show him the pages (tear them out if that's more convenient). He can look up the word in Spanish and point to the translation for you to understand.

English to Spanish translations

accelerator	*acelerador*	battery cable	*cable de acumulador*
adjust	*ajustar*	bearings	*metales*
air filter	*filtro de aire*	bearing, wheel	*cojinete de la rueda*
allen wrench	*llave de alá*	belt	*banda*
alternator	*alternador*	block	*bloque*
armature	*rotor*	bolt	*tornillo*
auto electric shop	*taller auto-electrico*	box end wrench	*llave ástria*
auto parts	*refacciones*	brake drum	*tambor*
auto parts store	*refaccionería*	brake fluid	*líquido de frenos*
axle	*eje*	brake line	*mangera de frenos*
ball bearings	*baleros*	brake pedal	*pedal de frenos*
ball joints	*rótulas*	brake shoes	*zapatas de freno*
battery	*acumulador, batería*		or *forros de freno*

brakes	*frenos*	gas tank	*tanque*
bumper	*defensa*	gasket	*empaque, sello*
bushing	*bushing, buje*	gasoline	*gasolina*
cable	*cable*	gear	*engranaje*
cable, wire	*cable, a]alambre*	gear shift	*palanca de cambios*
camshaft	*arbol de levas*	generator	*generador*
carburetor float	*flotador*	glove compart.	*cajuelita*
carburetor	*carburador*	grease	*grasa*
carburetor jet	*esprea*	grease job	*lubricación*
check, to	*revisar, chequear*	grease, to	*engrasar*
clamp	*abrazadera*	hack saw	*cegeta*
clutch	*embrague*	hammer	*martillo*
coil	*bobina de encendido*	head gasket	*empaque de cabeza*
coil springs	*resortes*	headlights	*los faros*
compressed air	*aire*	hood	*cofre*
compression ring	*anillo de compresión*	horn	*bocina, claxón*
condenser	*condensador*	hose	*mangera*
crankshaft	*cigüeñal*	intake manifold	*múltiple de admisión*
crescent wrench	*perico*	jack	*gato*
cylinder	*cilindro*	junk yard	*yonke*
differential	*diferencial*	leaf springs	*muelles*
distributor	*distribuidor*	leak, to	*tirar, gotar (but tirar*
drive shaft	*flecha cardán*		*agua means to piss!)*
exhaust pipe	*tubo de escape*	lug wrench	*llave de cruz*
exhaust manifold	*múltiple de escape*	manifold	*múltiple*
fan	*ventilador*	master cylinder	*cilindro maestro*
fan belt	*banda de ventilador*	motorhome	*motorhome (surprise)*
	or *corea de ventilador*	noise	*ruido*
feeler guage	*calibrador*	oil	*aceite*
fender	*guardafanga*	oil change	*cambiar de aceite*
file	*lima, escofina*	oil filter	*filtor de aceite*
filter	*filtro*	oil pump	*bomba de aceite*
fix, to	*arreglar, reparar*	open end wrench	*llave española*
flat tire	*llanta ponchada*	paint job	*pintura*
four-wheel-dr.	*doble tracción*	patch	*parche*
frame	*bastidor*	philips screwdriver	*desarmador de cruz*
fuel pump	*bomba*	pickup truck	*camioneta*
funnel	*embudo*	piston	*pistón*
gas station	*gasolinera*	pliers	*las pinzas*

pulley	*polea*	trailer	*casa rodante* or
rear suspension	*suspensión trasera*		*trailer* (pron. "try-lair")
ratchet wrench	*llave de trinquete*	transmission	*caja de transmisión*
rings	*anillos*	trunk (car)	*cajuela*
screw	*tornillo*	tune-up	*afinar motor*
screwdriver	*desarmador*	turn signals	*direccionales*
socket wrench	*llave de dado*	universal joint	*cruceta*
solder	*soldadura (not soldar)*	unleaded	*sin plomo*
spark plug	*bujía*	valve	*válvula*
start, to	*arrancar, prender*	valve cover	*tapa de pulerias*
starter	*motor de arranque*	vice grips	*pinzas de presión*
steering wheel	*volante*	voltage regulator	*regulador de voltage*
steering arm	*Varillaje de la dirección*	wash job	*lavado*
thermostat	*termóstato*	water pump	*bomba de agua*
tie rod ends	*barrillas de dirección*	weld	*soldar*
tighten, to	*apretar*	wheel	*rueda*
tire gauge	*calibrador*	wheel alignment	*alineanación*
tires	*llantas*	wheel cylinder	*cilindro de frenos*
tools	*herramientas*	windshield	*parabrisas*
top or cover	*tapa or tapón*	windshield wiper	*limpiadores*
torque wrench	*llave de torque*	wrench, key	*llave*
tow truck	*grúa*		

Anti-gravity and Inhumanity

I included this list of words because few pocket dictionaries ever have the technical terms you need. Once I used a pocket-sized traveler's dictionary that claimed to be full of "useful words and phrases for travelers." We searched through it in hopes of finding a translation for "clogged carburetor jet." Fat chance. Yes, I speak fairly good Spanish, but how many times in a lifetime of travels does the average person hear the words: "clogged carburetor jet"? Not often enough to remember them. But, we did find all sorts of other useful words in the dictionary. We found: *anti-gravity, inhumanity, torture,* and *etiquette,* among others. While driving through the Chiapas jungles, we spent several fun-packed hours competing to see who could come up with the best sentence using *anti-gravity* and *inhumanity* and etiquette together while speaking to an RV park manager or an automobile mechanic.

Spanish to English

Show these pages to your mechanic. This will be an easy way for him to communicate with you.

ESPANOL A INGLES

abrazadera	clamp
aceite	oil
acelerador	accelerator
acumulador, batería	battery
afinar motor	tune-up
aire	compressed air
ajustar	adjust
alineanación	wheel alignment
alternador	alternator
anillo de compresión	compression ring
anillos	rings
apretar	to tighten
arbol de levas	camshaft
arrancar, prender	to start
arreglar, reparar	to fix
baleros	ball bearings
banda o corea	fan belt
banda	belt
barrillas de dirección	tie rod ends
bastidor	frame
bloque	block
bobina de encendido	coil
bocina, claxón	horn
bomba de agua	water pump
bomba	fuel pump
bujía	spark plug
bushing, buje	bushing
cable de acumulador	battery cable
cable, a]alambre	cable, wire
cable	cable

caja de transmisión	transmission
cajuela	trunk (car)
cajuelita	glove compartment
calibrador	feeler guage
calibrador	tire gauge
cambiar de aceite	oil change
camioneta	pickup truck
carburador	carburetor
casa rodante	trailer
cegeta	hack saw
cigüeñal	crankshaft
cilindro de frenos	wheel cylinder
cilindro maestro	master cylinder
cilindro	cylinder
cofre	hood
cojinete de la rueda	bearing, wheel
condensador	condenser
cruceta	universal joint
defensa	bumper
desarmador de cruz	philips screwdriver
desarmador	screwriver
diferencial	differential
direccionales	turn signals
distribuidor	distributor
doble tracción	4-wheel drive
eje	axle
embrague	clutch
embudo	funnel
empaque de cabeza	head gasket
empaque, sello	gasket
engranaje	gear
engrasar	to grease
esprea	carburetor jet
filtor de aceite	oil filter
filtro de aire	air filter
filtro	filter
flecha cardán	drive shaft

flotador	carburetor float
frenos	brakes
gasolina	gasoline
gasolinera	gas station
gato	jack
generador	generator
grasa	grease
grúa	tow truck
guardafanga	fender
herramientas	tools
las pinzas	pliers
lavado	wash job
lima, escofina	file
limpiadores	windshield wiper
líquido de frenos	brake fluid
llanta ponchada	flat tire
llantas	tires
llave ástria	box end wrench
llave de alá	allen wrench
llave de cruz	lug wrench
llave de dado	socket wrench
llave de torque	torque wrench
llave de trinquete	ratchet wrench
llave española	open end wrench
llave	wrench, key
los faros	headlights
lubricación	grease job
mangera de frenos	brake line
mangera	hose
martillo	hammer
metales	bearings
motor de arranque	starter
muelles	leaf springs
múltiple	manifold
palanca de cambios	gear shift
parabrisas	windshield
parche	patch

pedal de frenos	brake pedal
perico	crescent wrench
pintura	paint job
pinzas de presión	vice grips
pistón	piston
polea	pulley
refaccionería	auto parts store
refacciones	auto parts
regulador de voltage	voltage regulator
resortes	coil springs
revisar, chequear	to check
rotor	armature
rótulas	ball joints
rueda	wheel
ruido	noise
soldadura	solder
soldar	weld
suspensión trasera	rear suspension
taller auto-electrico	auto electric shop
tambor	brake drum
tanque	gas tank
tapa de pulerias	valve cover
tapa o tapón	top or cover
termóstato	thermostat
tirar, gotar	to leak
tornillo	bolt
tornillo	screw
tubo de escape	exhaust pipe
válvula	valve
varillaje de la dirección	steering arm
ventilador	fan
volante	steering wheel
yonke	junk yard
zapatas de freno	brake shoes

Index

—A—
Acapulco, 117
  beaches, 118
  bus service, 118
  hotels, 118
  weather, 110
Agua Azul, 125
Akumal, 128
Alamos, 108
Antigua, 130
—B—
Bahía de Concepción, 89
Bahía de Los Angeles, 87
Bahia de Los Muertos, 91
Bahía de Palmas, 91
Bahía Kino, 105
Bahía San Carlos, 107
Baja California, 70 - 93
Baja California Sur, 86
bandidos, 35, 41
bargaining, 28
Barra de Navidad, 115
bass fishing, 108
beaches, public, 70
Belize, 129
boat permits, 64
bojuum trees, 77
boondocking, 70, 180
Bucerías, 114
Buena Vista, 91
bus drrivers, 38, 42
—C—
Cabo San Lucas, 93
Campeche, 127
Cancún, 127
Cañon de Cobre, 71, 109
car permit, 62
caravans, 36, 69, 169
Caribbean coast, 152
casa de cambio, 60
Catemaco, 130
CB radios, 65, 105
Central America, 124
Chamula indians, 123
Chiapas, 121
Chichén Itzá, 127
Chihuahua, 109
Children in Mexico, 37
Choya Bay, 105
Christmas gifts, 80
Ciudad Constitución, 90

Club Deportivo, 48, 169
Club Monarca, 169
Colorado river, 104
Comitán, 125
Conasupo, 143
cooking hygiene, 134
Copper Canyon, 109, 172
Costa de Oro, 111
Costa Rica, 124
Coyote Beach, 151
Creel, 109
crime, 32
Cuernavaca, 132
Cuidad Victoria, 130
—D—
desalinators, 71, 92
driving customs, 40
  in Baja, 80
  in Mexico, 39
drugs
  over-the-counter, 137
  prescription, 136
drugs and crime, 34
—E—
El Rosario, 52
electric
  connections, 58
  converters, 59
  hookups, 58
  solar, 58
  voltage, 58
Ensenada, 83
—F—
Ferry
  Cabo San Lucas, 95
  Puerto Vallarta, 95
  reservations, 98
  Santa Rosalía, 97
  Topolobampo, 95
Ferry, Baja, 95, 97, 99, 101
fidecomiso, 73
firewood, 61
fishing licenses, 64
flotation tires, 57
Free Zone, 80
—G—
gasoline, 51, 180
  additives, 52
  stations, 49
getting involved, 26

gifts, 167
  tools, 56
golf courses, 182
Golfo de Santa Clara, 103
Green Angels, 53
Guadalajara, 131
Guatemala, 124
Guerrero Lake, 130
Gulf Coast, 129
gun control, 182
guns, 63
—H—
habitual criminals, 34
handguns, 63
health care, 137
Hermosillo, 105
historical monuments, 108
hospitals, 138
Huatulco, 120
Hussong's cantina, 78
—I—
Inmigrado status, 154
Inmigrante Rentista, 154
Insurance, 36, 46, 48, 157, 179
  accidents, 49
  additional coverage, 159
  boats, trailers, 158
  brokers, 161
  group, 158
  protection, 36
  settlements, 36
  Texas travelers, 160
irrigation, 103
Ixtapa, 117
—J—
Johnny's Beach, 104
justice system, 34
—K—
Kino Bay, 105, 152
Klor DeAlva, 45
—L—
La Capilla, 91
La Paz, 90
La Playa, 93
Laguna San Ignacio, 77
Lagunas de Montebello, 124
Lake Catemaco, 130 - 131
Lake Chapala, 131
Lagarto Lagoon, 129
law and order, 34

laws, 61
leasing property, 72
legal matters, 61
legal system, 35
Loners on Wheels, 36
Loreto, 89
Los Barriles, 91
Los Cabos, 79, 93
Los Mochis, 109
    Topolobampo, 95
—M—
mail, 59
mail service, 59
maintenance, 54
Maneadero, 83
Manzanillo, 77, 115
markets
    native, 144
    supermarkets, 143
Matanchén, 113
Mazatlán, 111
    boondocking, 112
    Playa de Oro, 111
    transportation, 111
mechanics, 52
Medicare, 139
Mexicaneering, 52
Mexico City, 38, 132, 149
Mexico West, 48, 169
Ministry of Tourism, 35
mobile homes, 55, 82
Mocuzari Lake, 108
money changing, 60
mordidas, 45, 62
Mulegé, 87
—N—
Napoleonic Code, 34 - 35
New Kino, 105
—O—
Olmecs, 126
Operation Intercept, 33
Osingo, 125
Oviachic Lake, 108
—P—
Palenque, 125 - 126
Papantla, 130
passport, 61
petrified wood, 104
pets, 183
Playa Azul, 116
Playa de Carmen, 127
Playa de Juanito, 104
Playa de Oro, 91
Playa del Carmen, 128
Points South RV Tours, 172

police, 44 - 45
post office, 59
property
    lease-buy, 73
    purchase, 155
Puerto Angel, 121
Puerto Escondido, 119
    beaches, 120
Puerto Peñasco, 104
Puerto San Carlos, 90
Puerto Vallarta, 77, 114
    Bucerías, 114
    Pitillal, 114
Punta Banda, 33, 83
Punta Mita, 114
—Q—
Quintana Roo, 125
—R—
Ratings, 74
restaurants, 135
retirement, 149, 151, 153, 155
    full time, RV, 152
    legalities, 153
    Rio Grande Valley, 150
Rincón de Guyabitos, 115
RV cooking, 141, 143, 145
RV park ratings, 74
—S—
safety, 31 - 37
San Andrés Tuxtla, 131
San Blas, 112
San Carlos, 152
San Carlos Bay, 48, 107
San Cristóbal, 122, 125
    Indian tribes, 122
San Cristóbal de Las Casas, 155
San Felipe, 79, 84
San Franciscito, 115
San Ignacio, 87
San José del Cabo, 93
San Juan Chamula, 123
San Lucas Cove, 88
San Miguel de Allende, 132
San Vincente, 84
Santa Cruz, 113
Santa Rosalía, 88, 97
Santiago, 92
Santo Tomás , 84
Sayuita, 114
Sea of Cortez, 76
Seri Indians, 106
shopping
    butcher shops, 145
    food, 141
shotguns, 64

Sierra Madre, 108
solar cells, 58
Sonoyta, 62
Spanish
    classes, 174
    learning, 173
    TPR, 174
supermercados, 143
—T—
Tajín, 130
Tampico, 110, 130
Tapachula, 124
Tehuantepec, 122
telephones, 64
tennis, 182
Third Mexico, 24
Tiburón Island, 106
tires, flotation, 57
Todos Santos, 93
tool kits, 56
Topolobampo, 95
tourist cards, 61, 80, 83, 154
traffic fines, 45 - 46
traffic signals, 42
Transpeninsula Highway, 75
transportation
    bicycle, 72
    bus, 72
travel clubs, 169, 171
traveler's checks, 60
travelers' warnings, 32 - 33
Tropic of Cancer, 110
truck drivers, 41
Tuxpan, 130
—V—
Vagabundos del Mar, 48,
169 - 170
vehicle permit, 62
Veracruz, 130 - 131
    Antigua, 130
Verdugos, 91
Villahermosa, 38, 125 - 126
Visitante Rentista, 154
volunteer work, 165
—W—
water, drinking, 57
    purification, 134
water advice, 57
whale-watching, 76
working in Mexico, 182
—Y—
Yucatán, 127, 129
—Z—
Zihuatanejo, 116
zona libre, 80

COMMENT AND ORDER FORM

TO:
GATEWAY BOOKS
31 Grand View Avenue
San Francisco, CA 94114

FROM: _____

_____

_____

COMMENTS

(In this space we'd welcome your gripes as well as your kudos, but most of all we want your suggestions as to how we can make the next edition of RV TRAVEL IN MEXICO more helpful.

Order from reverse side.

GATEWAY BOOKS
31 Grand View Avenue
San Francisco, CA 94114

Our books for mature travelers and mature stay-at-homes are available in most bookstores. However, if you have any difficulty finding them, we will be happy to ship them to you directly.
Mail us this coupon with your check or money order and they'll be in the mail to you within days.

RV Travel in Mexico	$10.95	_____
The How-to-Do-It Book		
Get Up and Go:	10.95	_____
A Guide for the Mature Traveler		
Choose Mexico:	9.95	_____
Retire on $400 a Month		
Choose Latin America	9.95	_____
A Guide to Seasonal and Retirement Living		
Retirement Choices:	10.95	_____
For the Time of Your Life		
To Love Again:	7.95	_____
Intimate Relationships After 60		

Subtotal: _____

Add $1.50 for postage and handling for the first book, $ .50 for each additional one. (California residents add 6% sales tax.) _____

Total Enclosed..$_____

NAME_____

ADDRESS_____

CITY _____STATE _____ZIP_____

Mail to: Gateway Books, 31 Grand View Avenue, San Francisco, CA 94114